The Drama of
EASTER

An anthology of royalty-free Easter plays for all ages

Rh

MERIWETHER PUBLISHING LTD.
Colorado Springs, Colorado

Meriwether Publishing Ltd., Publisher
P.O. Box 7710
Colorado Springs, CO 80933

Typesetting: Elisabeth Hendricks, Sue Trinko
Cover design and illustration: Janice Melvin

Library of Congress Cataloging-in-Publication Data

The drama of Easter : an anthology of royalty-free Easter plays for all ages /
edited and compiled by Rhonda Wray. -- 1st ed.

      p.   cm.
   ISBN 1-56608-051-7 (pbk.)
   1. Easter Drama. 2. Christian drama, American.   I. Wray, Rhonda,
 1962-   .
 PS627.E37D73   1999
 812'.54080334--dc21

                                       99-36985
                                           CIP

1   2   3   4   5   6   03   02   01   00   99

If you've ever

Experienced the Easter story through drama

Worshiped at a sunrise service

Rejoiced in the hope of the Resurrection

Then this book is for you.

Special Thanks

To the authors:

Individually, your works sparkled.

Collectively, they're brilliant!

Thanks for sharing the light.

Contents

Preface

New life. That is the essence of Easter. I experienced new life in a literal way with the birth of a child during the time I was compiling and editing this book. What joy! And so it is with new, eternal life. Now *that* is worth celebrating!

The playwrights featured in this book explore Easter's promise of new life in many creative ways. My aim in selecting these scripts was to include a diversity of styles, age levels, and special days in the Lenten season. Imagine you are in a dusty carpenter's shop in Jerusalem, making the sign reading "This is Jesus, King of the Jews" for his cross. Or place yourself in a courtroom trial, where the prosecution has assembled six witnesses to prove that the "supposed resurrection of Jesus of Nazareth some 2,000 years ago is a fraud perpetrated on the public." Maybe you're a frustrated city official who is called on the carpet for letting an unauthorized parade of palm branch-waving fans to take place. And there's much more, from the shadowy candlelight of a reflective Tenebrae program to the exuberance of a sunrise service.

These twenty dramatic gems have been audience-tested in hundreds of churches nationwide. Production suggestions accompany each script to aid the director. They are appropriate for all denominations, for each has something compelling to say about the cornerstone of the Christian faith: the resurrection of our Lord.

It is my hope that as you direct or participate in these plays, you will find renewed and joyful meaning in the message of Easter. May these scripts remind you that Easter can be a way of life when good wins out over evil, when light triumphs over darkness, when faith replaces doubt.

He is risen as he said!

NOTE: The numerals running vertically down the left margin of each page of dialog are for the convenience of the director. With these, he/she may easily direct attention to a specific passage.

Lent and Holy Week

Give Us a Sign

A one-act play for Holy Week
by John Gillies

CAST

Malachi
Elderly Jewish sign painter

Justus
Roman soldier

PRODUCTION NOTES

Overview: This play was originally created as an Easter season television special. Action occurs within one setting and with two strong characters. It is a classically simple play with a clear and provocative message. A Roman soldier gives the order to an old Jewish sign painter to paint a sign for the head of the cross on which Jesus is to be crucified. The dialog between the sign painter and the soldier, as the sign is being prepared, brings light to the question of Jesus — man or king?

Set and Props: There is no formal set, only a suggestion of a first-century sign painter's shop. There is a table with several small jars (pottery) on top, in which we assume there is paint. Some brushes are placed in one jar. There are also several boards, an easel, and a stool. Everything except the boards appears old and worn. Justus needs a parchment scroll.

Lights: If theatrical lights are available, they may be used to suggest a rather high window on one side and to highlight an entrance on the other. If lights are unavailable, the window may be pantomimed.

Costumes: Malachi may wear a simple biblical robe, sandals, and *kaffiyeh* headpiece, preferably in an earthen tone. Justus should wear a *tunica*, or short-sleeved, knee-length garment, which is rust in color. Over this he wears the *cuirass*, a piece of armor consisting of a breastplate and backplate. This may be made of felt and spray-painted several times for stiffness with bronze-colored paint. In Roman times, this was hinged on one side and fastened with straps on the other. In place of the hinge in this case, both sides may be fastened with straps and buckles, making it adjustable for different actors. Fastened to the bottom of the cuirass is a leather (vinyl) waistband and the hanging leather straps. These are ornamented with cap bolts from the hardware store, and glued on with a "super" glue. At the shoulders of the cuirass are wide leather bands connecting the back and front sections of the armor. These are tacked in place except for one end, which has Velcro so it will slip on easily. Attached to these bands are shorter straps, also decorated with cap bolts. A plastic Roman short sword and sheath from the toy store is fastened to the waistband. The helmet is made from a bump hat, and sprayed with bronze paint. Attached to the inside of the helmet are the neck and forehead flaps and the chin straps. Two leather straps, 1½ inches wide, cross over the top of the helmet and a hook is screwed through the center. (Source for Roman soldier costume: *Costuming the Christmas and Easter Play* by Alice M. Staeheli, copyright © 1988 by Meriwether Publishing Ltd., page 47.)

Playing time: 15-20 minutes.

1   *(MALACHI, a white-bearded, energetic man, enters from the rear.*

2   *He walks toward the window, pausing in the light and, looking*

3   *up, murmurs a prayer. Two brief claps are heard outside the*

4   *entrance. MALACHI turns.)*

5 **MALACHI: Come in.** *(JUSTUS, a young Roman legionnaire, enters.*

6   *He has a parchment scroll inside his tunic. He has been here*

7   *before. MALACHI and JUSTUS know and like each other.)*

8 **JUSTUS: Good day, Malachi.**

9 **MALACHI: May this day bring you peace. How are you, Justus?**

10 **JUSTUS: Much as always, Old One. Tired of doing nothing. Bored.**

11 **MALACHI: Boredom is a terrible thing. Especially for a young**

12   **man.** *(With a twinkle)* **We Jews are not keeping you busy, is**

13   **that it?**

14 **JUSTUS: The centurion would not agree.**

15 **MALACHI:** *(Probing)* **And you? What do you say, Justus?**

16 **JUSTUS:** *(Walks to MALACHI, touches his shoulder.)* **I say — as I**

17   **have said so many times already — that you Jews have an**

18   **exaggerated opinion of yourselves.**

19 **MALACHI: You don't fear a rebellion?**

20 **JUSTUS: There isn't a thing we can't handle.**

21 **MALACHI:** *(Walks toward easel.)* **But others will have that**

22   **privilege, no?** *(Looking at JUSTUS)* **I imagine your thoughts**

23   **are with your home and family.**

24 **JUSTUS: Only two more months ... and I shall be with them!**

25 **MALACHI: It is good to be home. Whether your home be in**

26   **Judea or in Italia.**

27 **JUSTUS: But yours is such a strange home, Malachi! Paints,**

28   **brushes, boards ...**

29 **MALACHI: I live where I work. And now that I am alone, I like**

30   **to be near my tools. It is my home.**

31 **JUSTUS: And how long will you work, Old One? Will you never**

32   **cease?**

33 **MALACHI:** *(Looking up)* **As long as I am given strength, I shall**

34   **work.** *(To JUSTUS)* **I must work! I, too, would become bored**

35   **if I had nothing to do. And one must also eat.**

1   **JUSTUS:** *(Withdraws parchment from tunic.)* **Then you shall have**
2   **more work to do.** *(Smiles broadly.)* **On orders from Pontius**
3   **Pilate himself!**

4   **MALACHI:** *(Shrugging)* **I should be honored.** *(Caustically)* **I will be,**
5   **tomorrow, when you will return.**

6   **JUSTUS:** **Old One — the assignment I bring is for today.**

7   **MALACHI:** **Have you forgotten that today we celebrate**
8   **Passover? It is a holy day. A most holy day. Surely the**
9   **governor himself knows that Jews do not work on their**
10   **holy days ...**

11 **JUSTUS:** **Malachi, this is something which cannot be deferred.**

12 **MALACHI:** *(Takes parchment scroll from JUSTUS and begins to*
13   *unroll it.)* **Only last week I explained to you that the**
14   **Passover is, perhaps, our most important holiday!**

15 **JUSTUS:** **The governor wishes a simple sign. It will not take you long.**

16 **MALACHI:** *(Not looking at scroll, angry)* **You Romans have your**
17   **holy days, too!**

18 **JUSTUS:** **Old One, please! The Romans have been good to you.**
19   **You have made signs for the garrison. Inscriptions for the**
20   **buildings. Special proclamations.**

21 **MALACHI:** *(Subdued)* **And I am grateful for honest work.**

22 **JUSTUS:** **Then ... then do not force me to insist.** *(Turns aside.)* **I**
23   **do not have the desire for that. Not today.**

24 **MALACHI:** *(Turns and walks to light from window.)* **I'll have a look.**
25   *(MALACHI again unrolls the scroll. JUSTUS avoids looking at*
26   *him. MALACHI stares at the scroll, looks at JUSTUS, then stares*
27   *at scroll again, not trusting his eyes.)* **Surely this is some kind**
28   **of a joke!** *(Rushes to JUSTUS.)* **This is a joke?**

29 **JUSTUS:** *(Speaks cautiously but firmly.)* **The sign is to be made.**
30   **That is not a joke. The idea? I think it is cruel. And crude.**

31 **MALACHI:** **Why is this sign needed?**

32 **JUSTUS:** **You have heard of the crucifixion, no doubt.**

33 **MALACHI:** *(Slaps hands.)* **Crucifixions? There have been so many,**
34   **who can keep up with them?** *(Sarcastic)* **This is the Roman peace.**

35 **JUSTUS:** **Careful, Old One.**

1 MALACHI: I do not care who may overhear.

2 JUSTUS: I am a Roman. And I hear you, Malachi.

3 MALACHI: We have spoken of the matter many times. You know
4   how I feel about crucifixions.

5 JUSTUS: And I have reminded you, Old One, many times, that your
6   custom of stoning undesirables to death is itself rather cruel.

7 MALACHI: *(Nods.)* Agreed. There is too much cruelty
8   everywhere. *(Stares at parchment, shakes head.)* You spoke of
9   another crucifixion.

10 JUSTUS: Of the man called Jesus.

11 MALACHI: The Nazarene?

12 JUSTUS: I believe he is also known by that name.

13 MALACHI: *(Reading scroll)* "This is the King of the Jews."

14 JUSTUS: To be inscribed in three languages.

15 MALACHI: *(Nodding)* Hebrew, Latin, and Greek. *(Throws parchment*
16   *down.)* Justus, a man could be arrested for even jesting about
17   the "King of the Jews"! And you want me to make a sign,
18   announcing this to the world? It could be ... treason.

19 JUSTUS: You have the order of Pilate. Whatever he requests is
20   not treason.

21 MALACHI: *(Picks up scroll.)* When ... is this crucifixion?

22 JUSTUS: Tomorrow. Early tomorrow.

23 MALACHI: *(Sighs deeply.)* So we must make all preparations on the
24   day of our Passover. *(Walks to boards. Picks one and sights it.)*

25 JUSTUS: It does not have to be a large sign!

26 MALACHI: I know. I have seen your processions. Will he have
27   to wear the sign about his neck, as I have seen others do?

28 JUSTUS: I do not know, Malachi! Please get on with the sign. The
29   hours pass too quickly, and I must return to the garrison!

30 MALACHI: *(Places board on easel and sits on stool facing audience,*
31   *which will never see the completed sign. Slowly picks a brush,*
32   *stirs paint in pottery jar, looks at parchment, and starts to paint.*
33   *JUSTUS paces about but keeps MALACHI's work in view.)* In
34   three languages?

35 JUSTUS: Yes, Malachi! Latin, Greek, and Hebrew!

1 **MALACHI:** *(Refers to parchment as he speaks, occasionally glances*
2 *at JUSTUS, but mostly concentrates on his work.)* **So all may**
3 **understand.**
4 **JUSTUS: So all? Yes, I suppose so.**
5 **MALACHI: But I do not understand.**
6 **JUSTUS: About the sign?**
7 **MALACHI: I know about that. You Romans want everyone to**
8 **know the crime of a criminal sentenced to death. So he**
9 **wears an inscription telling it to the world.**
10 **JUSTUS: This sign is to be placed upon the cross.**
11 **MALACHI: Indeed. Your governor insults us, of course, with this**
12 **sign.** *(JUSTUS tries to protest.)* **I'll have my say, Justus. He**
13 **says that the only suitable king for the Jews is a criminal.**
14 **JUSTUS:** *(Looking at sign)* **Must you take so long?**
15 **MALACHI: I did not invent the Roman alphabet, my friend. Thick**
16 **strokes. Thin strokes. Serifs. An abomination for a sign painter!**
17 **JUSTUS: Your Hebrew letters utterly confuse me.**
18 **MALACHI:** *(Picks up earlier thought.)* **I understand, too, that Pilate**
19 **wishes to warn our younger revolutionaries. Incidentally,**
20 **why was Pilate in Jerusalem instead of Caesarea?**
21 **JUSTUS: Because of your Passover.**
22 **MALACHI: Indeed? Did he come to worship the one true God?**
23 **JUSTUS: Some say that his wife urged him to come.**
24 **MALACHI: Where will he be buried? This Jesus?**
25 **JUSTUS: On Golgotha.**
26 **MALACHI: That is a Hebrew name. Do you know its meaning?**
27 **JUSTUS: The skull.**
28 **MALACHI: A place of death. Romans do not crucify Romans, am**
29 **I correct?** *(JUSTUS nods.)* **Romans only crucify slaves and**
30 **criminals ... and Jews.**
31 **JUSTUS: Not because they are Jews! And Pilate did not wish to**
32 **sentence this man, Jesus!**
33 **MALACHI: Then why did he?**
34 **JUSTUS: Because so many of your own people clamored for it.**
35 **I heard them, Malachi! It was unbelievable.**

1 MALACHI: Led by the priests, no doubt.

2 JUSTUS: That's true. They did! How did you know?

3 MALACHI: The Levites do not like the Nazarene. Especially
4   since he drove the moneychangers out from the temple.
5   *(Chuckling)* I would have liked to have seen that.

6 JUSTUS: Old One, please hurry!

7 MALACHI: I will not hurry. Not even for a crucifixion. I will do
8   my work ... carefully. Do you know this Jesus?

9 JUSTUS: I saw him only at the trial.

10 MALACHI: I have never seen him. I have heard so much about
11   him. A good man, obviously. He feeds hungry people. He
12   heals the sick. He teaches as the prophets did! What does
13   he look like?

14 JUSTUS: He is a strong man. He was a carpenter, I believe.

15 MALACHI: *(Smiling)* I'm glad I chose a good board.

16 JUSTUS: He was very tired. Or sad. But his eyes have a kind of
17   glow to them. He looked my way once. I felt he was looking
18   right at me.

19 MALACHI: Perhaps he was. "The King of the Jews." Why does
20   Pilate wish this foolishness?

21 JUSTUS: Careful, Old One!

22 MALACHI: Did Jesus ever claim to be a king?

23 JUSTUS: There were people who shouted "Blessed be the King"
24   when he entered Jerusalem last week!

25 MALACHI: Yes. Riding that donkey.

26 JUSTUS: Why did he do that?

27 MALACHI: I don't know, Justus. Our kings rode horses when
28   they went to battle. When they wanted to show that they
29   came in peace, then they rode a donkey. Pilate shouldn't
30   worry so much about what a few fanatics might shout.

31 JUSTUS: Must you add a border?

32 MALACHI: I think the sign requires a border. Just a few
33   moments more.

34 JUSTUS: You have a steady hand, Malachi. I don't know how
35   you can paint a line as straight as that!

1   **MALACHI:** *(Stands and looks at sign on easel. Holds it carefully at*
2   *his side and walks to light, which has softened somewhat.*
3   *Audience still will not see the finished side.)* **What do you think?**
4   **JUSTUS:** **It is a very fine sign, Old One. Perhaps too good for**
5   **its purpose.**
6   **MALACHI:** **I like it, too.**
7   **JUSTUS:** **What do we owe you? I hate to rush you, Malachi, but**
8   **I must take the sign with me. Now.**
9   **MALACHI:** **The paint is wet!**
10 **JUSTUS:** **The crucifixion won't be delayed because of wet paint.**
11   **How much?**
12 **MALACHI:** *(Places sign on easel.)* **Nothing.**
13 **JUSTUS:** **Nothing? You could charge me twice as much.**
14   **Working so rapidly. On a holy day ...**
15 **MALACHI:** **I will not be paid for any part of a crucifixion.** *(Looks*
16   *at sign.)* **It is a good sign. If he is to be called a King, then**
17   **the sign should be worthy of a king.** *(Looks at JUSTUS.)*
18   **Justus, do you know what my name means? In Hebrew?**
19 **JUSTUS:** **The name ... Malachi?**
20 **MALACHI:** **Malachi means "messenger of Jehovah." Messenger of**
21   **the great God himself! Perhaps a sign painter is a messenger.**
22 **JUSTUS:** **It is a good name.**
23 **MALACHI:** **Justus, what if the sign is true?**
24 **JUSTUS:** **True?**
25 **MALACHI:** **In spite of the jest and the insults and Pilate's**
26   **confusion. What if my sign is true? What if he really is**
27   **King? Not only of us Jews, but of you Romans, too. What if**
28   **he is King of us all?** *(Lights fade to black as the two men exit.)*
29
30
31
32
33
34
35

Into the Light

A Lenten season drama
by Michael E. Dixon

CAST

Narrator
Man or woman

Shaphan
*A member of the council and
convener of the hearing*

Gaius
Roman investigating officer

Nicodemus
A member of the council

Sara
Nicodemus' maidservant

Mary of Bethany
(May be played by Narrator.)

PRODUCTION NOTES

Overview: The gospel of John presents a big story — one the narrator of this play says "can be seen in a small story — the story of one person. We call him Nicodemus." It was Nicodemus and Joseph of Arimathea who asked for Jesus' dead body for burial. As a member of the Sanhedrin, the ruling religious council of Israel, and as a Pharisee, Nicodemus had much to lose by following Jesus. Yet what he gained must have made it worth the risk. John's three brief references to Nicodemus show growing involvement, and they also show many of the most dramatic themes of the gospel: coming from darkness into light, being born anew ("If I be lifted up"), and Christ's kingship. The play is set after the body's disappearance. Nicodemus is on trial for his life as a blasphemer. The investigative hearing is enlivened with flashbacks linking Nicodemus' story with that of Lazarus, Mary, and Martha. The dialog reveals how a non-believer in Jesus slowly came out of the darkness into the light of Christ, the Messiah.

Scene: Jerusalem, a few weeks after the Crucifixion.

Set: Two areas are needed. In the first are three chairs and a table. The second area needs no furnishings and is used for flashback sequences.

Staging: The play is simple in construction and staging. Action flows between the investigative hearing and several flashback sequences. Transitions can be made more effective by dimming of lights and musical interludes. For the interludes, there are several possibilities: taped classical instrumental music, organ or piano music, a solo voice. Single verses of the hymns "Spirit of God, Descend Upon My Heart" and "Be Thou My Vision" lend themselves well to the meaning of the play. Like music, biblical costumes are helpful but not necessary. Performing the play as a reading is possible, but effective communication of the argument scenes would need minimum reliance on the scripts.

References: The play lends itself well to discussion. Passages which could form the basis for further discussion or study include John 1:1-18, 3:1-21, 7:32-52, 8:12, 11:1-57, 12:1-11, 19:28-42, and 20:1-23.

Playing Time: 35-40 minutes.

1   **NARRATOR:** *(Enters.)* **In the beginning was the Word; and the**
2   **Word was with God, and the Word was God** *(John 1:1).*
3   **Everything in all creation took shape from this creative,**
4   **powerful Word. Yet there was darkness in this creation, the**
5   **darkness of human sin, the darkness of human suffering. Into**
6   **the darkness came the light. Into its own creation came the**
7   **Word — and not as some high master of the universe, but as**
8   **one of us — living, breathing, sweating, worrying, suffering,**
9   **dying a little bit each day, the Word in human flesh.**
10   **Some received this Word as life and light, a new birth.**
11   **Others perceived the Word as one of judgment; the light as**
12   **a beam of exposure; the breath of new life as the wind of**
13   **revolution. That which loves darkness in each of us tried to**
14   **put out the light, but it continues to shine in the darkness.**
15   **This big story can be seen in a small story — the story of**
16   **one person. We call him Nicodemus.** *(NARRATOR retires*
17   *from scene. SHAPHAN and GAIUS enter in wary dignity and sit*
18   *at one end of table. SARA appears Upstage, timidly seeking*
19   *permission to enter. SHAPHAN nods, and she quietly moves a*
20   *few steps closer, still behind the two. NICODEMUS enters and*
21   *stands at a chair at other end of table.)*
22   **SHAPHAN:** **Thank you for coming, friend. It seems odd for us**
23   **to be at opposite sides of the table in a matter like this, but**
24   **I'm sure we can clear this question up quickly, quietly, and**
25   **in a friendly manner.**
26   **NICODEMUS:** **I am glad, Shaphan, that you still consider me**
27   **your friend. Indeed, we've spent many hours at the table**
28   **together, both enjoying food and wine and deliberating at**
29   **council hearings. I agree it does seem different to see you**
30   **from this end of the hearing table.**
31   **SHAPHAN:** **Nicodemus, sit down.** *(NICODEMUS sits.)* **You may**
32   **have met Gaius before. The governor requested that he sit in**
33   **on all hearings about the Nazarene's movement — possibility**
34   **of all kinds of political implications, as you might guess.**
35   **GAIUS: People out there are stirred up. Too easily excitable, too**

1   **many rumors floating around. Too many rumors cause**
2   **unrest. Unrest brings ... unpleasantness.**
3 **NICODEMUS: Yes, but what have I to do with all this? Have I**
4   **been spreading rumors? Have I been accused of heresy?**
5   **Am I suspected of sedition?**
6 **SHAPHAN:** *(Coolly)* **We don't know. That is why we have asked**
7   **you here. We want to find out the extent of your**
8   **involvement in this movement that is disrupting our faith**
9   **and even endangering civil peace.**
10 **NICODEMUS: Ask me your questions, then. I have nothing to**
11   **hide.** *(Notices SARA.)* **Sara! Is that you? Are you serving**
12   **Shaphan's table as well as my own?**
13 **SHAPHAN: She is here as a witness.**
14 **GAIUS: We may as well tell you now that we know she is a**
15   **member of the movement of this crucified "god" that's**
16   **raising the ruckus. We think she can be made to tell us of**
17   **your involvement.** *(SARA tenses.)*
18 **NICODEMUS: Your well-known methods of gathering**
19   **information will not be necessary, Gaius.** *(Turns.)* **Sara,**
20   **speak freely. Be loyal to the truth, and you'll be loyal to me.**
21   **Let everything out into the light.** *(Ponders, then softly.)* **Speak**
22   **freely ... Let everything be in the light ... It hasn't always**
23   **been that way, has it, Sara?**
24 **SHAPHAN: What about it, woman? Nicodemus may be wiser**
25   **than I thought. Since you are only a female, your evidence**
26   **will not damage your master's case. But it might help us**
27   **understand it.** *(SARA advances to NICODEMUS, curtsies, and*
28   *begins, timidly.)*
29 **SARA:** *(To SHAPHAN)* **If you please, sir.** *(Impulsively)* **Sir, if there**
30   **is punishment for following Jesus of Nazareth, let me be**
31   **punished in my master's place. If it were not for me, my**
32   **master would never have met Jesus.**
33 **NICODEMUS: Sara, remember I'm a grown man now. I'm fully**
34   **accountable for my own actions and decisions.**
35 **SARA: Yes, sir. It's just ... I can't help but feel responsible.**

1 GAIUS: Woman, we will make the decisions about who is
2   responsible. Get on with the story. You say you introduced
3   your master to Jesus?
4 SARA: No sir! I didn't introduce them! Who would I, an old
5   servant woman, be to introduce two great rabbis?
6 SHAPHAN: *(Angrily)* Jesus of Nazareth was *not* a rabbi! He had
7   not the credentials or ... *(Cooling)* What our esteemed
8   Roman friend means is that you knew of this Jesus first and
9   told Nicodemus about him. Tell us how it happened.
10 SARA: I am an old woman, sir, and I have seen many important
11   people, and heard of many strange and wonderful things.
12   But none were as strange and wonderful as the stories I
13   heard about the Galilean rabbi — *(SHAPHAN glowers.)*
14   Please forgive me, sir, the Galilean. Wonderful stories
15   spread through the marketplace: blind people that had
16   their sight restored, people with withered limbs walking,
17   even lepers cleansed! *(As SARA continues, SHAPHAN*
18   *mumbles, "Fantastic marketplace rumors.")* And his teachings!
19   The stories he told gave people a whole new way of
20   knowing about God! Poor servants he treated like princes!
21 SHAPHAN: And princes like beggars.
22 SARA: He treated us all like God's beloved children. And when
23   I heard he was coming to our town, I begged my master's
24   leave to go hear him.
25 SHAPHAN: And?
26 SARA: I went. It was crowded. One gentleman was so eager to
27   see him that he pushed a child out of his way. Jesus turned
28   to the child, leaned down, smiled, and whispered something
29   — and did that little boy's face glow!
30 GAIUS: Get to the heart of things. Your prattle is beginning to
31   bother me.
32 SARA: *(Enthusiastic, hardly skipping a beat)* And when he talked, it
33   was wonderful. He talked of simple things, like the seed of
34   a mustard plant that was near — how tiny it was, but how
35   it could grow — just like our faith in God! Well, I could go

1   on all day about what he said —

2 GAIUS: Please ... don't. The emperor didn't send me here to

3   attend seminars of eastern philosophy.

4 SARA: *(Only somewhat contritely)* I'm afraid I went on all day

5   telling my master about it; he's a *very* patient listener to an

6   old woman — Oh! not that you're not, m'lord.

7 SHAPHAN: You told him about this ... ah, teacher. How did he

8   respond?

9 SARA: Let's see. *(Lights dim and raise, music up briefly to signify*

10   *beginning of flashback. NICODEMUS and SARA move to*

11   *flashback area.)*

12   * * *

13 NICODEMUS: *(Responding to SARA's impassioned pantomimed*

14   *discussion)* Yes, Sara, I'm intrigued by what you tell me. This

15   Jesus fellow sounds rather remarkable. Funny, after all

16   these years, prophets seem to be sprouting out of the trees

17   like figs. This Jesus does sound a bit more likable than

18   poor old John — that priest's son who kept shouting and

19   calling people names. Quite a brave figure, but such a

20   doomsayer! Kept scaring folks out of their wits, then he'd

21   dip them in the Jordan.

22 SARA: You agree that Jesus is a prophet, then?

23 NICODEMUS: Wait, wait, wait. I didn't say "so-called prophet"

24   because I wanted him to have the benefit of the doubt.

25   Always remember, "prophet" and "madman" are both from

26   the same word. One's possessed by God, the other by ...

27   something less.

28 SARA: Oh! He's not crazy, sir. Many things he says are strange

29   and have more to them than I can perceive, but they're not

30   ramblings. They hold together. They have a center.

31 NICODEMUS: And what is that center?

32 SARA: I think — forgive me, sir, I'm obviously no scholar of the

33   law like you are — but I think they all center around what

34   we say whenever we worship: "You shall love the Lord your

35   God with all your heart, mind, soul, and strength." But

1   that's not all. He says that we can't love God and hate the
2   least of God's children. In order to love God, we must love
3   our neighbor as ourselves.

4 NICODEMUS: If that's the center of his teachings, Sara, he is
5   truly a child of the law. But when he teaches, which rabbi's
6   arguments does he use to prove his points? There are many
7   traditions in our faith, and I'm curious to know which he
8   follows.

9 SARA: No rabbis, sir. Sometimes he quotes Moses or another
10   prophet, but then he says, "But *I* say to you ..."

11 NICODEMUS: No one's authority but his own? Remarkable.

12 SARA: He knows the sacred books, sir, and makes them burn
13   with life. And it's ... it's as if he sees God in every bird, and
14   every bush is aflame, like the one that spoke to Moses!

15 NICODEMUS: Really? He sounds almost intoxicated with God.

16 SARA: He *is* very close to God. Sir, every day you spend hours
17   studying the words of the law and all those commentaries.
18   And — I don't want to offend — you always seem to find
19   more questions than answers. Couldn't you go see him?
20   Maybe he has something — some answers — that you've
21   been looking for.

22 NICODEMUS: *(Smiles.)* Some of us have learned to enjoy living
23   with the questions, and to suspect easy answers. Too many
24   answers take the mystery out of life. I must admit I'd like
25   to see Jesus, but he has many powerful enemies. There are
26   those who see him as a blasphemer, taking for himself that
27   which is rightfully God's. Even Shaphan thinks so. And
28   others see him as a threat to the peace and order — a
29   popular rabble-rouser that could bring the Romans down
30   tighter on our necks than they already are. Even to let you
31   go see him involved some risk on my part.

32 SARA: Sir, if you want to see him, why not go at night?

33 NICODEMUS: Hmmm. A private meeting under the cloak of
34   darkness. Not a bad idea. I could satisfy my own curiosity,
35   and remain ... very well, I'll do it!

1 SARA: Wonderful!

2 NICODEMUS: Make the arrangements, Sara ... quietly. I will

3   visit him at the home where he's staying.

4 SARA: I believe he is with Lazarus, sir.

5 NICODEMUS: Splendid! A man of integrity and discretion! Late

6   tomorrow, just before the rising of the moon. Three brief

7   raps on the door will be the signal. *(The two are left quietly*

8   *conversing. NARRATOR starts forward to Down Center on words*

9   *"Late tomorrow.")*

10 NARRATOR: On a dark spring evening, two strangers met and

11   shared from their deepest souls. Two strangers, each called

12   "rabbi" by their respective followers. Nicodemus — open

13   yet cautious, a beloved scholar of the Torah, one of the

14   wisest members of the council. Jesus — loved and hated

15   with equal intensity, a wandering teacher with no authority

16   except that strange light of his countenance when he talked

17   about his Father; no home except for the homes of friends

18   and the open countryside. The wind blew fiercely that

19   night, presaging the hot, dry winds of summer. Its whistling

20   was an ever-present reminder of the breath of God that

21   once breathed life into lumps of clay. The wind covered the

22   quiet conversation of Jesus and Nicodemus, so secrecy was

23   preserved. But not completely. The next day at the well,

24   two old friends would compare notes. *(NICODEMUS moves*

25   *back to table. MARY joins SARA in the flashback area.)*

26 SARA: What a wind! I'm afraid a hot summer is coming. My

27   master was covered with dust when he came back from ...

28   his walk last night.

29 MARY: You needn't be coy, Sara. Lazarus and Martha stayed on

30   the roof to discuss matters of business. I stayed quietly

31   near the stairs — just in case Jesus and your master needed

32   something.

33 SARA: *(Filling an imaginary bucket, dipping in a scoop for a sip)* I

34   had a feeling you would remain close by. What I wouldn't

35   have given to be there.

1   MARY: And what I wouldn't give to know what your master
2   thinks of Jesus.
3   SARA: I wish I could tell you, Mary. My master is cautious about
4   showing his feelings, even at best. Today, he's ... pensive.
5   MARY: You don't think his questions were answered?
6   SARA: Nicodemus always likes to say he's more interested in
7   playing with the questions and exploring them to the fullest.
8   But now I think even *his* appetite for questions is sated.
9   MARY: Jesus often has that effect on people. They come away
10   thinking, "I've just been given a wonderful gift. But what is
11   it? What do I do with it?"
12 SARA: Tell me what was said last night, Mary.
13 MARY: I couldn't hear well because of the wind, but Jesus was
14   delighted to see Nicodemus. Your master is a fair man. So
15   many make up their minds about Jesus without listening to
16   him, except to find the means to condemn him.
17 SARA: Nicodemus detests that narrow spirit. He always tries to
18   hold his judgments — always tries to be fair — and
19   sometimes he waits longer than he should before he makes
20   a decision about somebody.
21 MARY: Jesus tried to call Nicodemus to that kind of decision.
22   Remember how Jesus always talks about having to be like
23   children to truly follow God? He was calling Nicodemus to
24   a new birth — a birth from above.
25 SARA: A man giving birth?
26 MARY: No, a man *being born* anew ... starting afresh as God's
27   child, receiving God's Spirit. Just then the wind outdoors
28   really started howling, and Jesus said God's Spirit was like
29   that wind. No one knows where it comes from, or where it
30   goes. No one can see it. No one can make it blow and no
31   one can make it stop. Only God.
32 SARA: I'm beginning to see why my master was confused. Jesus
33   seems to talk of so many things at once.
34 MARY: Jesus said God was going to lift *him* up, and those that
35   looked up to Jesus in faith would be saved.

1 SARA: He couldn't mean that literally, could he? Mustn't Jesus
2   mean when he's lifted up to a position of leadership over
3   Israel?
4 MARY: Now *you're* talking like a rabbi. I honestly don't know.
5   All I know is that God's Son was being sent to the world to
6   show how much God loves the world, not to condemn it —
7   that God's Son would lead us from darkness to light.
8 SARA: God's Son — the Messiah?
9 MARY: I think that's what Jesus meant.
10 SARA: Is Jesus saying the Messiah is coming soon?
11 MARY: Or maybe something more.
12 SARA: What do you mean by that?
13 MARY: I'm not sure I know. But in that dark room, on that dark
14   night, I *think* Jesus was telling your master, "Come out into
15   the light. You are a child of the light. Don't hide in darkness
16   from the love of God."
17 SARA: A grown man being born, the wind, light, darkness,
18   God's Son being lifted up, ahhh! My poor master! How will
19   he ever sort that out? *(Lights dim; music rises; MARY leaves*
20   *scene; SARA returns to table. Music fades.)*
21   *   *   *
22 GAIUS: You people speak a strange language. It all seems so
23   meaningless. But when you all get so excited about it, I
24   wonder: Is it some code? Was the Galilean inciting people
25   to riot?
26 SHAPHAN: That's what we were afraid of, sir. Like so many
27   others, this Jesus had delusions about being a king of light.
28   He wanted to be lifted up to power, like Caesar's power.
29 GAIUS: He *did* get lifted up, didn't he?! Lifted up to what he
30   deserved. He surveyed his kingdom from a cross. But what
31   I don't understand is, why didn't that settle matters?
32 NICODEMUS: You wanted to settle matters. You wanted neat
33   answers. Perhaps it is God who is keeping things so untidy.
34 SHAPHAN: Perhaps it's the devil!
35 GAIUS: Gods, devils, who cares! Until this matter is settled,

1   nobody is going to be at peace. And when nobody is at
2   peace, we enforce peace. More than one person may have
3   to die because of that silly, idealistic preacher.
4 SHAPHAN: And that's what we wanted to avoid by having this
5   disturber of the peace put to death!
6 NICODEMUS: Jesus didn't come to offer death at Roman
7   spearpoint. He wanted to offer life — God's life — for Jew
8   and Roman alike.
9 SHAPHAN: Nicodemus! Once you had a fine mind. Once your
10   judgment was respected by all. But now this Galilean has
11   deluded you with his crude and simple heresies. Remember
12   what kind of life it brought him. His life was choked from
13   him on the cross. He was accused by our law and
14   condemned. He died a humiliating, tortured death. And you
15   spout on about him being able to offer God's life and light.
16 NICODEMUS: And "so must the Son of Man be lifted up" *(John*
17   *3:14, RSV)*. Shaphan, have you ever, in the wildest stretch
18   of your imagination, considered that the one we left
19   dangling on the cross, weak, dying, humiliated, hanging
20   like a puppet on a string, may have been crowned by God
21   as a new kind of king? Maybe you and the Romans were the
22   puppets in that little play. Maybe all your petty fury and
23   self-righteousness, your demand for law and order, was
24   powerless before the power of God's self-giving love. You
25   thought you were condemning him, but you were really
26   condemning yourselves by showing your true colors. For all
27   your professed love of God, you hated God, because God
28   threatened your power with a greater one.
29 SHAPHAN: Power? You prattle on about power? What power
30   did you have to prevent those despised forces of law and
31   order to carry out its duty against this false messiah of
32   yours? When the council met to try him, you proved that
33   your voice was not worth listening to, that your judgment
34   was not worth respecting.
35 NICODEMUS: Because I thought the law does not allow us to

1 condemn a man without a fair hearing!
2 GAIUS: Council? Law? When was this? Fill me in, please.
3 SHAPHAN: It was last autumn, not long after the Feast of
4 Tabernacles. Jesus had not only continually violated the law —
5 GAIUS: The law of Rome?
6 SHAPHAN: Primarily our religious laws, my dear Gaius. But
7 when one teaches disrespect of any law, all law suffers.
8 GAIUS: True. Go on.
9 SHAPHAN: He was leading the crowds on. Many people were
10 being duped — primarily the poor, the ignorant, the
11 unlettered, the superstitious — but it is from such scum
12 that civil unrest and rebellion come.
13 NICODEMUS: You've said all that before, Shaphan, at that
14 council meeting and at the one in the spring which
15 condemned him. But I have never heard report of any
16 teachings of Jesus, any actions of Jesus, that would
17 indicate he was calling the people to arms.
18 SHAPHAN: His disruption of the temple services — not only was
19 that inciting to riot, it was denouncing everything that
20 is holy.
21 NICODEMUS: Some might call it a prophetic protest against
22 corruption.
23 SHAPHAN: And that sham parade on his entry into Jerusalem
24 — people waving palm fronds, crying out, "Help save us,
25 Son of David!" Is that not a political statement?
26 NICODEMUS: He came on a donkey, a symbol of peace and
27 humility, not on a war horse.
28 GAIUS: Peace! Peace! I was sent here by Caesar to bring peace
29 and to keep peace, by military means or diplomatic. *(GAIUS*
30 *rises, moves around in agitation.)* But what happens? I spend
31 my time listening to silly squabbles between religious
32 fanatics. It's enough to turn my brain to gruel. First you
33 talked about a council meeting last fall, and now you're
34 quibbling over events this spring!
35 SHAPHAN: But it's our common concern that the unrest about

1   this Jesus business be taken care of.

2 GAIUS: Yes, but I have one other concern. In three years I plan
3   to retire, and I don't want to spend all three here in this
4   room! Shaphan, what is it about last fall's council that we
5   *need* to know?

6 SHAPHAN: *(Subdued)* We met because the Galilean was a threat
7   to the peace as well as to the true religion.

8 GAIUS: Did you meet with Jesus, bring charges against him,
9   and hear his witness?

10 SHAPHAN: We tried. Temple officers went out with a summons.

11 GAIUS: He eluded them?

12 SHAPHAN: He beguiled them.

13 GAIUS: He talked his way out of arrest? Slick!

14 SHAPHAN: We were bringing charges against him in his absence
15   when Nicodemus stood up for him.

16 GAIUS: Like a character witness?

17 NICODEMUS: No, I said nothing about Jesus. I just reminded
18   my colleagues that they were about to break the very law
19   they had spent their lives upholding.

20 GAIUS: How do you mean?

21 NICODEMUS: In two separate places in our law, it is stated that
22   an accused man has the right to face his accusers and give
23   his side of the story.

24 SHAPHAN: But this is ridiculous! We had asked — no, tried to
25   compel — Jesus to be there! He didn't appear, so we had
26   every right to —

27 NICODEMUS: Condemn him without a hearing?

28 SHAPHAN: Put a dangerous rebel and heretic out of the way!
29   Such rabble doesn't deserve the protection of the law.

30 GAIUS: Let us not bicker. This hearing is to see if there is any
31   connection between Nicodemus and this Jesus movement.
32   One visit in the night and one oblique reference to fairness
33   at a preliminary hearing would hardly indicate anything
34   suspicious to me.

35 SHAPHAN: Indeed, we had few suspicions of Nicodemus

1   **ourselves at that point. Errors in judgment, perhaps, but**
2   **little more. Near the end of the rainy season, though, the**
3   **situation became more tense. It began with the alleged**
4   **raising from the dead of one of the Galilean's local friends**
5   **and supporters — a friend of Nicodemus as well.** *(Music*
6   *rises, lights dim as MARY and SARA go to flashback area. Music*
7   *ends, lights raise.)*
8   *   *   *
9   SARA: Mary, why that look on your face? I thought the time for
10   sad faces had ended. Is the preparation for Passover
11   wearing you out?
12 MARY: Sara, you're such a good friend. I can never hide my
13   feelings from you.
14 SARA: I wouldn't blame you for being exhausted ... taking care
15   of your brother Lazarus when he was so sick, your grief
16   when he died ...
17 MARY: And my thunderstruck joy when Jesus bid him to come
18   out of the tomb, alive and well. From one extreme of
19   emotion to another, and all so soon! And now I'm
20   concerned for Jesus because of what the council might do.
21 SARA: Yes. Nicodemus tried again to call the council to fairness,
22   but he and Joseph of Arimathea and a few others were the
23   only ones present who felt Jesus might be a messenger
24   from God, one who should be listened to.
25 MARY: Did they speak out?
26 SARA: My master again tried to be sure that correct legal
27   procedures were followed, but he and the others didn't
28   speak out directly. They knew it was futile, that those who
29   lead the council had already made up their minds.
30 MARY: To condemn Jesus?
31 SARA: I'm afraid so. Too many members of the council were
32   afraid that Jesus would stir up so much political unrest that
33   the Romans would march in and destroy everything.
34   Caiaphas told them the answer was simple: "You do not
35   realize that it is better for you that one man die for the

1   **people than that the whole nation perish"** *(John 11:50).*
2   **MARY: Then death it will be. I've been obsessed with a sense of**
3   **doom whenever I see Jesus. Something terrible is going to**
4   **happen.**
5   **SARA: You think Jesus is to die, then?**
6   **MARY: I helped prepare him for his burial last night.**
7   **SARA: What?**
8   **MARY: They were at dinner — Jesus and the twelve, along with**
9   **Lazarus and a few others. Martha was serving. My feeling**
10   **about Jesus dying grew so strong that I felt I had to do**
11   **something to ...**
12 **SARA: To what?**
13 **MARY: To show Jesus, before he died, how we honor him —**
14   **how he is the most important thing in our lives.**
15 **SARA: How did you show him that?**
16 **MARY: I had purchased a whole pound of nard — top quality**
17   **ointment. We could ill afford it, but there it was.**
18 **SARA: I can only imagine what it cost. My master has been**
19   **purchasing ointments to honor several of his aging relatives**
20   **when they die.**
21 **MARY:** *(Rushes.)* **I took the ointment, ran to Jesus, rubbed it on**
22   **his feet, unwrapped my hair —**
23 **SARA:** *(Shocked)* **Mary! In front of men?**
24 **MARY: In front of my Savior. At my Savior's feet.** *(Catches*
25   *breath.)* **And I wiped his feet with my hair.**
26 **SARA: It was a foolish thing to do, but a wonderful thing. But**
27   **what did people think?**
28 **MARY: I was so caught up in devotion and grief, my eyes were**
29   **so filled with tears, I scarcely noticed. But I heard Judas**
30   **shouting, "Why wasn't this perfume sold and the money**
31   **given to the poor?"** *(John 12:5).*
32 **SARA: How did Jesus react? He loves the poor. Was he angry, too?**
33 **MARY: No, his face was filled with sadness. "Leave her alone,"**
34   **he said. "It was intended that she should save this perfume**
35   **for the day of my burial. You will always have the poor**

1   **among you, but you will not always have me"** *(John 12: 7,8).*
2   *(Music and light cue to draw attention back to the table as the*
3   *two women retreat.)*
4   *   *   *
5   **SHAPHAN:** *(As if concluding long speech)* **And so we carried out**
6   **the execution, and prepared to dispose of the remains in a**
7   **pauper's grave. But interestingly enough, two members of**
8   **the council went to see the governor.** *(Again, music and light*
9   *cue as GAIUS and NICODEMUS move to flashback area.)*
10   *   *   *
11   **GAIUS:** *(Facing NICODEMUS as if barring entrance to the door)*
12   **What may I tell Governor Pilate you want?**
13   **NICODEMUS:**   **Joseph of Arimathea** *(Indicates presence of*
14   *"companion")* **and I wish to ask permission to dispose of the**
15   **remains of one of the people executed today.**
16   **GAIUS:**   **You want a criminal's corpse? An odd pair of**
17   **undertakers you are!**
18   **NICODEMUS: We're not undertakers. We're ... friends of the**
19   **deceased.**
20   **GAIUS: And who might that be?**
21   **NICODEMUS: Jesus ... Jesus of Nazareth.**
22   **GAIUS: That preacher-type from up north? You're his friends?**
23   **You look more like members of the council that put him**
24   **away** *(Eyes their clothing)* **... and rich ones at that!**
25   **NICODEMUS: We are members of the council.**
26   **GAIUS: But the council said it wanted to have his body put in**
27   **the trench with those of the other criminals.**
28   **NICODEMUS: This is a ... personal matter.**
29   **GAIUS:** *(Suspiciously)* **And what are you going to do with the**
30   **body? I am the attaché for state security, and you're talking**
31   **about the body of one accused of politically sensitive crimes.**
32   **NICODEMUS: We are going to give a decent man a decent**
33   **burial. Joseph has offered his own rock-cut tomb. I have**
34   **the spices, ointments, and grave clothes for proper burial.**
35   **GAIUS: This Jesus gets stripped of all human dignity, and you,**

1   **members of the council that condemned him, want to bury**
2   **him with honor? I'll never understand you people.** *(Shakes*
3   *head.)* **Go ahead. See the governor.** *(Music and light cues*
4   *again, as NICODEMUS and GAIUS move back to the table.)*
5   *   *   *
6 GAIUS: *That's* where I've seen you before! I've been wondering
7   all day. Must be slipping, to forget an encounter like that.
8   Of course, it *had* been a long day, and I *did* have a bit of
9   a hangover.
10 SHAPHAN: And *that's* where our suspicions lie, Gaius. Do you
11   realize how they pulled the wool over your eyes?
12 GAIUS: What do you mean? It was an innocent enough request.
13   A bit peculiar maybe, but innocent.
14 SHAPHAN: Think! Joseph's rock-cut tomb was his pride and
15   joy. Not only that, but it was in the valley where we once
16   buried our kings. And the materials to prepare the body for
17   burial that Nicodemus kindly supplied? We know with
18   authority that he brought nearly a hundred pounds of the
19   most expensive spices and ointments — from Arabia,
20   maybe even India!
21 GAIUS: So?
22 SHAPHAN: Who gets that kind of burial, Gaius?
23 GAIUS: A governor, a princeling, maybe?
24 SHAPHAN: No, Gaius, a king — they gave an accursed criminal
25   a burial fit only for a king.
26 GAIUS: But why? It makes no sense. Would they have done it
27   out of spite, to make the council look foolish?
28 SHAPHAN: Maybe. But I wonder. Suppose they gave Jesus a
29   royal burial and showed us quite clearly where their
30   sentiments lie. But suppose they also bribed the guards —
31   they're the only followers of the Nazarene who would have
32   had enough money and power to do it — and stole the body
33   themselves?
34 NICODEMUS: That's preposterous. Why would we have done that?
35 GAIUS: Why? Yes, why? It doesn't make sense.

1 SHAPHAN: Don't you see? Those superstitious disciples would
2   believe — indeed, they say they *do* believe — that Jesus
3   rose from the dead. What if Nicodemus and Joseph, with all
4   the honor they showed Jesus after it was too late to really
5   *help* him any, were to say, "God rose Jesus from the dead.
6   Now Jesus wants us to be your new leaders. Overthrow the
7   temple priests. Overthrow the Romans! *We* are going to
8   inaugurate God's rule."
9 GAIUS: Could it be?
10 NICODEMUS: No, it couldn't. Shaphan, your imaginings are
11   distorted by your own lust for power. You want control and
12   power, so you imagined Jesus did, too. Now you imagine
13   that is our motivation. If it were, would we not have been
14   busy behind the scenes, working feverishly to consolidate
15   our power? Wouldn't we have made our move by now?
16 SHAPHAN: How dare you call it imaginings? How dare you try
17   to analyze my motives? You're on trial here, not me. My
18   theory fits the evidence — I believe you are part of a
19   conspiracy.
20 NICODEMUS: Your evidence fits your theory, perhaps — if your
21   mind invents evidence as well as it does theories. No, since
22   the death of Jesus, all of my actions have been in the
23   daylight. I have nothing to hide. Credible witnesses can
24   vouch for the both of us, and I am sure you will see that we
25   are not conspirators.
26 SHAPHAN: We will investigate that, you can be sure of it. But
27   you do not deny giving Jesus a king's burial?
28 NICODEMUS: Call it that, if you will. The human race has a long
29   history of honoring its prophets after they have killed them.
30   I only wish I could have given him more honor before.
31 GAIUS: You are a follower of Jesus, then?
32 NICODEMUS: It's hard for me to say. I respected him. I grew to
33   trust him. I could even see God in him, more than in any
34   other man I have ever known.
35 SHAPHAN: But surely you don't believe his claim to be God's Son?

1   **NICODEMUS:** I know of no other who could better make the claim.
2   **SHAPHAN:** You are writing your own ticket for expulsion from
3   the council — for public disgrace — possibly for death as a
4   blasphemer. I thought you were my friend at one time — a
5   bit too open to innovative ideas, but still my friend. I hardly
6   knew you though, did I?
7   **NICODEMUS:** You knew me, Shaphan. but you didn't allow for
8   growth; for change. God made someone new of me.
9   **SHAPHAN:** It must mean everything to you — for you are on the
10   verge of giving up everything for this so-called "Light of the
11   World."
12 **NICODEMUS:** A funny thing about that light ... I first met it in
13   darkness. That light showed me the light of God's love and
14   drew me to itself. I was fascinated with it, like a moth
15   fascinated by the flame of a lamp.
16 **SHAPHAN:** Moths often die when they get too close to the flame.
17 **NICODEMUS:** Maybe. Maybe the light will consume me. But if
18   it does, it doesn't matter. I will be a part of it.
19 **GAIUS:** It's become clear where you stand. I don't know much
20   about your beliefs. I don't know if we'll have to treat you as
21   an enemy of the state. But I must admit, you have courage.
22   Just like that one who died out there a few days back. One
23   question, though: When you heard that the body was
24   missing, when you heard the rumor from the disciples, what
25   did you do? How did you react?
26 **NICODEMUS:** Sara can answer that. She carried the news to me.
27 **GAIUS:** Sara, come over here. *(She comes.)* You heard the question.
28 **SARA:** Sir, I don't know how to say it. His reaction surprised me.
29 **SHAPHAN:** Why? What did he do?
30 **SARA:** He sat down on the step and cried. He cried and cried.
31 **SHAPHAN:** *(Thoroughly puzzled)* He was upset?
32 **NICODEMUS:** No, friend. I cried for joy. I cried like a baby — like
33   a newborn baby. Like a baby taking its first breath of life.
34 **NARRATOR:** The wind and the Spirit blow where they will. And
35   where the Spirit blows, new life is born. No one knows what

happened to Nicodemus. Maybe he was one of the early church's martyrs. Maybe he became one of the young church's respected leaders. Only one thing is for sure: He came out of the darkness and into the light. He became a part of the light that God sent into the world — a light all the forces of darkness can never extinguish.

It Is Finished

A dramatic sketch for Lent in six segments
by LeRoy Koopman

CAST

Speaking Parts:

Narrator (voice)
Jesus (voice)
Scribe
Pharisee
Disciple 1
Disciple 2
Disciple 3
Pontius Pilate
Claudia (voice)
Soldier 1
Soldier 2
Soldier 3
Soldier 4
Spectator
Scripture Reader (voice)

Crowd:

John
Mary, Mother of Jesus
Mary Magdalene
Mary, Wife of Clopas
Women
Townspeople

PRODUCTION NOTES

Overview: A dramatic interpretation of the Crucifixion for Lenten season presentation. In six segments the responses of witnesses are revealed, each with a separate interpretation: a scribe and a Pharisee, three disciples, four soldiers, Pilate and Claudia, and a spectator. The last segment recaps all the roles. Written in blank verse.

Set: Scenery is not essential to the production; a bare stage will do.

Props: Towel and wash basin on stand for Pilate, mallets, robe, bowl, and stick with sponge for Soldiers.

Lights: Although special lighting is not crucial to the script, if you have access to theatrical lighting, spotlights are highly desirable since the stage is to be dimly lit.

Costumes: The characters should wear biblical garb; however, the costumes may be as simple or elaborate as desired.

Sound Effects: Thunder, concluding music.

Playing Time: 30-40 minutes.

1 **SEGMENT ONE**
2 *(The opening reveals the entire cast, with the exception of*
3 *PILATE, CLAUDIA, NARRATOR, and SCRIPTURE READER.*
4 *They are sitting, standing, and kneeling, focusing their attention*
5 *on the crosses, presumably Off-Stage to the left. There is a ripple*
6 *of movement among them, and there is the low sound of*
7 *intermingled voices and sobbing. JOHN is comforting the three*
8 *WOMEN on the far left, near the cross. The SOLDIERS are*
9 *beside the cross. The PHARISEES and SCRIBES are in the*
10 *crowd. They are somewhat more noisy than the rest. The*
11 *DISCIPLES are on the fringe, some of them partially covering*
12 *their faces. When the NARRATOR begins speaking over the*
13 *public address system, the crowd noise fades. It is very dark.)*
14 **NARRATOR:** Except for the occasional thrashings and dry-
15 throated groans of the two coarse men on the end crosses,
16 there has been near silence on Golgotha for three hours. A
17 deep darkness has shrouded the hill since high noon, and
18 the blackness sinks into the very soul. Even the shouters
19 and the catcallers have lost their gusto.
20 It is nearly three o'clock in the afternoon. An eternal six
21 hours have elapsed since the blood first spurted from the
22 spike-holes in their wrists and feet. The spectators who are
23 experts in this sort of thing estimate that the men have
24 twenty hours yet to writhe between heaven and earth.
25 Most who suffer crucifixion have screamed away their
26 voices by now. One of today's victims has been different.
27 There were a few quiet words at first — to someone he
28 addressed as "Father" above him, to the thief beside him, and
29 to his mother below him. Since then there has been silence.
30 Then, without warning, the dark air is shattered by a full-
31 throated bellow.
32 **JESUS:** *(Voice from Off-Stage Left)* **My God, my God, why have you**
33 **forsaken me?** *(Matt. 27:46)* *(There is a pause; the crowd*
34 *shudders.)* **I am thirsty** *(John 19:28)*. *(The SOLDIERS dip a*
35 *sponge into a bowl, place it on a stick, and hold it up, as to his*

1   *mouth. There is silence for a moment.)* **It is finished** *(John 19:30).*
2   **Father, into your hands, I commit my spirit** *(Luke 23:46).*
3   NARRATOR: **His head wobbles to the side and his lungs stop**
4   **their spastic heaving. It is all over now. It is finished.** *(As if*
5   *making a public announcement)* **You can go home now, folks.**
6   **The show is over. Maybe we'll have a few more for you next**
7   **week.** *(A few begin to walk slowly away from the crowd. Thunder*
8   *sounds, and the people seem to have difficulty maintaining their*
9   *balance, grabbing each other. There is silence and the lights come*
10   *up.)* **What was it, do you think? An earthquake? Some kind**
11   **of sign from heaven? But it is over now. It was nothing,**
12   **perhaps. Again there is calm beneath your feet. The sun**
13   **shines warm and clear.**
14   **It is a rather pleasant day after all — now that it is**
15   **finished.**
16   **"It is finished," the man on the cross said. A mysterious**
17   **phrase. And a popular one, too, for it is mouthed by many**
18   **who are leaving the hill. Take those two clerics there ...**
19
20   SEGMENT TWO
21   *(Spot on the SCRIBE and the PHARISEES)*
22   NARRATOR: **"It is finished,"**
23   **Say the Scribe and Pharisee, holy men**
24   **Who daily pray and tithe.**
25   SCRIBE: **It is finished.**
26   **At last the Galilean dog is dead.**
27   PHARISEE: *(Taunting Jesus)* **King of the Jews!**
28   **Where are your subjects and your kingdom now,**
29   **O Monarch of the Dead?**
30   SCRIBE: **One so bold to name the Keepers of the Law**
31   **As "Whited Sepulchres" and "Broods of Vipers"**
32   **Deserves no more in his mouth than vinegar**
33   **To slake his foul tongue.**
34   PHARISEE: **Whatever was his magic power to heal**
35   **A withered hand on the Sabbath Day**

1   Could surely have been used at any other time!

2 SCRIBE: And how can one believe in God

3   And yet not purify one's cups and plates?

4 PHARISEE: Surely God was pleased to see

5   The deathly groans of one who dared

6   To claim equality with his own stern self.

7 SCRIBE: 'Twas blasphemy! No man of rational religion

8   Could think him but the son of Joseph,

9   The carpenter of Nazareth!

10 PHARISEE: *(Almost to himself, his doubts coming to the surface)*

11   What drew the multitudes to hear him speak?

12 SCRIBE: Perverted curiosity to see some wonder done.

13 PHARISEE: Whatever was the power for such strange deeds?

14   *(Pause)* He did make claim to rise again.

15 SCRIBE: *(Irritated)* Impossible, of course! But just the same,

16   We'll ask that soldiers guard the rotting corpse.

17 PHARISEE: *(Recovering from his doubts, shrugging)*

18   It is finished, once for all!

19   We'll never hear again of Jesus,

20   Son of Joseph, of Nazareth in Galilee.

21 SCRIBE: From whence no good thing has yet come!

22 PHARISEE: Back now to the corner of the street —

23   The time for prayer is nearly here!

24 NARRATOR: "It is finished,"

25   Say the Scribe and Pharisee, holy men

26   Who daily pray and tithe.

27

28 **SEGMENT THREE**

29   *(As the SCRIBE and PHARISEE move away, a group of three*

30   *DISCIPLES extricate themselves from the crowd and move*

31   *Downstage Center. They are dazed and confused. Each man is*

32   *preoccupied with his own thoughts, hardly listening to the others.)*

33 NARRATOR: "It is finished,"

34   Say the disciples,

35   Cringing at the fringe of the melting mob.

1   DISCIPLE 1: We thought he was Messiah, King,
2   Long-prophesied to Israel,
3   But now it is finished.
4   DISCIPLE 2: *(Bitterly)* It is from a throne one reigns,
5   Not from a cross with a crown of thorns!
6   DISCIPLE 3: What was he, then?
7   A sorcerer?
8   DISCIPLE 2: But by what magic are the dead raised up?
9   And blind men see and lepers cleansed?
10 DISCIPLE 1: At Nazareth they dared not touch him,
11   But at Olivet he stood, intent to die.
12   He who had such power over others' death
13   Was helpless at his own.
14 DISCIPLE 3: It is finished. A pleasant dream awaked,
15   A vision gone, hope drowned in dark despair.
16 DISCIPLE 2: When the shepherd's gone
17   The sheep are scattered far.
18 DISCIPLE 1: Back to the boats?
19 DISCIPLE 2: The seat of custom?
20 DISCIPLE 1: It's hard to say.
21 DISCIPLE 3: Things are so uncertain now.
22 DISCIPLE 2: He said he'd rise again —
23 DISCIPLE 1: No — no. Do not even mention that.
24   Let us not plague ourselves
25   With more false hope.
26 DISCIPLE 2: But just the same, we won't stray far.
27   Let's meet together in the upper room,
28   As formerly our custom was, the third day hence,
29   And speak again together of these things. *(DISCIPLES exit.)*
30 NARRATOR: "It is finished"
31   Say the disciples,
32   Cringing at the fringe of the melting mob.
33
34
35

1 **SEGMENT FOUR**
2 *(A few more of the people in the crowd leave. The spotlights go*
3 *to PONTIUS PILATE, who is standing to the front and side of the*
4 *stage. A bowl of water is on the stand in front of him, and he is*
5 *washing his hands and arms.)*
6 **NARRATOR:** **"It is finished"**
7 **Says Pontius Pilate,**
8 **Washer of his hands.**
9 **PILATE:** **It is finished.**
10 **My hands are washed of this man's blood.**
11 **Now back to state affairs of more importance.**
12 **A hundred uniforms must be asked of Rome,**
13 **And tax collections have been lagging.**
14 **These Jews are pains in any Roman neck!**
15 *(Pauses. CLAUDIA sobs Off-stage, behind him.)*
16 **Claudia, stop that female blabbering!**
17 **Those silly dreams of yours**
18 **Are just hallucinations; the gods don't speak.**
19 **CLAUDIA:** *(Weeping, Off-stage)* **He was innocent, Pontius;**
20 **He was a good man, that man from Nazareth!**
21 **PILATE:** **Yes, I know he did no crime deserving death.**
22 *(To himself)* **But it's not the first time or the**
23 **Last that the ends have justified the means.**
24 **Jerusalem's my stepping stone to higher things.**
25 *(Finishing his washing with a flourish)*
26 **Now it's finished. A week or two will pass.**
27 **And they'll forget he ever lived or died.**
28 **No doubt another will appoint himself as king**
29 **Or prophet or messiah, and try to teach.**
30 *(Flings towel over his shoulder.)*
31 **I hope he has the sense to stay in Galilee.** *(PILATE exits.)*
32 **NARRATOR:** **"It is finished"**
33 **Says Pontius Pilate,**
34 **Washer of his hands.**
35

1 **SEGMENT FIVE**

2 *(Now the last of the crowd at the cross leaves, including the*

3 *WOMEN and JOHN. Only the SOLDIERS are left, some sitting,*

4 *some standing.)*

5 **NARRATOR:** **"It is finished"**

6 **Say the strong men,**

7 **Skilled with swords and mallets,**

8 **Obedient to their commands.**

9 **SOLDIER 1:** *(Looking at the cross)* **It is finished.**

10 **Now if the others too will die**

11 **We can all go back to wash this crusted blood**

12 **And eat a good, warm meal.**

13 **SOLDIER 2:** **This one went fast!**

14 **Remember the murderer we nailed**

15 **Last month at Philippi?**

16 **He wiggled up there three days**

17 **Until we finally broke his legs.**

18 **SOLDIER 3:** *(Displaying Christ's robe with a flourish)*

19 **Yes, it is finished;**

20 **The Galilean's robe is now my own.**

21 **It's cheaply made and worn to the thread,**

22 **But it will do me well when sitting at my wine.**

23 **SOLDIER 4:** *(Stands by himself, looking at the cross.)*

24 **I had hoped the one he called Elias**

25 **Would yet come and take him down —**

26 **Or even that the Galilean**

27 **Might reveal himself to be a god,**

28 **As some have said he is.**

29 *(To the cross)* **Whoever you are, you'll leave memories**

30 **To creep back and haunt my nights.**

31 **A mouth that said no oaths**

32 **While we were driving in the spikes,**

33 **But prayed forgiveness for us all.**

34 **SOLDIER 2:** **What are you, man?**

35 **A soldier trained to kill, or a weepy woman?**

1   **SOLDIER 3: If so unhappy with this job,**

2   **Why not run home to Rome**

3   **And nurse the baby with your wife?** *(All laugh.)*

4   **SOLDIER 4: But he did no wrong!**

5   **You said yourself that Pilate said,**

6   **"I find no fault" —**

7   **SOLDIER 1: Shut your stupid mouth!**

8   **You ought to know by now**

9   **A soldier never questions orders.**

10   *(Pauses, looks at the cross and back again.)*

11   **Besides, we're finished with him now,**

12   **So let's return and tell them he is dead.** *(SOLDIERS exit.)*

13 **NARRATOR: "It is finished"**

14   **Say the strong men,**

15   **Skilled with swords and mallets,**

16   **Obedient to their commands.** *(Curtain begins to close.)*

17   **Stop! Stop the curtain! Just a moment, please.**

18   *(Curtain opens again.)*

19

20 **SEGMENT SIX**

21 **NARRATOR:** *(Calling)* **Soldiers! Soldiers! Will you come back for**

22   **a moment?** *(They appear again, hesitantly, On-stage.)*

23   **You who are so efficiently obedient to the orders of your**

24   **superiors — can you pause a moment before you go to**

25   **wash up, to hear exactly what it is you have finished?** *(They*

26   *shrug and come forward. NARRATOR calls.)* **Pontius Pilate!** *(He*

27   *appears.)* **You who are so quick to excuse yourself from all**

28   **responsibility — do you suppose those uniforms can wait**

29   **for a few more moments? More is finished than you think.**

30   *(He comes forward slowly. NARRATOR calls.)* **Disciples! May I**

31   **have the disciples, please?** *(They enter.)* **You who are so**

32   **quick to give up and to forget the promises of one you**

33   **worshiped — the fish will still be there tomorrow. Now I**

34   **want you to hear what is really finished.** *(They advance.*

35   *NARRATOR calls.)* **Scribe! Pharisee! Will you please return**

1   **to the place of your late triumph?** *(There is a pause.)*

2 **SPECTATOR:** *(Takes a few steps On-stage.)* **They are busy praying,**

3   **sir, but will be here in a minute.** *(They finally come, hands still*

4   *folded.)*

5 **NARRATOR:** Scribes and Pharisees — you who are so busy with

6   your religion — can you spare a few moments from your

7   holy acts to find out what was really finished today? *(They*

8   *step forward. NARRATOR calls.)* **Observers at the cross!**

9   **John! Mary, the Mother of Jesus! Mary Magdalene! Mary,**

10   **wife of Clopas! Townspeople! Whether you came today to**

11   **mourn or to jeer, can you linger here just a while longer?**

12   *(They come.)* **And to the members of this audience, who have**

13   **gathered in this place, before an empty bloody tree in early**

14   **spring, do you suppose you can take a few more minutes**

15   **before you return to your homes, your TV sets, and your**

16   **beds? If so, then please rise, stand up on your feet, and**

17   **hear what it is that is finished.** *(Audience rises. Members of*

18   *the cast again turn to gaze at the cross, Off-stage Left.*

19   *NARRATOR'S speeches are loud and bold.)* **Finished, O Man, is**

20   **the Savior's earthly life.**

21 **READER:** "And being found in human form he humbled himself

22   and became obedient unto death, even death on a cross"

23   *(Phil. 2:8)*.

24 **NARRATOR:** Finished, O Man, is the Savior's earthly work.

25 **READER:** "I glorified thee on earth, having accomplished the

26   work which thou gavest me to do *(John 17:4)*.

27 **NARRATOR:** Finished, O Man, is your sin and guilt.

28 **READER:** "He himself bore our sins in his body on the tree, that

29   we might die to sin and live to righteousness. By his

30   wounds you have been healed" *(1 Peter 2:24)*.

31 **NARRATOR:** Finished, O Man, is your spiritual death.

32 **READER:** "And you he made alive, when you were dead through the

33   trespasses and sins in which you once walked" *(Eph. 2:1,2a)*.

34 **NARRATOR:** Finished, O Man, is your condemnation.

35 **READER:** "There is therefore now no condemnation for those

1   **who are in Christ Jesus"** *(Rom. 8:1).*

2 **NARRATOR: Finished, O Man, is your lostness.**

3 **READER: "But to all who received him, who believed in his name,**

4   **he gave power to become children of God"** *(John 1:12).*

5 **NARRATOR: Finished, O Man, is your old life.**

6 **READER: "Therefore, if anyone is in Christ, he is a new**

7   **creation; the old has passed away, behold, the new has**

8   **come"** *(2 Cor. 5:17).*

9 **NARRATOR: Finished, O Man, is your troubled soul.**

10 **READER: "Let not your hearts be troubled; believe in God,**

11   **believe also in me. In my Father's house are many rooms;**

12   **if it were not so, would I have told you that I go to prepare**

13   **a place for you?"** *(John 14:1,2).*

14 **NARRATOR: Finished, O Man, is your eternal death.**

15 **READER: "O death, where is thy victory? O death, where is thy**

16   **sting? Thanks be to God, who gives us the victory through**

17   **our Lord Jesus Christ"** *(1 Cor. 15:55,57).*

18   *(The drama may conclude with an appropriate musical number*

19   *— by the organ, chorus, recording, or congregation. Especially*

20   *appropriate are "Crown Him with Many Crowns" or "The*

21   *Hallelujah Chorus" from Handel's* Messiah.)

22

23

24

25

26

27

28

29

30

31

32

33

34

35

Resurrection on Trial

A jury trial for the entire congregation
by Linda M. Goens

CAST

Judge
Prosecutor
Jury (the congregation)

Witnesses:
Peter
Joseph of Arimathea
Paul
Petronius
Ananias

World Lee Wise
Legion

FLASHBACK CAST
(additional characters)

First Flashback:
Maid 1
Maid 2
Man

Second Flashback:
Pilate
Centurion

Third Flashback:
High Priest

PRODUCTION NOTES

Overview: "Ladies and gentlemen ... you have been summoned to jury duty to determine whether the 'Christian Church' is guilty of misrepresentation. The prosecution has assembled six witnesses to prove that the supposed resurrection of Jesus of Nazareth some 2,000 years ago is a fraud perpetrated on the public." This play is a modern-day jury trial with an open ending to be decided by the church congregation, which serves as the final jury. Church members hear the testimonies of key witnesses, and they see the key events in dramatized flashbacks. This Lenten season presentation encourages total audience involvement.

Flashbacks: Everyone in your audience has seen flashbacks before, in movies, on TV, and in books. The flashbacks in this script are dealt with the same as in any of the above storytelling media. They are a reliving or a restaging of the event mentioned in the lead-in story. A flashback is like a recollection of something that has gone before. In this script, we use actors off to the side or on a stage apron to re-create the scene from the past. Or, as an alternative, you may pre-record on audio tape a voice dramatization of the scene. The tape may be played at the appropriate time.

Of the two alternatives, we suggest the live re-enactment of the flashback. A fading of the lights or a brief passage of music will assist the audience in making the imaginative readjustment to another time or place.

There are three flashbacks in this script. The lead-ins and lead-outs are indicated, along with the actors needed.

Set: The courtroom may be established by a bench for the Judge at Center Stage (a desk or table and chair may be used), a chair to the right of the Judge for the Witnesses, and a lectern or table and chair placed to the left of the Judge for the Prosecutor.

Props: Bible for Judge, letter for Prosecutor, note for Legion.

Costumes: The characters could wear either biblical or contemporary garb. The Judge should wear a black robe. World Lee Wise should wear glasses and a suit and tie. A cane is optional. Legion wears a long robe. Her face is painted half-black and half-white.

Sound Effects: Heavy footsteps and clanking mail, or flexible armor composed of small, overlapping metal rings, loops of chain, or scales, such as characterized Roman soldiers' uniforms. (Rhythmic footsteps, then troop snapping to attention just before Centurion's entrance.)

Playing Time: Up to 45 minutes.

1   *(The JUDGE sits at his bench. The PROSECUTOR walks back*
2   *and forth in front of the congregation or audience as if they*
3   *constituted the jury. In fact, they do.)*
4   **JUDGE:** *(To the jury)* **You have been summoned to jury duty to**
5   **determine whether or not Jesus of Nazareth arose from the**
6   **dead two thousand years ago as the Christian church**
7   **claims. During this trial, in which the people are accusing**
8   **the church of fraud, you will hear the testimony of a**
9   **number of witnesses. You are instructed not to discuss the**
10   **testimony or evidence with one another until the trial has**
11   **ended. It is requested that you abide by proper decorum by**
12   **standing when the judge enters the courtroom.**
13   **PROSECUTOR:**   **Ladies and gentlemen of the jury, the**
14   **prosecution is here today to charge the Christian church**
15   **with fraud and misrepresentation. The Christian church**
16   **teaches that Jesus of Nazareth is the Son of God. The**
17   **whole basis for this teaching relies on a supposed**
18   **resurrection of a man some two thousand years ago. In**
19   **order to challenge this, the prosecution has assembled six**
20   **witnesses who either claim to have seen this risen Jesus or**
21   **to have been closely associated with him before his**
22   **crucifixion. In addition to these eyewitnesses, the**
23   **prosecution will produce an expert witness to show how**
24   **these observations have logical and reasonable**
25   **explanations other than the resurrection of a dead man.**
26   **Once you have heard the testimony of these six witnesses,**
27   **I will have proved the teachings of this church are nothing**
28   **more than a clear case of misrepresentation and fraud**
29   **perpetrated on the public.**
30   **JUDGE: You may proceed.**
31   **PROSECUTOR: I call the first witness, Simon Peter.** *(PETER*
32   *takes stand.)*
33   **JUDGE: Do you swear to tell the truth, the whole truth, and**
34   **nothing but the truth, so help you God?**
35   **PETER:** *(Hand on Bible)* **I do.**

1   **JUDGE: You may be seated.** *(PETER sits.)*
2   **PROSECUTOR: Peter, would you explain your relationship to**
3   **Jesus before his death?**
4   **PETER: I was one of his disciples. It was I who Jesus chose to**
5   **be the founder of his church.**
6   **PROSECUTOR: Would you tell the court, please, what makes**
7   **you believe Jesus was resurrected?**
8   **PETER:** *(Smiling slightly)* **I had it on the best authority in the**
9   **world; Jesus himself told us that he would die on the cross**
10   **and return three days later. I was also present in the**
11   **courtyard of the high priest, Caiaphas, when Jesus**
12   **admitted to the authorities that this was so.**
13   **PROSECUTOR: Jesus told you he was the Son of God and would**
14   **be resurrected from the dead, yet you denied even knowing**
15   **him in that very courtyard you mention. Isn't that true?**
16
17   **FIRST FLASHBACK**
18   *(PETER drops head, lights dim, tape recorder plays flashback*
19   *scene or flashback scene can actually be performed on stage*
20   *apron. If live, MAID 1, MAID 2, and MAN join PETER On-stage.)*
21   **MAID 1: You! You were with Jesus, the Galilean, weren't you?**
22   *(PETER looks at speaker, drops head, remains silent.)* **Weren't**
23   **you with him?**
24   **PETER: I don't know what you mean.**
25   **MAID 2: Yes, I saw you, too.** *(MAID 2 turns to bystanders.)* **This**
26   **man was with Jesus of Nazareth.**
27   **PETER: I don't know what you are talking about. I don't know**
28   **this man, Jesus.**
29   **MAN: I know for certain you were one of his followers: there is**
30   **no question about it.**
31   **PETER: For the last time, may my soul be damned if I ever**
32   **spoke with the man Jesus!** *(Lights up; PETER goes back to*
33   *stand. Flashback over.)*
34
35

1 PROSECUTOR: Answer the question, please.

2 PETER: Yes, I denied him. I was frightened, a coward; I admit that.

3 PROSECUTOR: Isn't that rather strange behavior? You believe
4   that Jesus is the Son of God, the true Savior of humanity,
5   yet you haven't sufficient courage to stand by him in his
6   hour of need. You must have had very little real faith.

7 PETER: I did believe in him. But the hostile crowd surrounded
8   me. I was afraid if anyone knew how closely we associated,
9   the soldiers would arrest me, too.

10 PROSECUTOR: And you didn't feel this Son of God, this miracle
11   worker, would save you from prosecution?

12 PETER: Of course he could, but he ...

13 PROSECUTOR: But he made no effort to save himself, so you
14   figured he most certainly wouldn't bother to save you, is
15   that not so?

16 PETER: It wasn't like that. He knew he had to die.

17 PROSECUTOR: *(Stares silently at PETER for a moment.)* **All right,**
18   Peter; let's leave the scene of your denial for a moment.
19   Why don't you tell us exactly what *did* happen after Jesus
20   died on the cross?

21 PETER: After his death, we were all terribly depressed. We had
22   loved him so much. For three solid years, we spent
23   practically every moment with him, listening to him,
24   learning from him. We gave up our whole lives to follow
25   him. And then he was dead. We were utterly demoralized
26   and lost in grief. We didn't know where to go or what to do
27   except to hide, since the Jewish authorities considered us a
28   dangerous threat.

29 PROSECUTOR: Peter, you'll pardon me if I have some difficulty
30   understanding this situation. I presume the "we" you talk
31   about includes James, John, Thomas, and all the rest. Now,
32   you all claim to have loved and trusted this man. You said
33   that you listened when he spoke and learned. Now, Jesus
34   told you that he would rise from the dead; therefore, if you
35   did, indeed, listen to him, why would you mourn his death?

1   Yet you not only grieved, but you hid like a band of
2   criminals, fearing for your own lives. This does not sound
3   like the behavior of men who have faith.

4 PETER: *(Annoyed)* Would you believe it if someone told you he
5   would rise from the dead — no matter how much you loved
6   and trusted that someone?

7 PROSECUTOR: *(Smiling toward jury as if they are in on the joke)*
8   I'm not testifying, Peter; you are. Though, at this point, I'm
9   not certain what you are testifying to.

10 JUDGE: The prosecutor will keep such remarks to himself.

11 PROSECUTOR: Sorry, Your Honor. Peter, please go on.

12 PETER: We had decided to return to Galilee and try to pick up
13   life where we left off when the women, the two Marys,
14   arrived in a state of much excitement to tell us that Jesus
15   was not in the tomb. I ran to see, and sure enough, his body
16   was not there.

17 PROSECUTOR: You didn't believe your friends? You had to run and
18   see for yourself? You seem to have trouble trusting anyone.

19 PETER: *(Defensively)* The women were hysterical. I couldn't
20   count on them getting the story straight.

21 PROSECUTOR: All right, let's assume the body was not there.
22   Did it occur to you that the Jewish authorities might
23   remove the body themselves in order to prevent the tomb
24   from becoming a shrine to a martyr?

25 PETER: Jewish law pronounces a curse by God on any man
26   hung on a tree. Jews would have considered themselves
27   defiled had they removed the body. Besides, it wouldn't
28   occur to them that a man so cursed by God could become
29   a martyr to God.

30 PROSECUTOR: And his followers? Wouldn't they want the body?

31 PETER: For what? As I've already testified, we thought he had
32   died. We would want to anoint him properly for a burial,
33   not desecrate the tomb.

34 PROSECUTOR: Perhaps you're right, Peter. Perhaps no one
35   would remove a dead body. Jesus didn't hang on the cross

1   anywhere near as long as most crucified criminals. It is

2   distinctly possible that he was not dead at all, but had simply

3   fainted from the heat and exposure. I suggest that he awoke

4   in the coolness of the tomb, and walked out — unaided.

5 PETER: And I suggest, Mr. Prosecutor, that you are either

6   ignorant of Roman treatment of prisoners or grossly

7   insensitive to man's endurance, or both. Before being hung

8   on the cross, a prisoner was beaten so thoroughly by

9   sadistic Roman guards ...

10 PROSECUTOR: Objection: The word *sadistic* is prejudicial.

11 JUDGE: The jury will disregard the word *sadistic*. The witness

12   will adhere to the facts.

13 PETER: *(Now seething with anger which he barely keeps under*

14   *control)* A prisoner was beaten by efficient Roman guards to

15   the extent he might very well die before the cross was ever

16   raised. Jesus suffered just such a beating. If you recall, the

17   man was so weakened from pain and loss of blood that he

18   could not carry his own cross to the site of execution; he

19   had to be assisted. In addition, Roman guards were

20   charged with assuring the death of a prisoner before

21   removing his body from the cross. In fulfilling his duty, one

22   of the guards stabbed Jesus in the side. Now, this man

23   suffered hours of interrogation and torture, hung on a

24   cross in unbearable heat for six hours, and received a

25   piercing wound from a spear — all of this in addition to a

26   flogging. And you say he simply removed the stone which

27   sealed the tomb and walked out?

28 PROSECUTOR: None of this would be a problem for the Son of

29   God, now would it?

30 PETER: *(With poorly concealed triumph)* That's exactly what I'm

31   trying to tell you.

32 PROSECUTOR: *(Somewhat abashed, looks intently at PETER for a*

33   *moment.)* Peter, did you see this risen Jesus?

34 PETER: Yes.

35 PROSECUTOR: And did this ghost tell you anything — you

1   know, about heaven — or whatever?
2 PETER: It wasn't a ghost. He ate with us. We touched him. He
3   even gave us a message.
4 PROSECUTOR: A message? And what was this message?
5 PETER: There is forgiveness of sins for all who turn to him.
6 PROSECUTOR: Am I to understand that this man is going to
7   forgive me for something I do to someone else?
8 PETER: He said once that whatever we do to another person,
9   we do to him, because he is in all people. Therefore, he has
10   the right to forgive.
11 PROSECUTOR: Rather presumptuous, I'd say.
12 PETER: For a man, yes; for the Son of God — no.
13 PROSECUTOR: Did you see this risen Jesus again?
14 PETER: Yes — at the lake where I was fishing with my brother
15   James, Thomas, and a few others. We had caught no fish
16   after a whole night and were just about to give up when a
17   man appeared on the shore. He told us to cast our nets into
18   the water on the other side of the boat. We did and caught
19   so many fish we could hardly pull in the net. We recognized
20   Jesus then. After hauling in the fish, we all ate together and
21   talked. I remember Jesus asked me three times if I loved him.
22 PROSECUTOR: One for each denial, Peter?
23 PETER: Yes, one for each denial. He then instructed me to love
24   and care for others.
25 PROSECUTOR: Why did Jesus give you instructions? Since he
26   lived, or so you say, why didn't he deliver these messages
27   of love, caring, and forgiveness himself?
28 PETER: He had to go to be with our heavenly Father. He
29   provided me and all of us with the Holy Spirit to carry on
30   his work through the ages. In this way, we became active
31   doers with God working through us, instead of passively
32   letting God manipulate our lives. It is in doing that we gain
33   the joy of companionship with God.
34 PROSECUTOR: You speak for Jesus, then?
35 PETER: No, he speaks through me.

1 PROSECUTOR: I see. And after Jesus spoke with you each time,
2   he simply disappeared — vanished?
3 PETER: Yes.
4 PROSECUTOR: Peter, let me explain something to you here
5   about the psychology of men. You had already been told to
6   expect to see Jesus after he died. In your grief, you longed,
7   desperately, to see someone you loved, someone you had
8   depended on and needed. Your state of mind was exactly
9   suited to induce a vision — a vision not based on fact, but
10   on intense emotional desire.
11 PETER: *(With visible anger)* And all the others? They saw this
12   vision, too? Sir, you have called me and my brothers men
13   of little faith: you have called us cowards. I tell you, sir, in
14   this, and only this, I agree with you. Indeed, we were
15   cowards: weak men who, without our teacher, were
16   directionless and scared to death. But these men, the same
17   cowards, suddenly began to preach openly amidst hostile
18   territory. Now, why was that, counselor? Why would they
19   risk torture and death a dozen times a day to carry on a
20   mission that was based on some sketchy dream? Some of
21   us did meet horrible deaths that could have been avoided
22   by a simple denial of faith. We did not shrink from death or
23   persecution. We did not deny Christ. We could not deny
24   him. And you say our behavior, for many of us a rehearsal
25   of previous actions, was the result of a vision conjured up
26   in our distraught minds? I ask you, sir, which of us is
27   imagining things?
28 PROSECUTOR: *(Now visibly angry himself)* That will be all, Peter.
29   *(PETER steps down.)* I call Joseph of Arimathea as my next
30   witness. *(JOSEPH appears before bench.)*
31 JUDGE: Do you swear to tell the truth, the whole truth, and
32   nothing but the truth, so help you?
33 JOSEPH: *(Hand on Bible)* I do.
34 JUDGE: Be seated. *(JOSEPH sits.)*
35 PROSECUTOR: Joseph, you are an honored member of the

1   Jewish Supreme Court who sat in on the trials of the said
2   Jesus of Nazareth.
3 JOSEPH: I am.
4 PROSECUTOR: Yet you are the one who removed the body of
5   Jesus from the cross, is that correct?
6 JOSEPH: It is.
7 PROSECUTOR: Considering such an association with these
8   Christians would possibly lead to your removal from the
9   Supreme Court and to your own persecution, and would,
10   according to previous testimony, defile you in the eyes of
11   God, why would you take such a step?
12 JOSEPH: I did not think Jesus deserved to die in the first place.
13   I certainly considered a criminal's burial and injustice.
14 PROSECUTOR: Why didn't you proclaim the innocence of Jesus
15   during the trial, when it would have done him some good?
16 JOSEPH: I did speak for him.
17 PROSECUTOR: But not very loudly, right? Not enough to draw
18   attention to the fact that you had been a follower of this
19   man yourself.
20 JOSEPH: A lone dissident voice is seldom heard.
21 PROSECUTOR: Oh, really. Tell us, then, Joseph, did you hear
22   Jesus state he would rise from the dead?
23 JOSEPH: No.
24 PROSECUTOR: What did you hear him say?
25 JOSEPH: He said very little, actually. He never defended
26   himself. He admitted only to being the Son of God and
27   going to sit at the right hand of God.
28 PROSECUTOR: Should I assume that you believed in his claim?
29 JOSEPH: Yes. I believed him then, and I believe him now.
30 PROSECUTOR: You believed you had the Son of God on trial,
31   yet you did not have the strength or courage to save him
32   from your colleagues. If I were defending the Son of God, I
33   would expend every last ounce of my energy in a diligent
34   effort to save my client. You really didn't take a strong
35   stand, did you, Joseph?

1   **JOSEPH:** I'm taking a stand now.

2   **PROSECUTOR:** By admitting you removed a dead man's body

3   from a cross. That doesn't take much courage, does it?

4   **JOSEPH:** *(Annoyed)* No one else had the nerve to do it.

5   **PROSECUTOR:** No one else had access to Pilate, did they?

6   **JOSEPH:** No, I suppose not.

7   **PROSECUTOR:** Tell me, how did Pilate respond to a renowned

8   Jewish Supreme Court member asking permission to bury

9   the man convicted by that very court?

10

11   **SECOND FLASHBACK**

12   *(Live or tape recording. If live, PILATE and CENTURION join*

13   *JOSEPH On-stage.)*

14   **PILATE:** You wish to see me, Joseph of Arimathea?

15   **JOSEPH:** I do, sir. I ask your permission to remove the body of

16   Jesus and lay him to rest in my family tomb.

17   **PILATE:** You? But you are not a known follower of this man. You

18   are a member of the Jewish Supreme Court, are you not?

19   *(Hesitates while thinking.)* Ah, I think I see. Now that the Jews

20   have killed their enemy, they regret it.

21   **JOSEPH:** I am not representing the Jewish community. I come

22   to make this request only for myself.

23   **PILATE:** My good friend Joseph, there is no need to use space

24   in your family tomb. I am certain you know that the Roman

25   government provides a grave for executed criminals.

26   **JOSEPH:** It is nothing but a pit where bones are left to rot.

27   **PILATE:** And you think this Jesus deserves better. *(Pause)*

28   Perhaps. **Centurion!** *(Sounds of boots and mail clanking in*

29   *distance. Then sounds of soldiers nearby, snapping to attention.*

30   *CENTURION enters.)*

31   **CENTURION:** Sir!

32   **PILATE:** You guarded the cross of the crucified Jesus. Can you

33   confirm that the man is dead?

34   **CENTURION:** He is dead, sir. As was my duty in an execution,

35   after the man appeared to have drawn his last breath, I

1   ascertained his death with my spear.

2 **PILATE:** Then, Joseph, I see no reason to refuse your request.

3   Remove the body. Take it anywhere you wish and be done

4   with it. I sincerely hope this is the last I hear of the troublesome

5   Jesus. *(JOSEPH returns to the stand. Flashback over.)*

6

7 **PROSECUTOR:** *(In courtroom)* Joseph, should I repeat the question?

8 **JOSEPH:** No, I'll answer. Pilate expressed surprise when I made

9   the request.

10 **PROSECUTOR:** I'm sure he did. And did he readily hand over

11   the body?

12 **JOSEPH:** After verifying he was dead, yes.

13 **PROSECUTOR:** Then what did you do?

14 **JOSEPH:** I took the body down, wrapped it in fine linen cloth,

15   and carried him to my tomb. I had the entrance blocked

16   with a heavy stone. Later, it was ordered sealed to prevent

17   anyone from getting in. That's all there is to tell.

18 **PROSECUTOR:** Could anyone have removed that stone, Joseph?

19 **JOSEPH:** In view of the seal, it would have been a violation of

20   Roman law, subject to punishment. In addition, it would

21   have taken more than one man to remove the stone, and

22   the tomb was guarded by highly trained soldiers who would

23   permit no one near the tomb.

24 **PROSECUTOR:** Could these guards have been overpowered?

25 **JOSEPH:** By whom? The Jews didn't have the need or desire, and

26   as we have already seen, the Christians were running scared.

27 **PROSECUTOR:** Thank you, Joseph. *(JOSEPH steps down.)* My

28   next witness is Saul of Tarsus. *(PAUL approaches bench.)*

29 **JUDGE:** Do you swear to tell the truth, the whole truth, and

30   nothing but the truth, so help you?

31 **PAUL:** *(Loudly, full of confidence, hand on Bible)* I do.

32 **JUDGE:** You may sit down. *(PAUL sits.)*

33 **PROSECUTOR:** Saul, I suppose if I ask you, you will proclaim

34   loudly for all to hear that you are one of these Christians.

35 **PAUL:** I believe in Jesus Christ, the Savior of mankind, the Son

1   of God who died for our sins and arose from the dead to
2   give us life everlasting. It is because of this belief and my
3   new life in Christ that I am now called Paul.
4 PROSECUTOR: All right, Saul, may ...
5 PAUL: *(Turning to bench)* **Your Honor, I must insist that the**
6   **prosecutor address me by my Christian name, which**
7   **is Paul.**
8 JUDGE: Mr. Prosecutor, the witness has requested to be called
9   Paul. You will address him as such.
10 PROSECUTOR: Well, then, Paul, may I remind you that you are
11   on the witness stand, not in the pulpit? Please answer
12   questions directly. Are you a Christian?
13 PAUL: I have said so.
14 PROSECUTOR: Paul, *(Pause)* what if I were to tell you ... *(Begins*
15   *walking away from witness, looking at jury with a touch of*
16   *sarcasm in smile)* to tell you that this trial is a sham, and ...
17 PAUL: I would certainly agree to that.
18 PROSECUTOR: *(Wheels around angrily.)* Let me finish, please.
19   That this trial is a sham and that all of you who swear to
20   following this rebel, Jesus, will be convicted of treason and
21   executed immediately. Would you then so proudly proclaim
22   your dedication to this man you call the Son of God?
23 PAUL: I, sir, am a Christian. The fact that I could be threatened
24   with death means nothing, for Christ will be with me in
25   death just as he is in life. He who believes in Jesus Christ
26   has everlasting life.
27 PROSECUTOR: Strange words coming from a man who,
28   himself, set out to do away with the rebellious Christians
29   just a few years back. As a Roman magistrate and a Jew,
30   did you not request support from the high priest in your
31   effort to destroy these Christians?
32
33 THIRD FLASHBACK
34   *(Live or tape recording. If live, HIGH PRIEST joins PAUL On-stage.)*
35 HIGH PRIEST: Saul of Tarsus, you are to be commended for

1   your diligence in trying to rid the Empire of these insurgent

2   Christians.

3 PAUL: Thank you, sir, but I have not come for praise, but to

4   make a request.

5 HIGH PRIEST: Speak then.

6 PAUL: Some of the synagogue leaders in Damascus have

7   refused to convey the names of suspected Christians

8   because of public pressure. I feel I would have complete

9   cooperation if I could show these leaders a letter from you

10   — a letter requesting imprisonment of all suspected

11   followers of Jesus.

12 HIGH PRIEST: You shall have your letter, Saul, along with my

13   wish for your continued success. Come back tomorrow

14   morning and you will be on your way to Damascus with the

15   letter you requested. *(Flashback over.)*

16

17 PROSECUTOR: *(Back in courtroom)* You seem to have trouble

18   remembering your past. Perhaps this document will refresh

19   your memory. *(Shows PAUL letter.)* Would you explain to the

20   jury what this is, Paul?

21 PAUL: It is the letter I requested from the high priest demanding

22   identification of Christians for prosecution.

23 PROSECUTOR: Yet you now claim to be one of those you once

24   sought to kill. What changed your mind, Paul?

25 PAUL: On the way to Damascus to deliver the letter you hold,

26   Jesus visited me.

27 PROSECUTOR: He visited you? I was told by an earlier witness

28   that Jesus went to be with his Father — in heaven, I

29   presume. How could he visit you?

30 PAUL: I did not see him as man in flesh and blood. He came in

31   a bright light and spoke to me.

32 PROSECUTOR: The bright light spoke to you, did it? What did

33   the light say?

34 PAUL: The voice asked, "Saul, Saul, why are you persecuting

35   me?" I was very frightened. My knees shook so badly that I

1   fell to the ground. I asked who spoke to me and the voice
2   said, "I am Jesus, the one you are persecuting." He then
3   told me to go into the city and await instructions.
4 PROSECUTOR: I see. *(Pause)* Paul, I am going to ask you to
5   step down.
6 PAUL: But there is more to say. I ...
7 PROSECUTOR: I've heard you always have a great deal to say;
8   however, that will be all for now.
9 PAUL: *(Turns to JUDGE.)* But Your Honor, if the prosecutor
10   would just listen to the story, I could ...
11 JUDGE: You may step down.
12 PAUL: *(Reluctantly stands and looks around. Then, to*
13   *PROSECUTOR)* Christ is with us in this courtroom today,
14   you know.
15 JUDGE: The witness is excused. *(PAUL exits.)*
16 PROSECUTOR: I call to the stand the Roman officer, Petronius.
17   *(PETRONIUS stands at attention before bench.)*
18 JUDGE: Do you swear to tell the truth, the whole truth, and
19   nothing but the truth, so help you?
20 PETRONIUS: *(Hand on Bible)* Yes, sir.
21 PROSECUTOR: Petronius, I understand you were with Paul on
22   the road to Damascus on the day in question.
23 PETRONIUS: Yes. I usually accompanied Saul on his missions.
24 PROSECUTOR: Ah! So it's Saul now. All right, you heard Saul's
25   testimony just now?
26 PETRONIUS: I did.
27 PROSECUTOR: Now, think carefully, Petronius. Did you see an
28   extremely bright light that day?
29 PETRONIUS: No, I saw no light.
30 PROSECUTOR: Did you hear a voice saying, "Saul, Saul why
31   are you persecuting me?"
32 PETRONIUS: I didn't hear a specific voice. I did hear strange
33   sounds. And the atmosphere was different. I can't explain
34   it, exactly, but the total effect was to make me rather
35   lightheaded, almost dizzy, just for a moment.

1   PROSECUTOR: Was there any change in Saul's behavior?

2   PETRONIUS: Yes. Just as we heard the sounds, he threw his

3   hands over his head and fell to the ground. I heard him say,

4   "Who speaks to me?" I told him, "No one," but he didn't

5   seem to hear. After a while he got up, but he could hardly

6   walk, and he was completely blind.

7   PROSECUTOR: About what time of day was that?

8   PETRONIUS: Time? Oh, around noon, I'd say.

9   PROSECUTOR: It is very hot on the road in Israel around noon,

10   isn't it? Hot enough to produce sunstroke, wouldn't you say?

11   PETRONIUS: Yes, but Saul wasn't suffering from the sun, if

12   that's what you're getting at. He was used to traveling in

13   the heat of day; we all were. Besides, the symptoms were

14   not those of someone affected by the sun.

15   PROSECUTOR: Didn't Saul suffer a chronic illness? Epilepsy, or

16   a similar physical disorder? Could he not have had an

17   attack of that old familiar disease, perhaps brought on by

18   the hot sun?

19   PETRONIUS: He could have, but, again, the symptoms were not

20   like any I had ever seen before.

21   PROSECUTOR: But he could have suffered an illness, right?

22   PETRONIUS: Yes.

23   PROSECUTOR: In your opinion, did he, or did he not, see and

24   hear voices?

25   PETRONIUS: I'm no doctor, but I don't see how Saul's change in

26   attitude and behavior could be attributed to illness. I can't

27   say what he saw and heard, but he certainly acted like a man

28   who had seen something that frightened him half to death.

29   PROSECUTOR: Thank you, Petronius. That will be all.

30   *(PETRONIUS steps down.)* **I call Ananias.** *(ANANIAS takes stand.)*

31   JUDGE: Do you swear to tell the truth, the whole truth, and

32   nothing but the truth, so help you?

33   ANANIAS: *(Hand on Bible)* **I do.**

34   JUDGE: Be seated. *(ANANIAS sits.)*

35   PROSECUTOR: You are a Christian, is that correct?

1 ANANIAS: Yes.

2 PROSECUTOR: And you cured Paul of his blindness?

3 ANANIAS: No, God cured Paul, I was only the instrument to
4   carry out the cure. Paul had been sick for three days when
5   the Lord told me to go with him and lay my hands on him
6   so that he might see.

7 PROSECUTOR: And you, a Christian, went willingly to visit a
8   man who was known to persecute Christians? You must be
9   a very brave man — or a very foolish one.

10 ANANIAS: I did what the Lord told me to do. When one follows
11   the word of God, one knows no fear.

12 PROSECUTOR: Ah, another preacher. Are all you Christians
13   preachers?

14 ANANIAS: *(Smiling)* When we get the chance.

15 PROSECUTOR: *(Sternly)* Well, today is not your chance. Now,
16   you laid your hands on Paul and he could see. What
17   happened after he gained his sight?

18 ANANIAS: Paul went almost immediately to the synagogue to
19   tell everyone that Jesus was the Son of God. After that, he
20   dedicated his life to studying and preaching God's word
21   to others.

22 PROSECUTOR: Ananias, you feared Paul once, and then,
23   apparently, you trusted him instantly. Is that right?

24 ANANIAS: No, sir, I can't say I instantly trusted him. I did the
25   Lord's bidding because, as I said, one obeys God; but I
26   trusted God, not Paul, who I considered a murderer.
27   Gradually, however, I could see the radical change in him.
28   He simply wasn't the same man. I learned to love him and
29   trust him as a special messenger of God.

30 PROSECUTOR: Thank you, Ananias. *(ANANIAS steps down.*
31   *PROSECUTOR looks around.)* **Mr. World Lee Wise, would you**
32   **take the stand, please?** *(WORLD LEE WISE takes stand. He*
33   *smiles at everyone as he approaches and straightens his tie. He*
34   *may walk with a cane, though he would depend on it little, using*
35   *it more for effect. This man is a real character who is obviously*

1   *enjoying his moment in the limelight.)*

2 **JUDGE: Do you swear to tell the truth, the whole truth, and**
3   **nothing but the truth, so help you?**

4 **WORLD LEE:** *(Hand on Bible)* **Why certainly, Judge.** *(Smiles*
5   *broadly and greets PROSECUTOR before sitting down.)* **Good**
6   **afternoon, counselor.**

7 **PROSECUTOR: Mr. World Lee Wise, would you state your**
8   **occupation?**

9 **WORLD LEE: I am a historian.**

10 **PROSECUTOR: And as a historian, I'm sure you have studied**
11   **the information regarding the alleged Resurrection.**

12 **WORLD LEE: I have.**

13 **PROSECUTOR: Perhaps you would discuss with us today the**
14   **obvious discrepancies in the reports about various events**
15   **surrounding Jesus' death and supposed resurrection. For**
16   **example, there are several different reports regarding the**
17   **removal of the stone from in front of the tomb. There are**
18   **also discrepancies regarding who actually visited the tomb,**
19   **when, and what they found upon arrival. My question is**
20   **this: if the story that the body disappeared and then**
21   **reappeared as a risen Christ is true, wouldn't the reports**
22   **jibe? Doesn't it sound as if each person made up a story to**
23   **suit his or her own needs at the time?**

24 **WORLD LEE:** *(Takes off glasses and polishes lenses.)* **Let me tell you**
25   **about an incident that occurred in a sociology class that I**
26   **took in college a number of years ago.**

27 **PROSECUTOR: Mr. Wise, I would like you to answer the question.**

28 **WORLD LEE:** *(Turning to JUDGE)* **Judge, what I am about to**
29   **relate will answer the question if our impatient prosecutor**
30   **will give me the chance.**

31 **JUDGE: The prosecutor will allow the witness to answer the**
32   **question in his own way.** *(To WORLD LEE WISE)* **You may**
33   **proceed.**

34 **WORLD LEE: Professor Compton — I think that was his name —**
35   **yes, yes, it was Compton. He was lecturing on the effect of**

1   the Brown vs. Topeka decision on segregation. Or was it ...

2 PROSECUTOR: Judge, must we tolerate this?

3 JUDGE: Mr. World Lee Wise, do get on with it.

4 WORLD LEE: Professor Compton was lecturing when another
5   instructor entered the classroom, approached the lectern,
6   and announced right in the middle of class that he wished
7   to speak to the professor on a matter of importance to both
8   of them. He then invited the professor to step outside. The
9   professor declined the invitation. The two men commenced
10   to argue at great length and with much enthusiasm, when
11   suddenly, the instructor shoved the professor in the chest,
12   like — *(Stops and turns to JUDGE.)* **May I demonstrate?**

13 JUDGE: *(Smiles slightly.)* **Yes, you may.**

14 PROSECUTOR: *(Obviously dismayed as WORLD LEE WISE rises*
15   *and approaches him. He pleads.)* **Judge!** *(Takes step backward.)*

16 WORLD LEE: **He shoved him like this, see?** *(Shoves*
17   *PROSECUTOR in chest.)* **Then the professor shoved the**
18   **instructor right back.** *(Looks at PROSECUTOR.)* **Go ahead,**
19   **shove me. Go on.**

20 PROSECUTOR: *(Looks pleadingly at JUDGE again.)* **Judge!**

21 JUDGE: *(Practically shouting)* **Go ahead, shove him!** *(PROSECUTOR*
22   *shoves WORLD LEE WISE.)*

23 WORLD LEE: **The two argued some more, and the instructor hit**
24   **the professor in the arm.** *(Hits PROSECUTOR.)*

25 PROSECUTOR: *(Jumps back. Wails.)* **Judge!**

26 WORLD LEE: **Judge, I'm just trying to demonstrate so the jury**
27   **can clearly understand.**

28 JUDGE: **You may be seated now, Mr. Wise. I believe we have the**
29   **picture.**

30 WORLD LEE: *(Resumes seat.)* **Well, after the instructor hit the**
31   **professor, the two agreed to settle matters later, and the**
32   **instructor stomped out of the room.** *(PROSECUTOR is still*
33   *rubbing his arm.)* **You all right, counselor?**

34 PROSECUTOR: *(Somewhat humiliated by the whole episode)* **Yes,**
35   **I'm fine.**

1   WORLD LEE: Well, after the instructor left, the professor said
2   he was going to prosecute and asked the class to describe
3   what happened as accurately as possible to assist him with
4   an indictment. You should have heard them. The professor
5   got ten different descriptions of an incident they had all just
6   witnessed together. No two were alike, counselor. Some
7   students claimed they had been too stunned to observe
8   objectively. Some feared that violence would spread
9   throughout the classroom and were, thus, too nervous to
10   be objective. And, of course, many of the students
11   adamantly insisted they had reported truthfully and
12   accurately, even though all the reports differed.
13   PROSECUTOR: I presume that anecdote was designed to clear
14   up any questions the jury might have regarding the
15   discrepancies over the risen Jesus?
16   WORLD LEE: Why yes, indeed!
17   PROSECUTOR: Since you answered that question so directly
18   and clearly, let me ask you another. *(Aside)* Though I expect
19   I'm out of my mind. *(To WORLD LEE)* How could one
20   witness claim that Jesus appeared to the disciples for the
21   first time in Jerusalem while another insisted it was in
22   Galilee? The two cities are miles apart. Obviously, the
23   disciples could not be in both places at once. How might we
24   explain that?
25   WORLD LEE: I don't know that we can, but I have a question
26   for you.
27   PROSECUTOR: Judge?
28   JUDGE: I believe I'd like to hear the question.
29   WORLD LEE: Polybius, the Greek historian, and Livy, the Latin
30   historian, represent Hannibal, in his invasion of Italy,
31   crossing the Alps by two completely different routes, routes
32   that cannot be harmonized by any stretch of the
33   imagination. Now, my question — did Hannibal invade Italy?
34   PROSECUTOR: I'm enough of a scholar to know that he did.
35   WORLD LEE: Despite the contradictory reports? Even though

1   **two historians claim two different routes of travel as fact,**
2   **you still believe Hannibal did invade Italy? There is a**
3   **discrepancy here, counselor. Why don't you refuse to**
4   **acknowledge Hannibal ever arrived in Italy at all? Let's use**
5   **some logic here.**
6 **PROSECUTOR:** *(Disgusted)* **The witness may step down.**
7 **WORLD LEE:** *(Disappointed)* **No more questions?**
8 **PROSECUTOR: Not unless you have some.**
9 **WORLD LEE:** *(Looks at JUDGE and PROSECUTOR.)* **All right, then.**
10   *(He steps down, bows slightly when passing JUDGE, and exits.)*
11 **PROSECUTOR:** *(Approaches bench.)* **Your Honor, I believe that is**
12   **all I have for today ...** *(LEGION, in long robe, face painted half-*
13   *black, half-white, enters courtroom from back of church or*
14   *auditorium. She walks rather stately and slowly. JUDGE sees her*
15   *and puts up a hand to stop PROSECUTOR. LEGION hands a*
16   *note to JUDGE, who reads it and addresses PROSECUTOR.)*
17 **JUDGE: Counselor, it appears we do have another witness who**
18   **wishes to testify.** *(Hands note to PROSECUTOR.)*
19 **PROSECUTOR: This is highly irregular, but since I wish this to**
20   **be a totally fair and unbiased hearing, I am willing to let**
21   **this witness take the stand.**
22 **JUDGE: Approach the bench and be sworn in.** *(LEGION moves*
23   *forward and places her hand on the Bible.)* **Do you swear to tell**
24   **the truth, the whole truth, and nothing but the truth, so**
25   **help you?**
26 **LEGION: I do.**
27 **JUDGE: Then be seated.** *(LEGION sits.)*
28 **PROSECUTOR: Please state your name for the court.**
29 **LEGION: My name is Legion.**
30 **PROSECUTOR: You are the only witness I have placed on the**
31   **stand today about whom I know nothing. Tell the jury why**
32   **you wish to testify.**
33 **LEGION: Because, whether anyone listens or not, it is my duty**
34   **as a Christian to speak.**
35 **PROSECUTOR: Legion, you must forgive me if I sound**

1   **condescending, but all the witnesses today have either been**
2   **experts in the field of religion or have been eyewitnesses to**
3   **some event directly connected with Jesus of Nazareth. Who**
4   **or what, exactly, do you represent?**
5   **LEGION:**   **It is not who I represent that is important to this**
6   **hearing, but who I am.**
7   **PROSECUTOR: And who is that?**
8   **LEGION: I am a housewife in suburbia, a school teacher, the**
9   **coach of a football team, a plumber, a beggar in the street,**
10   **a prisoner behind bars. I am all of these and thousands**
11   **more. It is for this reason I am called Legion.**
12 **PROSECUTOR: Shall I assume, then, that you have met this so-**
13   **called risen Christ?**
14 **LEGION:** *(Smiles.)* **I have met Christ.**
15 **PROSECUTOR: Perhaps you will tell us the details. Spare us**
16   **nothing in your explanation, as we are accustomed to**
17   **hearing about blinding lights, voices from heaven, and**
18   **visitations of ghosts.**
19 **LEGION: I have seen no blinding lights, heard no voices from**
20   **heaven, and seen no ghosts.**
21 **PROSECUTOR: Ah, then you can no doubt testify to seeing this**
22   **Jesus in the flesh as Peter did.**
23 **LEGION: No. I have not had the privilege of seeing Christ in the flesh.**
24 **PROSECUTOR: I do not see, then, what you can possibly**
25   **contribute to the verification of the Resurrection.**
26 **LEGION: I come to tell you this: no one will believe in the truth**
27   **of the living Christ only from hearing the testimony of**
28   **others. Total belief comes from within the human soul, not**
29   **from without.**
30 **PROSECUTOR:** *(Pauses, looking around courtroom, obviously*
31   *somewhat perplexed.)* **You say you are a Christian, yet you**
32   **have not seen Christ in the flesh, nor witnessed any of his**
33   **miracles, and now you say you haven't been converted**
34   **through the testimony of others. How, then, did you**
35   **become a believer?**

1 LEGION: I believed when the joy of friendship lifted the despair
2   of loneliness, when the rose-tint of sunset colored a slum
3   with hope, when the sweet notes of a symphony carried
4   away the din of the city. I experienced Christ in my heart
5   when I gave my riches to a beggar on a lonely road in Italy,
6   when the walls of a prison no longer confined my soul,
7   when my spirit soared above the bombed-out dwelling of
8   my town in Germany.
9 PROSECUTOR: Poetic, very poetic. But how do you expect this
10   jury to accept any of what you say as proof of a living Christ?
11 LEGION: I ask you to look at me, sir. You are an investigator, so
12   ask questions. How can I, who once was shy and withdrawn,
13   suddenly speak so openly to groups of strangers? Why did I
14   become joyful when once I wallowed in the throes of
15   depression? A year ago, I lived only for the next shot, the
16   next drink. Why do I, today, eagerly seek the comfort of
17   people and nature and God, instead? Each day is an
18   adventure in living, not a living hell. Do you not believe in
19   the benefits of rain when you see a flower bud? Can you not
20   see the necessity of vitamins for life, though you know not
21   how they work in the body? There are hundreds of things
22   you cannot see, nor explain; but you believe because you've
23   seen the results. I tell you that once I was mentally and
24   emotionally sick — sick and near death. But I became well
25   because I received the risen Christ in my heart. Yet you do
26   not believe me. Why?
27 PROSECUTOR: I don't say that we doubt your testimony, nor
28   even that Jesus has changed your life. After all, none of us
29   questions the existence of Jesus or that he spoke profound
30   words of wisdom that, if studied and accepted, would
31   change a person's life.
32 LEGION: But I have not always studied. In fact, there were
33   instances when I could not even read.
34 PROSECUTOR: *(Exasperated)* Legion, you talk in riddles. This
35   jury is in session today to seek an answer to the question:

1   Did Jesus of Nazareth rise from the dead? If he did, he is

2   indeed the Son of God. Since you claim to be a Christian,

3   then you must believe the assertion that Jesus did rise from

4   the dead. What evidence can you place before this court to

5   support your belief?

6   LEGION: I've tried to give you that evidence.

7   PROSECUTOR: Yes, I know — sunsets over Harlem and roses

8   budding after rain. There are scientific reasons for the

9   phenomena you mentioned. Whether I can explain the

10   effects of vitamins on the body or not is irrelevant, because

11   someone else can.

12 LEGION: Someone can explain the effect of Christ on the human

13   being, too. Someone has, but you didn't listen.

14 PROSECUTOR: *(Smirking)* You said yourself, none of us listens

15   to testimony of Christ.

16 LEGION: No. I said we don't accept Christ solely from hearing

17   a testimony. However, someone else's story can open the

18   door to our hearts so Christ can come in.

19 PROSECUTOR: I see. Then you are now saying that if I believe

20   Peter and Paul, then I will also believe in Jesus Christ.

21 LEGION: Sir, would the people who testified here today have

22   undergone such radical changes in personality for a great

23   prophet who simply died and was forever gone? Consider

24   just the disciples alone — Thomas, the famous skeptic,

25   suddenly a firm believer; James and John, jealous of each

26   other, status-seekers, suddenly willing to be guided and led

27   by Peter. How can you rationally, logically explain the

28   changes in the disciples, and Paul, and the thousands upon

29   thousands of men and women since that time who have

30   dramatically altered their lives after accepting Christ as the

31   Son of God? I venture to say there is no reason for these

32   changed lives other than the one proposed — that I, and all

33   the others, received Christ from within through the Holy

34   Spirit which was released to us with the resurrection of

35   Jesus Christ.

1   **PROSECUTOR:** If the Holy Spirit from within oneself is the only
2   proof of a risen Christ, how can this jury learn the truth of
3   what you say?
4   **LEGION:** Jesus gave those instructions to Peter. We must only
5   ask Christ for forgiveness of our sins and believe that those
6   sins are, in fact, forgiven. Once we have received this
7   forgiveness, we become open to God's love and comfort.
8   We then have Christ in our hearts. No longer need we feel
9   guilty or inadequate because of past mistakes. The only
10   way our minds can see the truth of a living Christ is to open
11   the door to our hearts.
12   **PROSECUTOR:** Judge, I believe I have proven my case. This
13   last witness has openly admitted that the only proof of a
14   resurrected Jesus lies within the heart and soul of each
15   man and woman, which is an intangible that can never be
16   proved. The prosecution rests.
17   **JUDGE:** At this point, deliberation and judgment must be turned
18   over to the jury. You have heard the testimony. It is up to
19   you to make a decision — for the living Christ or against
20   him. He is alive within you, or he is not. You must decide.
21   *(Positions freeze. Lights off.)*
22
23
24
25
26
27
28
29
30
31
32
33
34
35

The Way of the Cross

A reader's enactment of Christ's ministry
by Beverly Guyton Rhymes

CAST

Leader
Should speak with authority

Seven Voices
*VOICE 2 carries a Bible
and will need to hold it forward
at times as if reading from it.
VOICE 3 is the voice of Jesus
when this is appropriate.*

Cross Bearers
See "Optional Staging" in the Production Notes

PRODUCTION NOTES

Overview: Seven readers follow a leader on the path of Jesus' life and ministry. The path is marked by cross bearers from all walks of life, each representing one of the crossroads of Jesus' ministry. The leader announces each crossroad (station) as the readers portray the lessons Jesus taught. The journey begins with the boy Jesus' awareness that he is different and has a prophecy to fulfill. It continues through his baptism and his ministry, culminating in the events of Holy Week and his crucifixion.

Set: Three risers would be helpful.

Props: A large but lightweight wooden cross. It needs to be large enough so as to be visible to the congregation, yet lightweight enough so it may be held easily. The cross may be the traditional one used in services. Voice 2 needs a Bible.

Costumes: Choir robes give the seven Voices visual unity. The others may dress as they wish.

Staging: If there are limitations of space or of available cast members, the Voices can also act as Cross Bearers.

There does need to be movement. The Cross Bearer enters, takes the cross, and finds a position — this done at the beginning of each station. The positions of the Cross Bearers should vary. If possible, the first and last Cross Bearers should be very young. They stand Downstage Center. As the Cross Bearers give up the cross, they are to find positions behind and between the Voices.

Optional Staging: Cross Bearers — Fifteen people who reflect the diversity of our world. If possible, they should be young and old, male and female, and of various ethnic backgrounds. Their apparel could also vary — professional, maintenance person, housewife, rich, poor. Cross Bearers may remain on stage and join in the chorus.

This play does not intentionally reflect the practice of any religious denomination. Some denominations may be more comfortable substituting the word "crossroad" for "station" throughout the performance. It is the author's wish that the drama reflect the diversity of our humanity, as well as the potentiality of our spirituality. *The Way of the Cross* did not begin with the path to the hill of Golgotha, nor did it end there. The paths we walk today are interwoven with the path of Jesus. We meet him in our way stations, our crossroads. When our path becomes his way, we may well come to the last of our intersections, and with the Voices cry "Hope," "Faith," "Love," and with the Chorus sing out "Life Everlasting."

It is also the author's intention to make this work as flexible as possible. Staging can be done in a simple church setting or on an elaborate stage with music and lighting.

Playing Time: 30-40 minutes

1   **SETTING:** *The staging area is vacant. VOICES 1, 3, 5, and 7 enter*
2   *from the left. From the right the LEADER enters, followed by*
3   *VOICES 2, 4, and 6. VOICE 2 carries a large Bible. These*
4   *VOICES make up the CHORUS. The LEADER takes position*
5   *right forward center.*
6
7   **LEADER:** We ask thy mercy in the name of the Trinity. Lord,
8   have mercy.
9   **CHORUS:** Christ, have mercy.
10 **LEADER:** Lord, have mercy. Help us, O God, as we, in our
11   human frailty, walk the path of your son, Jesus; the path,
12   which for him was the way of the cross. Open our eyes;
13   enlarge our understanding; teach us, Lord, as we
14   contemplate the perfect pilgrimage, and in so doing
15   strengthen us in our journey, and join our path to his. This
16   we ask in his name. Amen.
17 *(A young BOY with the cross enters from the left and takes his*
18   *position Down Center near the LEADER. He may join the*
19   *CHORUS in responses.)*
20   **Our journey begins along the crude, rocky pathways of**
21   **Galilee. We come to our first crossroad, or way station**
22   **along this road. Jesus, as a boy, feels isolated, different,**
23   **and lonely.**
24 **VOICE 1:** We worship you, O Christ!
25 **CHORUS:** By your cross you have redeemed the world.
26 **VOICE 2:** *(Holds Bible as if reading.)* **"For he shall grow up before**
27   **him as a tender plant, and as a root out of a dry ground"**
28   *(Isa. 53:2, KJV).*
29 **LEADER:** The ground of that countryside was dry indeed. The
30   growing of the small boy was nurtured by love and fed by
31   strange stories.
32 **VOICE 3:** The stories told were tales of shepherds and a star;
33   of wise men and gifts; of prophecy; of flight.
34 **VOICE 4:** There was the dreadful story of the killing of other
35   babies, the bewilderment of being saved from this

1   slaughter, the feeling of lingering guilt and disquieting
2   responsibility.
3   VOICE 5: For some time Jesus did not fully understand that he
4   was in any way different from the other boys and girls with
5   whom he played.
6   VOICE 6: At first he thought everyone heard the silent voice
7   that he heard and took pleasure in this heavenly Father's
8   company.
9   VOICE 7: Jesus knew that his mother and his earth father had
10   great faith. He felt they, at least, shared with him this all-
11   consuming love for the God-Father-All.
12 VOICE 1: For that reason he thought they had understood when
13   he stayed in Jerusalem — that this was natural and right.
14 VOICE 2: Jesus didn't intend to frighten them or to sound
15   reproachful when they found him in the temple. He was
16   honestly surprised that they had not understood.
17 VOICE 3: Jesus grasped then that they must not have this silent
18   voice always loving, always teaching, in the same way that
19   he did.
20 VOICE 4: If others did not know this Inner Person as he did,
21   what did this mean for him? Why was he different? He
22   besieged this God — this All — with endless questions.
23 VOICE 5: Jesus knew that he bore some kind of responsibility
24   in this; that he had a central role to play. He wanted to do
25   well for his heavenly Father's sake. He wanted with all his
26   being to honor him.
27 VOICE 6: If only there was someone who would understand.
28 VOICE 7: Jesus was very, very lonely.
29 VOICE 1: *(Steps forward.)* "Son, why have you treated us so?
30   Behold, your father and I have been looking for you
31   anxiously" *(Luke 2:48).*
32 VOICE 3: *(Steps forward.)* And he said to them, "How is it that
33   you sought me? Did you not know that I must be in my
34   Father's house?" *(Luke 2:49).*
35 VOICE 2: *(Holds Bible as if to read.)* And they did not understand

1   **the saying which he spoke to them. And he went down with**
2   **them and came to Nazareth, and was obedient to them; and**
3   **his mother kept all these things in her heart** *(Luke 2:50-51).*
4   **VOICE 4: God sent his Son to us in the fullness of our humanity.**
5   **CHORUS: Jesus grew in love and obedience to his heavenly**
6   **Father and to his parents on earth.**
7   **LEADER: Let us pray:**
8   **Almighty God, whose Son walked this earth as we walk,**
9   **grant us growth in loving obedience to our heavenly Father.**
10   **In Christ's name we pray. Amen.**
11   *(The young BOY hands the cross to the CROSS BEARER who*
12   *has entered from Stage Right. The BOY may now be part of the*
13   *CHORUS — true of all those who enter to take the cross. If there*
14   *are not enough participants, the cross may be passed from one to*
15   *another of the VOICES. However, positions should move back*
16   *and forth, forward and backward.)*
17   **We come to our second crossroads: Jesus is baptized.**
18   **VOICE 1: We worship you, O Christ!**
19   **CHORUS: By your cross you have redeemed the world.**
20   **VOICE 2:** *(Holds Bible as if reading.)* **John the baptizer appeared**
21   **in the wilderness, preaching a baptism of repentance for**
22   **the forgiveness of sins. And there went out to him all the**
23   **country of Judea, and all the people of Jerusalem; and they**
24   **were baptized by him in the river Jordan, confessing their**
25   **sins** *(Mark 1:4-5).*
26   **VOICE 4: Now John came clothed in camel's hair, and had a**
27   **leather girdle around his waist, and ate locusts and wild**
28   **honey** *(Mark 1:6).*
29   **VOICE 5: And he preached, saying, "After me comes he who is**
30   **mightier than I, the thong of whose sandals I am not worthy**
31   **to stoop down and untie. I have baptized you with water;**
32   **but he will baptize you with the Holy Spirit** *(Mark 1:7-8).*
33   **VOICE 6: Then Jesus arrived at the Jordan from Galilee, and**
34   **came to John to be baptized by him.**
35   **VOICE 7: John tried to dissuade him. "Why do you come to me?"**

1   he asked. I am the one who should be baptized by you."

2 VOICE 1: But Jesus was baptized by John.

3 VOICE 2: At the moment that Jesus came up out of the water,

4   the heavens tore open and the Spirit, like a dove,

5   descended upon him.

6 VOICE 4: And a voice spoke from heaven: "Thou art my beloved

7   Son; with thee I am well pleased" *(Mark 1:11)*.

8 LEADER: Let us pray:

9   We thank you, O God, for this affirmation and anointing of

10   your Son. We thank you that we also feel your affirming

11   love, and we ask for the gift of your grace, that we may

12   participate with Jesus in the making of your kingdom. In

13   Christ's name we pray. Amen.

14   *(The MAN hands the cross to the CROSS BEARER who enters*

15   *and takes position.)*

16   We have arrived at the third crossroads, where Jesus faces

17   endless continuing temptations in every disguise.

18 VOICE 1: We worship you, O Christ!

19 CHORUS: By your cross you have redeemed the world.

20 VOICE 2: *(Holds Bible as if reading.)* **And Jesus, full of the Holy**

21   **Spirit, returned from the Jordan, and was led by the Spirit**

22   **for forty days in the wilderness, tempted by the devil. And**

23   **he ate nothing in those days; and when they were ended, he**

24   **was hungry. And when the devil had ended every**

25   **temptation, he departed from him until an opportune time**

26   *(Luke 4:1-2, 13)*.

27 LEADER: If only the devil and temptations had always been as

28   recognizable!

29 VOICE 1: There are the little insidious temptations.

30 VOICE 2: It is the subtle bending of the truth —

31 VOICE 3: The attractive appeal of the argument —

32 VOICE 4: The logic of the suggestion that digs the pit.

33 VOICE 5: It is easy to recognize the large, blatant temptations

34   for what they are, and it is just as easy to turn aside from

35   them. The small digressions are ever the snare. It is fairly

1   simple to tell the devil "No" when one can recognize him as

2   such, but it is harder, much harder, when he is disguised —

3 VOICE 6: As a beautiful girl —

4 VOICE 7: An old woman —

5 VOICE 1: A graying grandfather —

6 VOICE 2: An abused child —

7 VOICE 3: An angel.

8 VOICE 4: There were the ploys — promises of healing, of good

9   done, of famine prevented, nature's havoc harnessed.

10 VOICE 5: There were the threats — of fire, and death, and

11   torture, and these not to be done to Jesus — but suffered

12   by the least of those he loved.

13 VOICE 6: There were the opportune times of weariness, of

14   discouragement, of despair, of sickness, of mourning, and

15   there were the temptations that mounted on the crest of

16   exhilaration.

17 VOICE 7: The Evil One knew all the tricks. The Lord of the Darkness

18   relentlessly pursued the greatest challenge — and lost.

19 LEADER: *(Moves Downstage.)* "If you are the Son of God,

20   command this stone to become bread" *(Luke 4:3).*

21 CHORUS: "It is written, 'Man shall not live by bread alone'"

22   (Luke 4:4).

23 LEADER: *(Moves farther Downstage Center.)* "To you I will give all

24   this authority and their glory; for it has been delivered to

25   me, and I give it to whom I will. If you, then, will worship

26   me, it shall all be yours" *(Luke 4:6).*

27 CHORUS: "It is written, 'You shall worship the Lord your God,

28   and him only shall you serve'" *(Luke 4:8).*

29 LEADER: *(Mounts center riser, two steps up.)* "If you are the Son of

30   God, throw yourself down from here; for it is written, 'He

31   will give his angels charge of you, to guard you,' and 'On

32   their hands they will bear you up, lest you strike your foot

33   against a stone'" *(Luke 4:9-11).*

34 CHORUS: "It is said, 'You shall not tempt the Lord your God'"

35   *(Luke 4:12). (LEADER steps down from riser.)*

1   LEADER: Let us pray:

2   O God, may we take courage in the example of your Son as

3   he daily faced temptations, just as we do. May we recognize

4   enticements as the temptations that they are and discern

5   their source. Give us strength and wisdom, and the grace

6   to withstand the onslaughts of evil. This we ask in his

7   name. Amen.

8   *(The fourth CROSS BEARER enters and takes the cross.)*

9   At crossroads four, Jesus struggles to find the will of his

10   heavenly Father for his life.

11 VOICE 1: We worship you, O Christ!

12 CHORUS: By your cross you have redeemed the world.

13 VOICE 3: *(Steps forward.)* "Lo, I have come to do thy will, O God"

14   *(Heb. 10:7).*

15 VOICE 2: Finding the will of his God was not easy for Jesus. He

16   begged his Father to be more specific. What did he want of

17   Jesus? Where was he to go? Over and over, directions and

18   words seemed to form in his soul, only to dissipate in the

19   crispness of the morning, in the bustle of the village.

20 VOICE 3: *(Again steps forward.)* What would you have me do?

21   What, O Father, what?

22 VOICE 4: If only this heavenly Father would have spoken more

23   clearly. Jesus agonized over what he was to do. Did this God

24   Father not understand the confusion and static of mortals?

25 VOICE 3: *(Moves right forward.)* Am I on the right course? Is this

26   the path you want?

27 VOICE 5: Jesus hurt. There was foreboding, and there was the

28   fear. Fear that he would not be strong enough or brave

29   enough or loving enough. He was terrified of his weakness,

30   of his humanity.

31 VOICE 3: Jesus shouted, "Abba, Abba," and this God Father

32   seemed far away at times. Then Jesus felt only the

33   desolation, the loneliness, and the fear.

34 CHORUS: And Jesus kept on. He kept on.

35 VOICE 6: Jesus knew the bewilderment of seeking to know the

1   will of God. He prayed and questioned, asking for
2   discernment and guidance, and he kept on keeping on.
3 LEADER: Let us pray:
4   God, help us in the example of your Son to see that he,
5   also, in his humanity had to seek your will through dark
6   silence. Help us to remain open to your way for our lives as
7   we walk this path he trod. In his name — Amen.
8   *(Fifth CROSS BEARER enters and takes the cross.)*
9   Crossroads five: Jesus feels that he has disappointed John
10   and sorrows in John's death.
11 VOICE 1: We worship you, O Christ!
12 CHORUS: By your cross you have redeemed the world.
13 VOICE 2: *(Steps toward center.)* Now, John had come eating no
14   bread and drinking no wine. He was a larger-than-life
15   prophet who was loyal and disciplined, and he expected an
16   equally competent Savior to follow him — powerful,
17   forceful, majestic, strong, law-keeping, and exhorting
18   sinners to repentance.
19 VOICE 4: What John got was Jesus with his ministry of love and
20   forgiveness, one who ate and drank with sinners.
21 VOICE 5: John sent disciples to ask, "Are you he who is to
22   come, or shall we look for another?" *(Matt. 11:3)*.
23 VOICE 3: And Jesus answered them, "Go and tell John what you
24   hear and see. Truly, I say to you, among those born of
25   women there has risen no one greater than John the Baptist
26   — for John came neither eating nor drinking, and they say,
27   'He has a demon'; the Son of Man came eating and drinking,
28   and they say, 'Behold, a glutton and a drunkard, and a
29   friend of tax collectors and sinners!'" *(Matt. 11:4, 11, 18-19)*.
30 VOICE 6: Jesus loved his cousin, and felt keenly the
31   disappointment that he must have given John. His sorrow
32   was overwhelming when told by his disciples of the mighty
33   John's ignoble death —
34 VOICE 7: His head was brought on a platter and given to the
35   girl, and she brought it to her mother —

1   **VOICE 1:** *(Moves two or three steps as if to go Off-stage.)* **Now when**
2   **Jesus heard this, he withdrew from there in a boat to a**
3   **lonely place apart.**
4   **LEADER: Let us pray:**
5   **Our Father, your son Jesus felt he had betrayed John in not**
6   **living up to his expectations. Daily we betray the**
7   **expectations of those we love and who love us. Daily we**
8   **must ask your forgiveness for these defeats, for being less**
9   **than you made us. We take comfort in the knowledge that**
10   **Jesus understands, that he felt keenly the disappointment**
11   **of John and sorrowed in this, and that he knew grief in the**
12   **death of this loved one. May his example lead us to**
13   **renewed endeavor in our ministries of love and witness. In**
14   **Christ's name — Amen.**
15   *(CROSS BEARER 6 enters and is given the cross.)*
16   **Crossroads six: Jesus meets slander, rejection, persecution,**
17   **and unbelief, and he keeps on keeping on.**
18   **VOICE 1: We worship you, O Christ!**
19   **CHORUS: By your cross you have redeemed the world.**
20   **VOICE 2:** *(Holds Bible forward.)* **And he came to Nazareth, where**
21   **he had been brought up; and he went to the synagogue, as**
22   **his custom was, on the sabbath day. And he stood up to**
23   **read; and there was given to him the book of the prophet**
24   **Isaiah. He opened the book and found the place where it**
25   **was written** *(Luke 4:16-17).*
26   **VOICE 3: "The Spirit of the Lord is upon me, because he has**
27   **anointed me to preach good news to the poor. He has sent**
28   **me to proclaim release to the captives and recovering of**
29   **sight to the blind, to set at liberty those who are oppressed,**
30   **to proclaim the acceptable year of the Lord"** *(Luke 4:18-19).*
31   **VOICE 4: And he closed the book, and gave it back to the**
32   **attendant, and sat down; and the eyes of all in the**
33   **synagogue were fixed on him. And he began to say to them**
34   *(Luke 4:20, 21),*
35   **VOICE 3: "Today this Scripture has been fulfilled in your**

1 hearing. Truly, I say to you, no prophet is acceptable in his
2 own country" *(Luke 4:21, 24)*.
3 VOICE 5: All in the synagogue were filled with wrath. And they
4 rose up and put him out of the city, and led him to the brow
5 of the hill on which their city was built, that they might
6 throw him down headlong *(Luke 4:28-29)*.
7 VOICE 6: And he did not do many mighty works there, because
8 of their unbelief *(Matt. 13:58)*.
9 VOICE 7: *(Moves up.)* And behold, all the city came out to meet
10 Jesus; and when they saw him, they begged him to leave
11 their neighborhood *(Matt. 8:34)*.
12 VOICE 1: *(Steps up.)* "This man is blaspheming" *(Matt. 9:3)*.
13 VOICE 2: *(Strident)* "Why does your teacher eat with tax
14 collectors and sinners?" *(Matt. 9:11)*.
15 VOICE 4: *(Hostile)* "He casts out demons by the prince of
16 demons" *(Matt. 9:34)*.
17 VOICE 5: They were filled with fury and discussed with one
18 another what they might do to Jesus *(Luke 6:11)*.
19 VOICE 6: So Jesus met rejection and denial. The taunts and
20 allegations paved the long road to the cross. They were not
21 new during the final days.
22 VOICE 7: They had been met — and conquered.
23 CHORUS: And Jesus kept on through rejection and fear,
24 through doubt and discouragement.
25 LEADER: Let us pray:
26 We know, God, that Jesus met hostility and rejection. He
27 was misunderstood, just as we are. We gather courage in
28 his victory. We are grateful. In Christ's name — Amen.
29 *(Seventh CROSS BEARER comes to take the cross and place.)*
30 Crossroads seven: Jesus used everything at his disposal to
31 make his Father understood. He healed and taught,
32 preached and lived.
33 VOICE 1: We worship you, O Christ!
34 CHORUS: By your cross you have redeemed the world.
35 VOICE 2: The loneliness continued. There were the nagging

1   doubts, the terrible premonitions.

2 VOICE 3: *(Seated on bottom step of center riser.)* **"Now is my soul**
3   **troubled. And what shall I say, 'Father, save me from this**
4   **hour'?** *(Stands.)* **No, for this purpose I have come to this**
5   **hour. Father, glorify thy name"** *(John 12:27-28).*

6 VOICE 4: He renewed his efforts to make his God — his Father
7   — his Mother — his All — visible. He spoke in parables, he
8   used signs and stories. He felt that time was running out,
9   and he wondered if even the Twelve understood. He had
10   gone through everything he could think of, and still he felt
11   they didn't grasp the significance of his life, or of the
12   coming events.

13 VOICE 3: "The kingdom of heaven may be compared to a man
14   who sowed good seed in his field" *(Matt. 13:24).*

15 VOICE 5: "The kingdom of heaven is like a grain of mustard
16   seed which a man took and sowed in his field" *(Matt. 13:31).*

17 VOICE 6: "The kingdom of heaven is like treasure hidden in a
18   field" *(Matt. 13:44).*

19 VOICE 7: Here is another picture of the kingdom of heaven.
20   "The kingdom of heaven is like a merchant in search of fine
21   pearls ..." *(Matt. 13:45).*

22 VOICE 1: "Again, the kingdom of heaven is like net which was thrown
23   into the sea and gathered fish of every kind" *(Matt. 13:47).*

24 VOICE 2: "Therefore the kingdom of heaven may be compared
25   to a king ..." *(Matt. 18:23).*

26 VOICE 3: "For the kingdom of heaven is like a householder who
27   went out early in the morning ..." *(Matt. 20:1).*

28 VOICE 4: But Jesus was answered in misunderstandings, in traps
29   that were set with his own words, with riddles and in tests.

30 VOICE 3: *(Seated again)* "O Jerusalem, Jerusalem, killing the
31   prophets and stoning those who are sent to you! How often
32   would I have gathered your children together as a hen
33   gathers her brood under her wings, and you would not!"
34   *(Matt. 23:37).*

35 VOICE 5: And they were deaf to his words —

79

1   VOICE 6: And blind —

2   CHORUS: As we are deaf — and blind.

3   LEADER: Let us pray:

4   Open, God, our ears that we may hear and understand; our

5   eyes that we may see. Give us grace to say in truth, "Blessings

6   on him who comes in the name of the Lord." Amen.

7   *(Eighth CROSS BEARER takes cross.)*

8   Crossroads eight: Jesus is drained. He heals. He works

9   miracles. He feels a vast tiredness.

10 VOICE 1: We worship you, O Christ.

11 CHORUS: By your cross you have redeemed the world.

12 VOICE 2:   *(Holding Bible)* Though he had done so many signs

13   before them, yet they did not believe in him; it was that the

14   word spoken by the prophet Isaiah might be fulfilled:

15   "Lord, who has believed our report, and to whom has the

16   arm of the Lord been revealed?" *(John 12:37-38)*.

17 VOICE 4: Simon's mother-in-law was in the grip of a high fever

18   — and he rebuked the fever.

19 VOICE 5: At sunset, all who had friends suffering from one

20   disease or another brought them to him — and he laid his

21   hands on them and cured.

22 VOICE 6: And he cleansed lepers, and made blind men see.

23 VOICE 7: The lame walked.

24 VOICE 1: The unclean were made clean; the dead were made alive.

25 VOICE 2: Still they did not believe, nor did they understand.

26 VOICE 3:   *(Standing — forcefully)* "He who believes in me,

27   believes not in me but in him who sent me. And he who sees

28   me sees him who sent me" *(John 12:44-45)*.

29 LEADER: Let us pray:

30   Heal us, Lord, of our disbelief. Give us faith that we may

31   know that through Jesus we see the Father, and through

32   him is eternal life. Amen.

33   *(Ninth CROSS BEARER takes the cross and position.)*

34   Crossroads nine: Jesus has terrible premonitions of his

35   death, but his concern is for those who follow him.

1 **VOICE 1: We worship you, O Christ!**

2 **CHORUS: By your cross you have redeemed the world.**

3 **VOICE 2:** *(Holds Bible.)* **From that time Jesus began to show his**

4   **disciples that he must go to Jerusalem and suffer many**

5   **things from the elders and chief priests and scribes, and be**

6   **killed, and on the third day be raised** *(Matt. 16:21).*

7 **VOICE 3: Little children, yet a little while I am with you. You will**

8   **seek me, but where I am going you cannot follow. One day**

9   **you will. Only for a little longer am I with you.**

10 **VOICE 4: Peter said, "Lord, what is the reason I cannot follow**

11   **you now? Why, I will lay down my life for you."**

12 **VOICE 3: Will you lay down your life for me, Peter?** *(Pause)*

13 **LEADER: Let us pray:**

14   **O God, we pray that we can be faithful through the power**

15   **of your Holy Spirit. We know that alone, we are weak and**

16   **afraid. Only with your help can we make visible your**

17   **kingdom. Give us, we ask, what you know that we need.**

18   **This we ask in your son Jesus' name. Amen.**

19   *(Tenth CROSS BEARER takes the cross and position.)*

20   **Crossroads ten: There is affirmation.**

21 **VOICE 1: We worship you, O Christ!**

22 **CHORUS: By your cross you have redeemed the world.**

23 **VOICE 2:** *(Holding Bible)* **And after six days Jesus took with him**

24   **Peter and James and John and led them up a high**

25   **mountain apart by themselves; and he was transfigured**

26   **before them, and his garments became glistening, intensely**

27   **white, as no fuller on earth could bleach them. And there**

28   **appeared to them Elijah with Moses; and they were talking**

29   **to Jesus** *(Mark 9:2-4).*

30 **VOICE 4: A cloud appeared, and cast its shadow over them, and**

31   **out of the cloud came a voice: "This is my Son; my beloved**

32   **Son. Listen to him."**

33 **VOICE 3: "I have come down from heaven, not to do my own**

34   **will, but the will of him who sent me ... This is the will of**

35   **my Father, that everyone who sees the Son and believes in**

1   **him should have eternal life"** *(John 6:38-40).*

2   **VOICE 5: For God had said to Moses, "I** *am* **who I** *am.* **Say this**

3   **— I** *am* **has sent me to you."**

4   **VOICE 3: And Jesus said, "I am the bread of life"** *(John 6:48).*

5   **VOICE 6: And Jesus said, "If any one thirst, let him come to me**

6   **and drink** *(John 7:37).*

7   **VOICE 7: I am the door —**

8   **VOICE 1: I am the vine —**

9   **VOICE 2: I am the way —**

10   **VOICE 3: I** *am* **—**

11   **VOICE 4: I** *am* **—**

12   **VOICE 5: I** *am* **—**

13   **LEADER: Let us pray:**

14   **Lord, we thank you for all the consolations and the**

15   **affirming joys of this life, and for the promise of eternal life**

16   **with you. Amen.**

17   *(Eleventh CROSS BEARER enters and takes the cross.)*

18   **Crossroads eleven: Jesus loved his own who were in the**

19   **world, and now he was to show the full extent of his love.**

20   **VOICE 1: We worship you, O Christ!**

21   **CHORUS: By your cross you have redeemed the world.**

22   **VOICE 2: It was before the festival of the Passover, and Jesus**

23   **knew that the hour had come for him to pass from this**

24   **world to the Father. He had always loved those who were**

25   **his in the world, but now he longed to find some way to**

26   **demonstrate the magnitude of his love.**

27   **VOICE 4: They were at supper. The mind of Judas Iscariot, son**

28   **of Simon, was already set upon betrayal.**

29   **VOICE 5: Jesus knew that time was running out. He wondered**

30   **yet if those twelve understood.**

31   **VOICE 6: Jesus had tried every way he knew to teach them. He**

32   **had told them stories about things they knew well, and then**

33   **he had explained the stories.**

34   **VOICE 7: There were the acts of healing — and, again, the**

35   **explanations.**

1 VOICE 1: Jesus went through everything he could think of and
2   still felt they didn't grasp the significance of his life — or of
3   the coming events.
4 VOICE 2: Jesus wondered how he could demonstrate in some
5   way what this was all about — the great love and mercy of
6   the Father, made visible in the Son.
7 VOICE 4: The inspiration came.
8 VOICE 5: Quickly Jesus got up from the table, removed his
9   outer garment and, taking a towel, wrapped it around his
10   waist. He then poured water into a basin and began to wash
11   his disciples' feet.
12 VOICE 6: Tenderly he took the feet of the men he loved. Gently he
13   washed those hard, callused feet. Carefully he dried them.
14 VOICE 7: The men were strangely silent, a little embarrassed.
15   Perhaps this action *had* been enough!
16 VOICE 4: But Peter — Peter, impetuous as ever, said, "Lord, are
17   you going to wash my feet?"
18 VOICE 3: Yes, Peter. At the moment you don't know what this
19   means. Later you will remember this and understand.
20 VOICE 4: Never! You shall never wash my feet.
21 VOICE 3: If you don't let me wash your feet, you cannot have
22   anything in common with me.
23 VOICE 4: Oh, Lord, if you feel that way, don't stop with my feet
24   — wash all of me.
25 VOICE 3: Peter, you have had all of me — with you. You are
26   clean all over — all but one here is clean.
27 VOICE 5: Do we dare remember that he also washed the feet
28   of Judas?
29 VOICE 6: And Jesus prayed:
30 VOICE 3: "I have manifested thy name to the men whom thou
31   gavest me out of the world ... I am praying for them; I am
32   not praying for the world but for those whom thou hast
33   given me, for they are mine, and I am glorified in them. And
34   now I am no more in the world, but they are in the world,
35   and I am coming to thee. Holy Father, keep them in thy

1   name ... I do not pray for these only, but also for those who
2   ... believe in me through their word, that they may all be
3   one; even as thou, Father, art in me, and I in thee, that they
4   also may be in us, so that the world may believe that thou
5   hast sent me ... that the love with which thou hast loved me
6   may be in them, and I in them" *(John 17:6, 9-11, 20-21, 26).*
7   VOICE 6: And they understood not.
8   LEADER: Let us pray:
9   Lord, nor do we understand. Our finite minds cannot grasp
10   the love you bear for us. We cannot comprehend it. Please
11   give us the gift of your spirit, that we may love fully, that
12   we may grow in service, and that we may in some way
13   glorify you, our God. In Christ's name we pray. Amen.
14   *(Twelfth CROSS BEARER enters and takes the cross.)*
15   Crossroads twelve: His hour is at hand.
16   VOICE 1: We worship you, O Christ!
17   CHORUS: By your cross you have redeemed the world.
18   VOICE 2: Jesus was troubled in spirit.
19   VOICE 3: "Truly, truly, I must say to you; one of you will betray me."
20   VOICE 5: Tell us, who is it of whom you speak?
21   CHORUS: Lord, who is it?
22   VOICE 3: "It is he to whom I give this morsel when I have
23   dipped it."
24   VOICE 6: And, when he had dipped the morsel, he gave it to Judas.
25   VOICE 3: "What you are going to do, do now and quickly."
26   VOICE 7: As soon as Judas had received the bread, he went out.
27   It was night.
28   LEADER: Let us pray:
29   Lord, we continue to betray you. We still do not understand
30   the mercy and love you offer. We are sorry for our
31   betrayals, for all the things we have done that we should
32   not have done, and for all the things we have not done that
33   we should have done. Forgive us, Lord, for we sin. Amen.
34   *(Thirteenth CROSS BEARER enters and takes the cross.)*
35   Crossroads thirteen: The way of the cross continues

1 throughout the long night.

2 VOICE 1: We worship you, O Christ!

3 CHORUS: By your cross you have redeemed the world.

4 VOICE 2: Jesus took Peter and James and John with him to

5   Gethsemane.

6 VOICE 3: Sit here and be near while I pray.

7 VOICE 5: In anguish he cried out once again to his Father.

8 VOICE 3: "Abba, Father, all things are possible to thee; remove

9   this cup from me; yet not what I will, but what thou wilt"

10   *(Mark 14:36)*.

11 VOICE 6: And he came back and found them sleeping.

12 VOICE 3: "[Peter] are you asleep? Could you not watch one

13   hour?" *(Mark 14:37)*.

14 VOICE 7: And again he went away and prayed, saying the same

15   words. And again he came and found them sleeping, for

16   their eyes were very heavy *(Mark 14:39-40)*.

17 VOICE 1: And he came the third time.

18 VOICE 3: "Are you still sleeping and taking your rest? It is

19   enough; the hour has come; the Son of Man is betrayed into

20   the hands of sinners. Rise, let us be going; see, my betrayer

21   is at hand" *(Mark 14:41-42)*.

22 VOICE 6: And Judas came, and with him a crowd with swords

23   and clubs.

24 LEADER: Judas said, "Master," and kissed him.

25 VOICE 7: Everything happened all too fast now. The arrest was

26   made. There was flogging and jeering and more betrayal.

27   There were the cries of the crowd.

28 CHORUS: Crucify him! Crucify him!

29   *(Lights dim. Fourteenth CROSS BEARER enters and slowly*

30   *takes the cross.)*

31 LEADER: Crossroads fourteen: Jesus is taken to Golgotha

32   where they crucify him, and with him two others.

33 VOICE 1: We worship you, O Christ!

34 CHORUS: By your cross you have redeemed the world.

35 VOICE 2: So they took Jesus, and he went out, bearing his own

1   cross, to the place called the place of a skull, which is
2   called in Hebrew, Golgotha.
3   VOICE 5:   There they crucified him, and with him two others,
4   one on either side, and Jesus between them.
5   VOICE 6:   Pilate wrote a title and put it on the cross, "Jesus of
6   Nazareth, the King of the Jews," and he would not change this.
7   VOICE 7:   When the soldiers had crucified Jesus, they took his
8   garments and made four parts, one for each soldier; also
9   his tunic. But the tunic was without seam, woven from top
10   to bottom.
11 VOICE 1:   And they cast lots for this.
12 VOICE 2:   At the foot of the cross were his mother, and his
13   mother's sister, and Mary Magdalene. Jesus saw his
14   mother, and the disciple whom he loved.
15 VOICE 3:   Mother, there is your son.
16 VOICE 2:   And to the disciple —
17 VOICE 3:   There is your mother.
18 VOICE 2:   And she was cared for. He said:
19 VOICE 3:   I thirst.
20 VOICE 2:   He was given sour wine — and finally —
21 VOICE 3:   It is finished! *(Lights down.)*
22   *(Fifteenth CROSS BEARER, a young child, enters and takes the*
23   *cross. During this station the lights should gradually go up.)*
24 LEADER: Crossroads fifteen.
25 VOICE 1:   We worship you, O Christ!
26 CHORUS: By your cross you have redeemed the world.
27 LEADER: Of course, the way of the cross did not end there.
28 VOICE 2:   Of course not — for on the third day —
29 VOICE 3:   He conquered death.
30 VOICE 4:   There is life after what we call death.
31 VOICE 5:   And there is still pain
32 VOICE 6:   Betrayal
33 VOICE 7:   Evil and death
34 VOICE 1:   Hope
35 VOICE 2:   and Hopelessness

1 VOICE 3: Hate
2 VOICE 4: Abuse
3 VOICE 5: Murder
4 VOICE 6: Hope
5 VOICE 7: Violence
6 VOICE 1: Poverty
7 VOICE 2: Hunger
8 VOICE 3: Hope
9 VOICE 4: Despair
10 VOICE 5: Bitterness
11 VOICE 6: Suffering
12 VOICE 7: Hope
13 VOICE 1: Loss
14 VOICE 2: Emptiness
15 VOICE 3: Loneliness
16 VOICE 4: Hope
17 VOICE 5: Ugliness
18 VOICE 6: Discrimination
19 VOICE 7: Beauty
20 VOICE 1: Selfishness
21 VOICE 2: and Generosity
22 VOICE 3: Filth
23 VOICE 4: Defilement
24 VOICE 5: Pollution
25 VOICE 6: Inhumanity
26 VOICE 7: War
27 VOICE 1: Care
28 VOICE 2: Hope
29 VOICE 3: Ignorance
30 VOICE 4: Superstition
31 VOICE 5: Friends
32 VOICE 6: Bombings
33 VOICE 7: Peace
34 VOICE 1: Faith
35 VOICE 2: Hope

1   **VOICE 3:**   Love *(Lights bright by now)*
2   **LEADER:**   Eternal life
3   **CHORUS:**   LIfe everlasting.
4   **LEADER:**   Let us pray:
5   **Thank you, O God, for the path Jesus walked. Forgive us**
6   **as we stumble, as we fall, as we take other paths and lose**
7   **our way. Bring us back, please, to the path you have**
8   **chosen for us as our way to you, and our way to life**
9   **everlasting. This we pray in Christ's name. Amen.** *(Curtain*
10   *— or lights out and CAST files out in silence.)*
11
12
13
14
15
16
17
18
19
20
21
22
23
24
25
26
27
28
29
30
31
32
33
34
35

Who Am I?

A chancel play for Lent or Easter
by Arthur L. Zapel

CAST

Guest

A man about forty, dressed in a well-tailored suit — not too conservative. An intense person. He speaks well but has trouble controlling his instant thoughts. Unquestionably he's a take-charge personality; someone accustomed to command. There's an impatience about him stemming from his unhappiness with himself and what he represents.

Man (Mr. Johnson)

Someone about the same age as the guest. Could be older but not over sixty. Could be almost any church-going husband in any congregation today.

Woman (Mrs. Hoffer)

An attractive person, about thirty, dressed as any middle-class church-going housewife.

Teen

About nineteen years old. Tall, intelligent. He or she is interested in the game all the way.

PRODUCTION NOTES

Overview: An unknown man appears in the chancel area of your church. He is well-dressed, articulate, and carries himself proudly as a man of importance. As he speaks, glimpses of a deep remorse are seen through his seeming bravado. He suggests that the audience join him in a game of twenty questions which he calls *Who Am I?* Selected members of the congregation are chosen to participate. Using them as a foil for his troubled message, he explores the true essence of Christianity. On the twentieth question, one participant guesses that he is Pontius Pilate! The guess is both right and wrong. A surprise ending reveals that he is really all of us who, like he did, worship false gods even as we profess a belief in Jesus, the Christ.

Set: Only a tall stool for the Guest and three chairs for the Man, Woman, and Teen are needed.

Props: Large mirror and coat for Guest.

Lighting: Although theatrical lighting is not essential, it, together with the staging, can enhance the production by highlighting the players and keeping them slightly more than life-size. On the next page is a diagram of the set-up with optional lighting instructions.

Additional Considerations: In these days of fierce competition for minds, or merely for attention, it is essential that our communication has substance and, hopefully, originality. It's difficult to achieve both in one go-around, but it is possible. They can be mutually compatible. At least we tried to make them so in this playlet.

    Who Am I? was written as both a game and a spectator sport. Admittedly, writer's tricks force audience involvement, but not at the expense of our message, we hope. "What is a Christian?" remains the hub of all action. All lines, however trivial, lead back to this single query. All lines carry the action forward, even though they carry a double-edged meaning.

    The entertainment should be played with this always in mind. Fun with a point. A spectator event, and a rather cruel one at that. We witness a sensitive man revealing himself publicly. We hear him repent out loud. Then we are shocked to hear that he's been talking about us, and that he's not too far wrong!

    Obviously, the effectiveness of this presentation depends on the lead player. Anyone with stage presence should do well. He should create the character for himself, for the personality of Pilate is generally unknown. We were guided in our development of the character by some biographical information which indicated him to be a glib-speaking man of many moods, proud and imperious. But perhaps the creative talents of the player will discover a personage distinctly his own. Better that he does. Though it is our intention that this "game" be played as if it were really happening, a touch of the theatrical might have to be added to keep the fantasy real in this perspective.

Undoubtedly you will create things along the way that never occurred to the author. If they "feel right," put them in. You know your congregation better than the writer. If local names help — put them in. If some lines are better deleted — do so. Only remember this: Say something. And keep the audience interested. Make them think!

Playing Time: 20-30 minutes

Explanation: The simple single-source lighting set-up below can be achieved with two spotlights placed nearly side by side. We recommend placing them both to the left as indicated to avoid cross shadows on faces. This is a basic but effective lighting arrangement. Spotlights are better raised than on the floor unless you want to add a little mystery to all faces.

Lighting Diagram

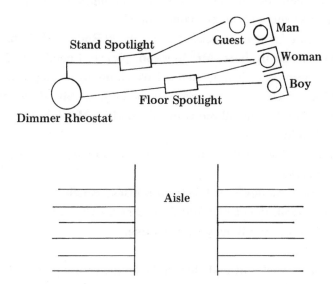

91

1   *(A single figure, GUEST, is seated on a tall stool in the center of*
2   *the chancel area. As the congregation is being seated, he quite*
3   *obviously is looking on, evaluating everyone. No explanation is*
4   *made about his presence. MAN, WOMAN, and TEEN are seated*
5   *at different places in the congregation.)*
6   **Call to Worship**
7   **Invocation**
8   **Hymn** *(Sung by congregation)*
9   **Introduction by pastor or priest**
10   *(Spotlight fades up on figure in chancel area.)*
11   **GUEST:** *(Easily)* **Well, now ... I suppose you're all wondering just**
12   **who I am sitting up here so importantly, looking you all**
13   **over. Yes, who ... am ... I? Fair question. You'll know soon**
14   **enough, and I daresay you won't be overjoyed to meet me**
15   **when you do know me ... But now, who ... are ... you? What**
16   **sort of person are you?** *(Pointing to one, then another in the*
17   *congregation)* **You Christian there ... and you and you. Do**
18   **you really belong here, or are you an impostor in spirit like**
19   **me?** *(Pointing)* **You, sir, your name?**
20   **MAN:** *(Seated in pew; somewhat taken aback)* **Roger Johnson.**
21   **GUEST: Come up here, Mr. Johnson, please. I need your help.**
22   *(He gestures to him insistently.)* **We're going to play a game.**
23   **Fine.** *(GUEST places chair flanking his.)* **Sit right here.**
24   **Excellent! Now tell me your occupation, Mr. Johnson.**
25   **MAN: Builder.**
26   **GUEST: And what do you construct ... buildings, bridges, or**
27   **fortresses?**
28   **MAN: Small homes — subdivision houses, mostly.**
29   **GUEST: Good.** *(Suddenly)* **And do you serve Christ?**
30   **MAN:** *(Unprepared)* **Why, yes, of course.**
31   **GUEST: How?**
32   **MAN: Uh ... well, I attend church. Keep my yearly pledge. I help**
33   **some with the church building program ...** *(Can't quite think*
34   *of anything else.)*
35   **GUEST:** *(Commenting more with an attitude)* **Uh-huh!** *(Pauses.)* **And**

1   the resurrection, sir ... how do you feel about the trial,
2   crucifixion, and resurrection of Christ?
3 MAN: I believe in it.
4 GUEST: In what?
5 MAN: In Christ resurrected. That he died for our sins.
6 GUEST: Why?
7 MAN: *(Suspiciously)* Why what? Why do I believe? Or why did he
8   die for our sins?
9 GUEST: Either and both.
10 MAN: Well I believe that *(In the middle of his response, his anger*
11   *overcomes his civility.)* ... now just a minute, you ... I don't
12   see why I should have to answer all this ...
13 GUEST: Ashamed?
14 MAN: I resent that, sir, and your impertinent questions.
15 GUEST: *(Grandly)* Of course you do, and you're entirely right. My
16   apologies. It's my characteristic high-handed manner. Too
17   much authority spoiled me years ago. Anyway, it was my
18   thought you would ask me questions. It would be a game
19   we could play. You ask questions to discover who I am if
20   you can. Like one of your modern TV panel shows. *(The*
21   *possibilities strike him.)* Yes, yes ... now there's a capital idea!
22   We'll have our own TV panel show right here in church —
23   *What's My Name?* Excellent! *(Thinking rapidly)* But we'll
24   need two more players to make a panel. *(Turning quickly to*
25   *audience)* Volunteers! Come now, who will volunteer? *(No one*
26   *does.)* Now look here, *you* must. *(Ingratiates.)* This will be
27   splendid fun. *(Peevishly)* I will have volunteers. *(Finding a*
28   *WOMAN in the congregation whose appearance pleases him.)* You
29   there! Say now, there's a twinkle of brightness in those eyes!
30 WOMAN: No, no thank you.
31 GUEST: *(He will not be denied. He gently lifts her from her seat as*
32   *he talks, leading her to a chair beside the MAN. Oh, he can be so*
33   *charming and commanding when he chooses.)* Now, good lady,
34   don't be that way. I promise not to be discourteous. I shall
35   ask no embarrassing questions — indeed, I will only answer

1   your questions, whatever they may be. *(Pauses.)* **However ...**
2   **allow me but two polite questions of acquaintance ... your**
3   **name and occupation?**
4 **WOMAN:** *(She is now being seated beside MAN.)* **I'm Lucille Hoffer,**
5   **housewife.**
6 **GUEST: Our pleasure, Mrs. Hoffer.** *(To audience)* **Now, one more**
7   **volunteer for our panel.** *(Points again.)* **Yes, you. We'll need**
8   **a young mind fresh to decision-making and direct in inquiry**
9   **... a mind not yet stiffened by years of experience and**
10   **method. Do sit right here.** *(Pleased)* **There we have it!** *(He's*
11   *an announcer now.)* **Ladies and gentlemen,** *(Your church name)*
12   **presents the popular TV panel show,** *Who Am I?* **brought**
13   **to you by ... uh ... by the Christian Council of the**
14   **Brotherhood of ... yes, the Brotherhood of Men, Women,**
15   **and Children ... and spirits Holy and Unholy.** *(Pleased with*
16   *himself)* **Now that's a perfect do-good group name — don't**
17   **you agree?** *(Snaps fingers.)* **But on with the game. Rules!**
18   **Twenty questions or twenty minutes, whichever comes first.**
19   **You must guess who I am.** *(Pauses.)* **Now how do we start?**
20   **Oh, yes, animal, vegetable, or mineral?** *(Reflects.)* **Yes,**
21   **mineral.** *(Thinks aloud.)* **Something hard ... its entire make-**
22   **up crystallized ... unyielding ... inflexible ... well, could that**
23   **be me? Maybe. But it isn't. No, I'm not a mineral.** *(Pauses.)*
24   **Vegetable?** *(Pauses.)* **A living thing ... a worshiper of sun,**
25   **rain, seasons, nature unaltered, unconditioned ... a living**
26   **thing without intelligence and unconcerned about free will,**
27   **ultimate purpose, hope ... something that reproduces with**
28   **abandon, blossoms, and dies, forgotten? Vegetable! No,**
29   **that's not what I am. Thankfully, no. Which leaves ...**
30   **animal! The only being with a sense for — no, correction ...**
31   **a feeling for truth ... the being that acts free but is not ...**
32   **the being that lives forward but understands backward.**
33   **Animal ... Homo-sapien ... that is I! Now who am I? Come**
34   **now. Start asking questions.**
35 **TEEN: Are you a living man?**

1 GUEST: No, I'm dead — long dead and full of remorse. Next.

2 WOMAN: Did you do anything that made history?

3 GUEST: I kept my appointment ... with circumstance. Yes, I made

4   history, but a wiser man would say that history made me.

5 MAN: Are you a person famous for his good works?

6 GUEST: Now there's a question! To whom shall I direct my

7   answer? The righteous? Answer: No! They would say no

8   because my good works would not fit the limits of their

9   lopsided geometric boundaries of what is precisely good.

10   *(Pauses.)* The getters and holders? Answer: Yes! I did well. I

11   served with loyalty to achieve a position of authority and

12   importance. I believed as I was told to believe to advance

13   my party's cause. I acted and reacted to my times to

14   achieve good works of a sort. *(Pauses.)* Enough! There's

15   your answer, and that's three questions down.

16 TEEN: Do you live in biblical times?

17 GUEST: Yes. Four questions.

18 WOMAN: B.C. or A.D.?

19 GUEST: Both. Five questions.

20 MAN: Did you ... uh ... have anything to do with Jesus?

21 GUEST: Jesus, the man ... or Jesus, the Christ?

22 MAN: Well ... uh ... I suppose I mean ...

23 GUEST: *(Interrupting)* No matter. I did, indeed play a role in the

24   life of Jesus, the man and Jesus, the Christ. I helped him,

25   in my fateful way, to prove that the human situation is

26   linked with divine eternity. Six questions.

27 TEEN: Were you one of the twelve disciples?

28 GUEST: *(Now a glimpse of the man behind the bravado)* No, but a

29   million light years of my eternity I would give to have been

30   one. The disciples were blessed by circumstances, but I was

31   not. The disciples suffered in body for Christ to bring faith

32   to others. I suffered in soul emptiness. *(Snaps back.)* Answer!

33   No, I was not one of the twelve of Christ.

34 WOMAN: *(Making a subtotal of the facts now known)* You were not

35   a disciple, yet you helped prove Jesus' promise to man.

1   *(Pauses.)* **Are you Paul?**

2   **GUEST: Disbeliever I was. A convert I have been, but I am not**

3   **Paul of Tarsus.** *(Reflects.)* **Lucky Paul! We called him Saul.**

4   **Blessed was he with insight that overcame his education.**

5   **Lucky Paul with his penetrating eye ... an eye so keen that**

6   **all man's overlaid layers of logic could not keep him from**

7   **seeing through to the truth. Lucky Paul ... I am not he!**

8   **Again unlucky I! Next question.**

9   **MAN: You said something about being a convert ... then you**

10   **were an early Christian?**

11   **GUEST: Hold on there, Mr. Johnson. I said, "A convert I have**

12   **been." If from that you draw the inference that I was an**

13   **early Christian, disabuse yourself of this falsity. I was not**

14   **an early Christian ... but, then, what is a Christian, Mr.**

15   **Johnson, early or late?**

16   **MAN:** *(Chiding)* **You promised no more questions — only answers,**

17   **remember?**

18   **GUEST: Correct! Then I'll answer my own question and not**

19   **charge you for it.** *(Defining pedantically)* **An early Christian:**

20   **a soul who would be meat for lions.** *(Pauses.)* **A late**

21   **Christian: a lion who would be a soul. I am a late Christian.**

22   **Still eight questions. Your turn, dear lady.**

23   **WOMAN: Did you see the living Jesus?**

24   **GUEST: Jesus lives still, I am told, or is this not so?** *(Politely)*

25   **May I rephrase your question to ask, "Did I see Jesus in the**

26   **flesh?" Answer ... yes, I did, and I will tell you what I saw:**

27   **A thin man. Fifteen palms and a half tall. Your measure,**

28   **about five feet ten inches. His features cleanly formed.**

29   **Quiet in repose. Eyes deep-set ... dark ... no questions in**

30   **them. Mouth — full lipped, suggestive of wisdom unspoken.**

31   **His hair, wood-brown, wavy. His beard, thin and parted in**

32   **the middle in the manner of the Nazarenes. His demeanor**

33   **— composed. His total presence — humble. Yes, I saw**

34   **Jesus in the flesh, but flesh was all I could see. Jesus of the**

35   **spirit I missed seeing, though I sensed my failure even as I**

1   **was failing. Nine questions.**

2   **TEEN: Are you some kind of a philosopher or a prophet?**

3   **GUEST: Neither, but I have been a seeker after truth ... when**

4   **not too busy with other things. I have asked: "What is**

5   **truth?" only to forget my question as other thoughts**

6   **impinge on the inquiry. Like: "Will truth hurt me if I learn**

7   **more about what it is? Will truth upset my world of creature**

8   **comforts? Will it disturb my boss? My competitive position?**

9   *(Pauses.)* **Was I ... am I, a prophet?** *(Pauses.)* **No. Was I ... am**

10   **I, a philosopher? Yes. Not by fame ... not by title, but**

11   **philosopher I am. Now! This day!** *(Pauses.)* **Your attention,**

12   **please. Editorial comment from your philosopher looking**

13   **back across the two-thousand years of Christianity.**

14   *(Measured words)* **It's ... a ... mess!** *(Pauses to reflect again.)*

15   **Still, it holds together ... the whole crazy quilt of it! Tribute**

16   **to the Founder! And grateful thanks to the Owner!**

17   *(Suddenly, to someone in the audience)* **And you, sir, how do**

18   **you serve Christ?** *(Catches himself.)* **Sorry. Back to *Who* ...**

19   ***Am ... I?* Nine ... ten ... eleven ... yes, now question twelve.**

20   **Let's speed this game along. I want you to know who I am**

21   **... if you cannot guess already.**

22   **MAN: Were you a military figure?**

23   **GUEST: No, I could not properly answer affirmative to that, yet**

24   **... well, let's leave it a simple "no."**

25   **WOMAN: Were you a religious leader?**

26   **GUEST: Again, no. Thirteen ... fourteen questions.**

27   **TEEN: Were you a pagan?**

28   **GUEST: Now what, young soul, is a pagan? A non-worshiper?**

29   **TEEN: A non-worshiper of Christ.**

30   **GUEST: Then pagan I was, my young Christian friend, but you**

31   **draw such a tight little circle for worshipers. You leave so**

32   **many of us out in the pagan cold. Yet we are all worshipers.**

33   **Now my wife and I were never really pagans in our own**

34   **sight. We worshiped many gods. In our youth we began**

35   **with the gods of our fathers: Janus, Jupiter, Juno, Mars,**

1   **and Vesta, to name the popular ones. They represented the**
2   **powers of nature. My dear wife's family believed differently.**
3   **More advanced. They worshiped Cybele, Isis, Mithras, and**
4   **Serapis. But after we were married, our gods changed. The**
5   **new gods we shared were called Success, Power, Influence,**
6   **Prestige ... You know them: they're still popular contenders.**
7   **A person needs to worship. When I was flesh, it pleased me**
8   **to worship winners. You worship** *(Name a prominent sports*
9   *figure)* **... I worshiped Petruno, the gladiator. My, what a**
10   **fighter he was. And I worshiped Juleeah, the exotic dancer**
11   **... you worship** *(Name the current sex goddess).* **A person**
12   **needs a subject to worship. Something perfect to the eye.**
13   **But worship of the heart — the soul — for the pagans, that**
14   **comes hard. Question sixteen, please.**
15 **MAN: You were not a military figure or a religious leader, and you**
16   **were a pagan.** *(Pauses to reflect.)* **Were you, then, an evil man?**
17 **GUEST: Is an objective man ... a politic man ... a practical man,**
18   **an evil man? Sorry ... I answered your question with my**
19   **question. Let me say instead** *(Deferring to Mr. Johnson)* **that I**
20   **was a builder, too, of sorts. Among my works was an**
21   **aqueduct twenty-one miles long to bring health-giving**
22   **water from the Pools of Solomon to the Temple Cisterns.**
23   **Also among my constructive efforts, I kept the peace for the**
24   **many by killing the few. I honored my country and paid**
25   **homage through loyal service. Was I an evil man having**
26   **done all this? Yes! Question seventeen?**
27 **WOMAN: You were a Roman, then?**
28 **GUEST: Yes.**
29 **TEEN: You were a governor for Rome in Judea?**
30 **GUEST:** *(Nods affirmatively.)* **Eighteen questions.**
31 **MAN:** *(Closing in)* **You sat in judgment of Jesus?**
32 **GUEST:** *(Nods again.)* **Nineteen ... and my name?**
33 **MAN: Are you Pontius Pilate?**
34 **GUEST: Twenty questions!** *(Long pause)* **And wrong! You lose!**
35   **You are tragically mistaken! I was Pontius Pilate, but still**

1   you are wrong. That's only part one of this game. My true
2   identity you have missed completely, and that is what really
3   counts in this game. Unless you really know me, you will be
4   the loser — the tragic loser. Are you ready to face reality?
5   Then I will tell you who I really am. *(He goes off to the side*
6   *and returns with a mirror which he faces to the audience so that*
7   *all can see themselves.)* **There, I am you! Every one of you**
8   **that is a seeker of status ... of false gods ... that murders**
9   **Christ every day ... you have sat in judgment of Christ as**
10   **much as I, and you have washed your hands of his blood as**
11   **I did. And I say to you ... he who is not for Jesus Incarnate**
12   **is against God, the Almighty! I say most of you put him on**
13   **the cross as I did ... not by choice but by weakness! You**
14   **must follow his way with a will. He suffered and died to**
15   **prove that belief is more important than life. And he**
16   **returned on the third day to prove that belief transcends**
17   **death. Believe and be of joy and peace. Man in life is more**
18   **than a chance combination of atoms. Man in death is more**
19   **than a displacement of atoms. If atoms can combine and**
20   **displace, they can replace themselves. This is Christ's**
21   **message of Easter. God's mind is eternal. Man is of God.**
22   **Man is eternal. Believe, and be of joy and peace. Accept**
23   **Christ as the authority. Follow him in life. You and I are the**
24   **same. Listen to me, a sinner, but follow him in his promise:**
25   **"He that believes in me, although he be dead, shall live.**
26   **And everyone that lives and believes in me shall not die,**
27   **forever"** *(John 11:25-26, author's paraphrase).* *(Pauses.)* **I've**
28   **enjoyed your company. If you will excuse me, I have other**
29   **places to go. The Lord be with you.** *(He reaches for his coat,*
30   *lying folded in a corner, then quietly walks down the aisle of the*
31   *church sanctuary and disappears out the door. There is a pause*
32   *for thought, then the church choir begins a hymn. Closing*
33   *benediction.)*
34
35

1	***Alternate Ending***
2	
3	**GUEST:** **Twenty questions!** *(Long pause)* **And wrong! You lose!** *(To*
4	*audience)* **You all lose! You are all tragically mistaken! True,**
5	**I was Pontius Pilate, but you are still wrong. That's only**
6	**one part of this game. You have completely missed my true**
7	**identity, and that's what really counts in this game. Unless**
8	**you really know me for who I am, you will be the loser, the**
9	**tragic loser. All right, are you ready to face reality? Then I**
10	**will tell you who I really am! I am you! Every one of you.**
11	**And you, each and every one of you, are Pontius Pilate!**
12	**And you're Judas, and you're Peter. We who lived with**
13	**Christ are not one bit different than you. Yes, I**
14	**compromised what I believed was right just to save my own**
15	**skin but so do you. I was a coward in the face of their**
16	**threats, but which one of you has not backed down the**
17	**same way? I sat in judgment of Christ and then washed my**
18	**hands of his blood, but so have you, each time you've**
19	**decided that your way is better than his. And Peter. How**
20	**tragically he denied Christ. Even lost his temper and swore**
21	**an oath. But isn't that just like you, you with your words or**
22	**your actions or your attitudes giving the lie to your**
23	**Christian faith? I think if you look at Peter very closely,**
24	**you'll see yourself. Take Judas, Judas Iscariot, the great**
25	**betrayer. You despise the man for what he did, but you**
26	**might as well despise yourself, for have not all of you, as**
27	**well, betrayed Christ and the faith into evil hands by your**
28	**indifference, by not defending the faith, by not insisting**
29	**upon the right and the good? Haven't you, too, played into**
30	**the hands of those who would turn Christ over to his**
31	**enemies by winking at the evil that would destroy people's**
32	**faith in God? Sure, you're Pontius Pilate and Peter and**
33	**Judas. Those men are symbolic of people in all ages,**
34	**people just like you; he who is not clearly for Jesus is**
35	**against him. And the whole miserable story of Christ's**

1   suffering is just as real today as it was two thousand years
2   ago, and it's happening in your lives! But thank God, so is
3   the message of forgiveness and resurrection! Every one of
4   you can rise above your failures, your denials, and your
5   betrayals and be faithful, just as sure as Easter follows
6   Good Friday! Don't follow Judas down his dead-end street.
7   He was aware of his failure, but he lost hope. Follow Peter.
8   He failed, too, and he knew it. But he experienced Christ's
9   forgiveness and built a new life for himself. Tonight, only
10   you can answer the most important question, because you
11   are Pilate and Pilate is you. The bridge between him and
12   you, and you must answer. How will you answer? Which
13   way will you go?
14 MAN: Sir, may I ask —
15 GUEST: *(Interrupts sharply.)* No more questions! The game is
16   over. It's time now for answers. You must give your answer!
17
18
19
20
21
22
23
24
25
26
27
28
29
30
31
32
33
34
35

Palm Sunday

Parade Without a Permit

A one-act play for Palm Sunday
by Ernest R. Stair

CAST

Chief
David
Messenger
Agent 1
Agent 2
Agent 3
Aide 1
Aide 2
Joanna
Jonathan

PRODUCTION NOTES

Overview: Although we think of Palm Sunday as a joyful occasion, it may have also held disappointment and misunderstanding for some. This play focuses on the familiar story of the Triumphal Entry from the viewpoint of a frustrated city official who is responsible for issuing parade permits. He is called on the carpet for letting this unauthorized parade happen. Although the official does not become a committed follower of Christ, he does speculate on what the future holds for the unlikely hero who rode the streets on a donkey amid shouts of "Hosanna!" And we, with the long view of history, gain a glimpse of what might have happened on that momentous day.

Set: All action takes place at the Police Department. This may be done as simply as a desk for Chief, a table, assorted chairs, and a bench for the children to sit on by the Chief's desk. The script refers to a window, but this may be pantomimed.

Props: You will need a lot of papers: a stack for Chief, various papers scattered across Chief's desk and the table, a bundle for each of the two Aides, two small pieces of paper (memos) for the Messenger, and two stacks for David, in addition to a pad of paper and a pencil. The children, Joanna and Jonathan, each need a palm branch.

Costumes: The characters may wear either biblical or contemporary garb. If using contemporary costumes, we suggest police uniforms for Chief and David, suits and ties for the Agents and Aides, a shirt, tie, name tag, and hat for Messenger, and colorful children's clothing for Joanna and Jonathan.

Sound Effects: The shouts from the parade on page 107 may be taped or performed into an Off-stage microphone by the cast members not On-stage at that time.

Playing Time: About 20-25 minutes.

1   **CHIEF:** *(Sitting at desk, rummaging frantically through a stack of*
2   *papers; goes to window and looks out, shaking his head,*
3   *obviously distressed at what he sees; then returns to desk to*
4   *resume the search through papers.)* **It must be here**
5   **somewhere.** *(Pause)* **I don't understand it.** *(Walks to table and*
6   *continues rummaging through papers there.)* **If I've told them**
7   **once, I've told them a thousand times: white copy to me,**
8   **yellow copy to the Department of Police, and pink copy for**
9   **the files. Nothing difficult about that.** *(Pause)* **If they would**
10   **just follow the system, nothing would go wrong.** *(Raises voice*
11   *to a shout.)* **David! Come here.** *(Pause)* ***Today,*** **David!** *(DAVID*
12   *enters, carrying a new stack of papers to put on the desk.)*
13 **DAVID:** **You called, sir?**
14 **CHIEF:**   **Don't put those there! I'm having enough trouble**
15   **straightening out this mess as it is without adding more to it.**
16 **DAVID:** **Mess, sir?**
17 **CHIEF:** **Just put those over there out of the way, and help me**
18   **go through these papers. Something is missing, and we've**
19   **got to find it now. What has gone wrong with our system,**
20   **David? When I put you in charge of things around here, I**
21   **thought I could count on you.**
22 **DAVID:** *(Laying down his stack of papers on the table)* **I'm sorry, sir.**
23   **Something is missing, you say?**
24 **CHIEF:** **An application — for a parade permit. It's just not here.**
25 **DAVID:** **That's strange. We always file the pink copy, send the**
26   **yellow copy to the Department of Police, and the white**
27   **copy comes right here to your desk.**
28 **CHIEF:** **Well, it's not here. And that makes me, the Chief in**
29   **charge of issuing parade permits, look pretty foolish!**
30 **DAVID:** **But how do you know an application is missing? If I may**
31   **dare to sound a bit facetious, there is really no way to tell when**
32   **an application for a parade has been misplaced until that day,**
33   **when suddenly there is an unexpected and unauthorized**
34   **parade marching through the streets!** *(Grins momentarily, then*
35   *straightens his face as he sees the CHIEF does not share his humor.)*

1 **CHIEF: That's exactly my point. You *do* have an ounce of sense**
2 **in your head after all. Have you looked outside lately?**
3 **There is a parade today. It's forming now, in the middle of**
4 **the street. And we have issued no permit for it!**
5 **DAVID:** *(A bit shaken)* **Sir? You mean to say ...**
6 **CHIEF: I mean to say that for the first time in my thirteen years**
7 **in this office, we have lost a parade! Now get busy and help**
8 **me find it.**
9 *(Both rummage through papers. DAVID takes a quick glance out*
10 *the window, winces, then returns to the search. Knocking at the*
11 *door. They don't move to answer immediately, since both are*
12 *engrossed in their search. A second knock. Still unanswered.*
13 *Then the door slowly and tentatively opens to admit an*
14 *obsequious MESSENGER.)*
15 **MESSENGER: Uh ... excuse me.** *(Not heard, he clears his throat for*
16 *attention.)*
17 **CHIEF: Well, what it is?** *(CHIEF abruptly looks up with an*
18 *expression fierce enough to send the MESSENGER back a step.)*
19 **Never mind! Whatever it is, it can wait.**
20 **MESSENGER: I'm ... I'm a messenger from the Captain of**
21 **Police, sir.** *(Holds up a small piece of paper.)* **A memo for you**
22 **— from the Captain.**
23 **CHIEF:** *(Sarcastically)* **Great — just what I needed.** *(Snatches the*
24 *paper from the MESSENGER's hand and reads it, groaning.*
25 *Goes to the window for another look outside and groans again.)*
26 **DAVID: The memo, chief ... It's about the parade, I presume?**
27 **CHIEF:** *(Perusing the memo again)* **The Captain of Police has**
28 **gotten a message from the Governor's office. The Governor**
29 **reports that he was not aware of any parade scheduled in**
30 **the city for today. He wonders whether he has mislaid his**
31 **notification of it.** *(Groans.)* **The Captain has also been**
32 **caught off-guard, since he has no extra officers on duty for**
33 **the day. He wants to know whether the parade permit has**
34 **been issued and, if so, why he has not been properly**
35 **notified himself.** *(Pause)* **Where *are* the papers on that**

1   **parade?** *(Shouting, banging his fist on the table and sending the*
2   *MESSENGER back two more steps.)* **What has happened to the**
3   **system? Every parade must have a permit. Application**
4   **must be made to this office at least thirty days in advance**
5   **of the date of the parade — in triplicate! No permit, no**
6   **parade. It's that simple.** *(Sounds from the street outside:*
7   *yelling, cheering. A confusion of sounds at first, then a ringing*
8   *unison chant, "Hosanna! Hosanna! Blessed is he who comes in*
9   *the name of the Lord! Hosanna in the highest!")*
10 **DAVID:** **Perhaps we need to evaluate the system, sir.** *(A remark*
11   *which earns a glare from the CHIEF)*
12 **MESSENGER:** **Uh, excuse me ...**
13 **CHIEF:** **Oh, what is it now?**
14 **MESSENGER:** **Is there a ... a ... m-m-message to take back to**
15   **the Captain? A reply, sir?** *(CHIEF sits down, dejectedly.)*
16 **DAVID:** *(Consolingly)* **Really, Chief, aren't you making a little too**
17   **much of this whole incident? I'm sure it will all blow over**
18   **in time ...**
19 **CHIEF:** **Blow over?** *(Laughs ironically.)* **Blow over! You are naive,**
20   **David. Aren't you aware of political realities? This job is a**
21   **political appointment, and I'm in the wrong party. The**
22   **Governor is just looking for an opportunity to put me out**
23   **of here.** *(From outside, the shouting again: "Hosanna," etc. ...)*
24   **And I believe somebody is giving him that opportunity.**
25   *(Pause)* **What are they shouting about, anyway?** *(His question*
26   *goes unanswered as the conversation is interrupted by the entrance*
27   *of three AGENTS coming through the door without knocking.)*
28 **AGENT 1:** **We're here to see the person in charge of parade permits.**
29 **AGENT 2:** **It's urgent.**
30 **AGENT 3:** **Is he or she here?**
31 **CHIEF:** **Oh, Lord, this is it.** *(Puts his hands over his heart and looks*
32   *upward toward heaven.)* **Honey, I'm on my way. I'm coming to**
33   **meet you, honey!**
34 **DAVID:** *(Trying to bring the CHIEF back to reality)* **Sir! I think these**
35   **gentlemen want to have a word with you, and it might be**

1   wise for you to give them your attention.

2 CHIEF: I'm all ears.

3 AGENT 1: The three of us came separately, actually, but we

4   arrived at precisely the same moment ...

5 AGENT 2: And, ironically, with business of a similar nature.

6 CHIEF: Don't tell me, let me guess.

7 AGENT 1: I'm afraid we've come to file complaints with you. I'm

8   from the OAP.

9 AGENT 2: I'm from the PBM.

10 AGENT 3: And I'm from the CEC.

11 CHIEF: I flunked the alphabet in first grade. Could you run that

12   by me again?

13 AGENT 1: The OAP — Office of Administrative Procedures.

14 AGENT 2: PBM — Political Buttons Manufacturers.

15 AGENT 3: And the CEC — Commission on Environmental Concerns.

16 CHIEF: *(His mouth open wide at hearing this)* **And you've come to**

17   register complaints about the parade?

18 AGENTS: *(Together)* **Yes!**

19 AGENT 1: As you know, the OAP, Office of Administrative

20   Procedures, has the responsibility of evaluating the

21   efficiency of office operations among the various

22   governmental agencies. When it was brought to our

23   attention that a parade was forming in town which did not

24   have the proper permit from this office, naturally we

25   though it necessary to investigate to see whether proper

26   administrative procedures are being followed.

27 CHIEF: Naturally.

28 AGENT 1: According to the Procedures Manual — and I assume

29   you have a copy and are thoroughly familiar with its

30   contents — you should see that every parade is authorized

31   by proper application thirty days in advance. Do you follow

32   that procedure?

33 CHIEF: In pink, yellow, and white?

34 AGENT 1: Well, somewhere there is a piece missing in your

35   system, and it is my job to have a look around and find it.

1   *(Immediately he begins looking about the office, examining*
2   *papers and "systems.")*
3   **DAVID:**   *(To AGENT 2)* **You said you were with the Political**
4   **Buttons Manufacturers. What, possibly, could your**
5   **complaint about the parade be?**
6   **CHIEF: That's what I wanted to know but was afraid to ask!**
7   **AGENT 2:   As you may know, our firm manufactures political**
8   **buttons which advertise and boost the names and slogans of**
9   **persons running for office. It's a good business, but we depend**
10   **heavily on tips from offices such as yours to tell us when a**
11   **person of political importance is coming to town, so that an**
12   **ample supply of buttons can be ready for sale to the crowds.**
13   **CHIEF: I think I'm beginning to see the awful light. That parade is ...**
14   **AGENT 2:   ... Is political, or at least that's my understanding.**
15   **Those people are cheering for their candidate. And I've been**
16   **told he is a real reformer — out to change a lot of things.**
17   **CHIEF:** *(Groans and looks to heaven again.)* **Get ready, honey, I'm**
18   **coming to meet you!** *(Then back to reality)* **David! Get out**
19   **there to the streets. Now! Find out what is going on. Take**
20   **some of the office aides with you. I want to know who is**
21   **leading that parade and what he is trying to do here! Find**
22   **out everything you can. Now, get going!** *(DAVID leaves*
23   *quickly with pad and pencil.)* **I can't believe this. It started out**
24   **to be such a beautiful day.** *(Then looking toward AGENT 3)*
25   **And you! You're with the Commission on Environmental**
26   **Concerns. Now, what is your complaint? How in heaven's**
27   **name could that parade be a concern to environmentalists?**
28   **AGENT 3: The trees, sir. I'm here on behalf of the trees.**
29   **CHIEF: Of course! How forgetful of me! The trees!**
30   **AGENT 3: Yes, you see, the people in the crowds are breaking**
31   **branches off the trees to use in waving to their hero as he**
32   **comes riding through the streets. If we had been notified**
33   **that a parade was planned, proper preventative measures**
34   **might have been taken. Apparently, the yellow copy never**
35   **made it to the Department of Police.**

1   **CHIEF:** Apparently! Apparently! *(Goes to the window.)* **Yes, they**
2   **are being hard on the trees, all right. And look at that!**
3   **Some of the people are taking off their coats and putting**
4   **them down on the ground for that man on the donkey to**
5   **ride over! That's the only bright spot in the whole mess.**
6   **MESSENGER: How's that, sir?**
7   **CHIEF: My brother runs a dry-cleaning shop down the street.**
8   **MESSENGER: I see, sir.**
9   **CHIEF:** *(Firmly to everyone in the room)* **All right, I get your**
10   **messages. I know you want explanations — action. But I**
11   **need time. Give me a chance to get to the bottom of this,**
12   **and I'll answer your complaints. Now, please, go away and**
13   **leave me alone!** *(All leave respectfully. CHIEF paces the floor,*
14   *goes to the window, and returns to the desk to thumb vacantly*
15   *through some of the papers, slipping into a reflective mood.)* **I'm**
16   **a pretty decent fellow. I think I always have been. I've done**
17   **my work, never took anything that didn't belong to me, and**
18   **sometimes I've helped out people in trouble. I'm no saint,**
19   **now. But you could do worse. I mind my own business and**
20   **try to get along with people. I'm not a bad guy! So, what's**
21   **this all about? I could name officials in every agency of the**
22   **government who deliberately use other people and are only**
23   **out to get what they can for themselves. And they never get**
24   **what's coming to them. But me, I'm a decent fellow. I really**
25   **am.** *(Looks out the window again.)* **And here into my peaceful**
26   **and well-organized life comes trouble — and he is riding on**
27   **a donkey.** *(Pause)* **Whoever you are out there, do you have**
28   **any idea what you are doing to me? Do you care? And what**
29   **sort of hero are you anyway? If you are a political reformer,**
30   **you surely don't look like one. I've never seen a political**
31   **hero come riding into town on a donkey. What are you up**
32   **to? What do you want? Suddenly, from out of nowhere, you**
33   **come riding into the city — into my life — and you mess up**
34   **everything.** *(Ironic grin)* **At least you could have been**
35   **considerate enough to file an application — in triplicate!**

1   *(He exits slowly, shoulders drooping. Some signal suggesting a*
2   *lapse of time is needed here: perhaps a brief closing of a curtain,*
3   *if available, or a fading and brightening of lights, or a brief choral*
4   *bridge or hymn. DAVID and two AIDES enter, each clutching a*
5   *small bundle of papers containing notes taken from interviews*
6   *on the street.)*
7   **DAVID: Chief! We're back, and we've got something on that**
8   **parade — and on the man on the donkey. Chief?** *(Pause)*
9   **Guess he isn't here. Well, maybe that's just as well. We'll**
10   **have a chance to go over our notes and pull together a**
11   **better report for him. Sit down and let's see what we have.**
12 **AIDE 1: It is quite a bit. The man's name is Jesus, the teacher**
13   **from Nazareth who has been traveling up and down the**
14   **countryside for some time now.**
15 **AIDE 2: And he draws a crowd everywhere he goes. It's no**
16   **wonder there's such a commotion out there today. It's been**
17   **the same story everywhere he goes.**
18 **DAVID: I'm not surprised. Jesus has been saying some pretty**
19   **spectacular things ...**
20 **AIDE 2: And *doing* some spectacular things. What do you make**
21   **out of the stories that he has healed people who were sick?**
22 **DAVID: I honestly don't know. But I got the distinct impression**
23   **from people I talked to that he isn't interested in being**
24   **known as a wonder-worker. It's what he says that really**
25   **counts. Like this, for example:** *(Looks at notes.)* **He quoted**
26   **the law against killing — the one we've all heard since we**
27   **were this high** *(Gesturing).* **I always figured I was doing OK**
28   **on that score, since I never killed anybody. But Jesus talks**
29   **about another kind of killing. He says that anybody who is**
30   **angry with another person has done serious injury to that**
31   **person — in his heart. So, I may not be a murderer in one**
32   **sense, but I certainly have done a lot of violence to my**
33   **neighbors in my heart. I never really thought of it that way**
34   **until now.**
35 **AIDE 1: And listen to this. He once quoted the law about getting**

1   even with somebody who takes advantage of you. The law
2   says it's OK to settle the score — "an eye for an eye, and a
3   tooth for a tooth." But Jesus says it shouldn't always work
4   that way. If anybody strikes you on the right cheek — get
5   this! — he says you should turn the other cheek also!
6 AIDE 2: Just stand there and take it, is that it?
7 AIDE 1: I guess so.
8 AIDE 2: I wonder whether he would stand by that if he is ever
9   caught in a dark alley alone. Jesus looks like a pretty
10   healthy guy to me, and my guess is that he would be the first
11   to fight back if somebody ever tries to give him trouble.
12 AIDE 1: Could be.
13 DAVID: I've got a note here about the kind of people Jesus has
14   been seen with. Did you get anything on this? He claims to
15   be a religious teacher, and you would expect a religious
16   teacher to be careful about the company he keeps. But Jesus
17   has made friends with anybody — even people whose
18   personal lives are really messed up. There has been some
19   controversy over that, some thinking he ought to be setting an
20   example by staying away from people with bad reputations.
21 AIDE 1: Yes, and the thing that bugs me is that he's quick to
22   criticize people like us who are trying to live the right way.
23   We say our prayers, make our offerings, and fast when
24   we're supposed to, but Jesus suggests that our motives are
25   not what they should be, or something like that. It makes
26   you wonder whether he is trying to undermine the moral
27   fiber of the country.
28 AIDE 2: It does seem he is always taking up for the poor and
29   the down-and-out. It seems to me that he might have more
30   to say to support people who have made a success out of
31   their lives and who have come out on top.
32 DAVID: I can see how you might react that way. But maybe the
33   problem is with us. Maybe we need to hear what Jesus is
34   saying. As I see it, he is trying to bring us together. And I
35   know a lot of people aren't really in favor of that! Some

1   **would have us separate permanently into the rich on one**
2   **hand, the poor on the other.**
3   **AIDE 1:** And they want to keep the different races of people
4   from getting too close together.
5   **DAVID:** Exactly! And Jesus is trying to bring us together as
6   people who are all alike — citizens of what he calls the
7   "kingdom of God."
8   **AIDE 1:** Where do you suppose all of this will take him?
9   **DAVID:** That's a good question. *(CHIEF enters, still drooping in*
10   *spirit.)* **Oh, Chief. We were just going over some of the**
11   **things we learned about the parade.** *(Gathers up the papers*
12   *from the AIDES and hands them, with his own, to the CHIEF,*
13   *who looks them over with distracted interest.)* **I was hoping to**
14   **write it up in better form** *(Pause)* **... I can still have that**
15   **done, of course.**
16 **CHIEF:** *(Softly)* **No, no. This is fine.** *(Pause)* **Good job.** *(DAVID and*
17   *AIDES show pleasure at his reaction, but then disappointment as*
18   *he continues.)* **But there is something omitted.**
19 **DAVID:** Omitted? Of course, I'm sure there is more to learn
20   about Jesus than this, but is there something in particular
21   that you're thinking of?
22 **CHIEF:** *(Sitting down, appearing exhausted)* **I found out a few**
23   **things myself out in the street. Didn't mean to, really. I just**
24   **couldn't help it. I was wandering around and overheard**
25   **some disturbing things. All I had to do was listen. I'm**
26   **surprised you didn't pick up any of it yourselves.**
27 **AIDE 1:** What sort of things?
28 **CHIEF:** All that cheering we've been hearing is deceptive. You
29   get the idea that Jesus is a man riding a wave of
30   tremendous popularity.
31 **DAVID:** And isn't he?
32 **CHIEF:** Up to a point he is. But he has about as many enemies
33   as friends — people who are afraid of him and how he
34   might use his popularity.
35 **AIDE 1:** I'm not sure I understand.

1   CHIEF: This political talk — there isn't anything to it. Jesus is
2   no more running for office than you are. But a lot of people
3   think he is here to straighten out the government.
4   DAVID: Overthrow it, you mean?
5   CHIEF: Something like that.
6   AIDE 1:   Then Jesus isn't out to lead a popular revolution
7   against the government?
8   CHIEF: No. At least I don't think so. That's why he's riding that
9   donkey. That's his way of telling the people that he isn't
10   about to come riding in as a conqueror about to lead an
11   uprising. The donkey represents his humility, I heard.
12   AIDE 2: Then what is he trying to do?
13   CHIEF: I'm not sure. Somebody close to him said that the only
14   kingdom he wants to rule is the hearts of people. Figure
15   that out.
16   AIDE 1: You said something about those cheers being deceptive.
17   CHIEF: I mean that some of the people who are cheering today
18   don't know what they're cheering for. They're in for a
19   disappointment when they find out that Jesus isn't going to
20   lead a tough political reform ... And then there's the
21   conspiracy. I see you didn't mention that.
22   DAVID: Conspiracy?
23   CHIEF: What did you expect? The people on top of things in this
24   town aren't going to stand by and let this upstart teacher move
25   in here and make trouble. They've got their heads together
26   right now to figure out what can be done about Jesus.
27   AIDE 2: Are you saying what I think you're saying?
28   CHIEF: I'm saying that unless Jesus backs off now, people at
29   the top will stop at nothing to get rid of him.
30   DAVID: Nothing?
31   CHIEF: Nothing. *(Pause)* And for the life of me, I can't understand
32   what they are so afraid of. This Jesus isn't going to hurt
33   anybody! That's the furthest thing from his mind. That is
34   what the donkey means: He doesn't intend to use force
35   against anybody. But if he stays in town too long, there will

1   be trouble. You can count on it. And it will be a sad day. As
2   far as I'm concerned, Jesus is guilty of only one infraction:
3   He failed to submit an application for a parade permit. But,
4   then, I don't think he even meant to have a parade in the first
5   place. It just happened. This whole thing is just happening,
6   and I'm afraid to think where it is all going.

7 DAVID: Chief, do I detect in you a note of sympathy for this man
8   **Jesus?** *(The CHIEF and DAVID exchange significant glances, but*
9   *there is no opportunity to reply, since at this moment DAVID's*
10   *two children come bursting in, each holding a palm branch.)*

11 JOANNA: Daddy! Daddy! Have you been outside? Did you see
12   the parade?

13 JONATHAN: You never told us there was going to be a parade
14   today. You never saw so much excitement!

15 DAVID: Children! Please! Not so much noise. This is a busy
16   place, and we can't take time now to listen to what you've
17   been up to all day. Now, please, go outside. You are
18   bothering the Chief.

19 CHIEF: Nonsense, David. They aren't bothering me. Let them
20   come in. Why, they are just what I need right now. Come
21   over here, Joanna, Jonathan. It's been a long time since
22   I've seen you. *Too* long. *(The CHILDREN sit on a bench next*
23   *to the CHIEF.)* So, you saw the parade, did you?

24 JOANNA: It was a lot of fun. So many boys and girls were there
25   to see it and join in the cheering.

26 CHIEF: Why were they cheering?

27 JONATHAN: It was for Jesus. You've heard of him — the
28   teacher from Nazareth.

29 CHIEF: Oh, yes. *(Innocently)* I've heard of him. So the parade
30   was a happy one?

31 JONATHAN: Yes! Everybody was having such a good time.

32 CHIEF: And the man Jesus — he was having a good time?

33 JONATHAN: I think he was! Why wouldn't he? Everybody in town
34   was cheering for him. *(JOANNA looks down, silent and sad.)*

35 DAVID: Joanna, what is it?

1   JOANNA: Oh, nothing I guess.

2   CHIEF: You have something on your mind. Can't you tell us?

3   JOANNA: Well, it's just that ... I was standing right on the curb

4   and I got a good look at Jesus. *(Pause)* I'm not so sure he

5   was having a good time at all. I think he looked kind of —

6   sad. *(The CHIEF and DAVID look at each other. There is*

7   *knocking at the door. DAVID lets in the MESSENGER from the*

8   *Department of Police, who holds a memo in his hand.)*

9   MESSENGER: Uh, ... er ... excuse me again.

10 CHIEF: Well, what is it? I told you I'd get back to you with some

11   kind of information that you could report to the Captain.

12 MESSENGER: *(Holds out the memo, hand shaking.)* **Something**

13   from the department, sir.

14 CHIEF: *(Turns head away from the MESSENGER in disgust.)* **You**

15   read it, David.

16 DAVID: *(Taking the memo and perusing it)* **Chief, the Captain says**

17   that the Governor's office has been in touch with them again

18   over the parade, and they want to talk to you about it.

19 CHIEF: *(Jumping to his feet)* **The parade! The parade! What's all**

20   this about the parade? So we had a parade we weren't

21   expecting. Is that the end of the world? It's over by now.

22   Why can't everybody just forget it and get back to work?

23 DAVID: The Captain writes here that there is a fear among a

24   number of officials that the man Jesus is dangerous.

25 CHIEF: Dangerous! The whole town has gone mad!

26 DAVID: *(Hopefully)* **Chief, we never did finish our search through**

27   the papers here. Perhaps we can find the forms which give

28   authorization to the parade. If we find them, you could take

29   them to the Captain and he could tell the Governor's office,

30   and that would clear up this whole thing.

31 CHIEF: David! Do you honestly believe that would make any

32   difference? I told you that they are going to make trouble

33   for Jesus. The fact that he was part of an illegal parade will

34   be used against him, but I can assure you, even if I should

35   come up with the pink, yellow, and white copies of permit

1   papers properly processed, it wouldn't help. They are out
2   to get him. Don't you understand? But never mind that
3   now. Does the memo say when the Captain wants to talk to
4   me? I could see him first thing in the morning.
5   DAVID: He wants to see you — immediately.
6   CHIEF: Oh. I see. Well, then, I guess immediately means ...
7   immediately. I'd better be going. *(Goes toward the door, but*
8   *stops in his tracks as DAVID calls after him.)*
9   DAVID: Have you thought ... what will you say to them?
10   CHIEF: *(Feigning a lighthearted mood)* **Why, there is nothing to**
11   **think about. I'll simply tell them that there was a parade**
12   **today — a parade without a permit!** *(The CHIEF turns and*
13   *goes out the door. JOANNA jumps up with her palm branch in*
14   *her hand, takes the other branch from JONATHAN, and runs*
15   *toward the door. Looking in the direction the CHIEF has gone,*
16   *she calls after him.)*
17   JOANNA: Wait! Wait, sir! *(Waving the branches)* **Here, take these**
18   **with you ... for good luck!**
19
20
21
22
23
24
25
26
27
28
29
30
31
32
33
34
35

Maundy Thursday

To Serve One Another

A Maundy Thursday service of
Holy Communion and Foot-Washing
by Joanne Owens

CAST

Twelve Adults
(Eleven speakers and pastor)
One vocal soloist
Organist or pianist
Ushers as needed

PRODUCTION NOTES

Overview: The pastor and several lay readers present this service celebrating the ancient tradition of foot-washing, established by Christ himself. With narrative, music, and prayers, the neglected sacrament of foot-washing is explained and demonstrated. Those in a group of twelve symbolically wash each other's feet; then the same opportunity is offered to all who wish to participate. This service allows for a flexible adaptation of the text to fit the situation of any individual church.

Props: One large table (long enough to seat twelve comfortably), twelve chairs, a white tablecloth, twelve plates of broken bread pieces, twelve goblets of wine (grape juice), twelve bowls of water, twelve small white towels, two candles in candlesticks and hymnbooks for congregation.

Procedure: If possible, this service should be held in the sanctuary or in a place conducive to reverence and worship. The room should be dimly lit. At the front of the sanctuary, there is a long table covered with a white cloth. Around the table are twelve chairs. On the table are two large burning candles. At each of the twelve places at the table, there is a goblet of wine (grape juice), a plate of broken bread pieces, a bowl of water, and a small white towel. As the service begins, quiet music is being played. The twelve worship leaders take their places at the table and bow their heads in silent prayer. If at all possible, Leader 12 should be the minister of the church. Each leader stands and faces the congregation as he/she speaks.

A Word About the Mechanics of Foot-Washing: Jesus took the common, ordinary act of washing feet and made it an act of worship. Foot-washing is a symbol of humility, self-giving, and spiritual cleansing. Because it is a symbolic act of worship, there is no one right way to do it. Just as Christians around the world have various approaches to baptism, e.g., total immersion, pouring, or sprinkling; likewise there can be several methods of foot-washing. The important thing is to handle the act in a way that is conducive to dignity, reverence, and worship.

Some may choose to have basins of water available at each chair so that the participant's foot is actually placed down in the water and literally washed. Others may simply want to sprinkle a few drops of water on the foot as a symbol of the ancient custom. Some may decide to use a damp towel to wipe the foot and a dry towel to dry it. Because we live in a modern society where shoes, socks, and pantyhose have replaced the open sandals of Palestine, it will be important for those planning a service of foot-washing to take the mechanics of foot-washing into consideration in order to maintain a worshipful atmosphere.

Music: All hymns are in *The Methodist Hymnal,* available from the Methodist Publishing House, Nashville, Tennessee. The verses included in the script are used by permission. The pastor's closing thought is also taken from *The Methodist Hymnal,* in the benediction section of "General Aids to Worship."

Playing Time: One hour with music.

1   **LEADER 1:** Our first act of worship will be joining together to
2   sing a hymn. This hymn is a prayer that God will speak to
3   us, strengthen us, teach us, fill us, and use us. Let us
4   thoughtfully and prayerfully open our hearts and minds to
5   the presence of God as we stand and sing together hymn
6   number ____, "Lord, Speak to Me."
7

8   Lord, speak to me that I may speak
9   In living echoes of thy tone;
10   As thou has sought, so let me seek
11   Thine erring children lost and lone.
12

13   O strengthen me, that while I stand
14   Firm on the rock, and strong in thee,
15   I may stretch out a loving hand
16   To wrestlers with the troubled sea.
17

18   O teach me, Lord, that I may teach
19   The precious things thou dost impart;
20   And wing my words, that they may reach
21   The hidden depths of many a heart.
22

23   O fill me with thy fulness, Lord,
24   Until my very heart o'er flow
25   In kindling thought and glowing word,
26   Thy love to tell, thy praise to show.
27

28   O use me, Lord, use even me,
29   Just as thou wilt, and when, and where;
30   Until thy blessed face I see,
31   Thy rest, thy joy, thy glory share.
32   Amen.
33

34

35

1   LEADER 2: Let us pray. Our most gracious God and heavenly
2   Father, we come before thee with praise and adoration for
3   thy goodness and mercy to us. We recognize that all we
4   have comes from thee. We come into thy presence keenly
5   aware of our own human frailties and shortcomings, and we
6   pray, O God, for thy forgiveness for all we have done that
7   falls short of your intentions for us. We have done what we
8   should not have done, and we have failed to do much that
9   we should have done. Forgive us, we pray. We give thee
10   thanks for bringing us together in this service of worship.
11   We are grateful for this church, for its leadership, and for
12   thy children who compose its congregation. We earnestly
13   pray for a renewal of your Holy Spirit among us. Speak to
14   us, strengthen us, teach us, fill us, and use us, we pray, that
15   we may better serve thee and truly love and serve one
16   another. We make our prayer in the name of our Lord and
17   Savior, Jesus Christ, who taught us to pray together, saying
18   *(To be said by all)*, "Our Father, who art in heaven, hallowed
19   be thy name. Thy kingdom come, thy will be done on earth
20   as it is in heaven. Give us this day our daily bread. And
21   forgive us our trespasses, as we forgive those who trespass
22   against us. And lead us not into temptation, but deliver us
23   from evil. For thine is the kingdom, and the power, and the
24   glory, forever. Amen."
25   LEADER 3: We are here to worship God and to renew our
26   dedication to serve and love him and one another. Maundy
27   Thursday is a holy day, rich in history and tradition in the
28   Christian church. It is sometimes known as Holy Thursday.
29   On Maundy Thursday, we commemorate the Last Supper,
30   which Jesus shared with his disciples before his crucifixion
31   on Good Friday. During that meal Christ washed the feet of
32   his disciples and instructed them to follow his example in
33   that act of humility and servitude. Sharing the bread and
34   wine of the Last Supper has become a sacrament
35   universally accepted throughout Christendom, but the

1 practice of foot-washing has not had so wide an acceptance.
2 It has even been called the neglected sacrament. However,
3 some churches today still follow the ancient custom.
4 Traditionally, the priest girded himself with a towel and,
5 using a vessel of water, washed the feet of the faithful. In
6 some European countries, the emperor or king washed the
7 feet of twelve poor people on Maundy Thursday. In
8 England, the king watched as servants washed the feet of
9 the poor. In some Roman Catholic cathedrals, the bishop
10 washes the feet of twelve young men. Pope John the
11 twenty-third revived the custom of foot-washing by a pope
12 in 1961. When done with reverence and understanding, the
13 foot-washing service can be one of the tenderest and most
14 meaningful worship services available to Christians. As we
15 enter into this worship experience, let us take care to
16 preserve the sacredness of the moment. May this ceremony
17 be a visible token of our love for God and for one another
18 as we participate in this act of humble service, which our
19 Lord instructed us to perform.
20 LEADER 4: It has been said that true worship has not really
21 taken place unless actions of service result. May the words
22 of our next hymn help us to prepare ourselves to serve God
23 through our daily lives. This hymn emphasizes that a daily
24 walk with God is a walk of service to one another. Through
25 our words of love, through fellowship, and through work,
26 we can serve the Lord and find the patience, hope, and
27 peace that only he can give. Let us continue our worship
28 with the singing of hymn number _____, "O Master, Let Me
29 Walk With Thee."
30
31　　　　　O Master, let me walk with thee
32　　　　　In lowly paths of service free;
33　　　　　Tell me thy secret; help me bear
34　　　　　The strain of toil, the fret of care.
35

1   Help me the slow of heart to move
2   By some clear, winning word of love;
3   Teach me the wayward feet to stay,
4   And guide them in the homeward way.
5
6   Teach me thy patience; still with thee
7   In closer, dearer company,
8   In work that keeps faith sweet and strong,
9   In trust that triumphs over wrong;
10
11   In hope that sends a shining ray
12   Far down the future's broadening way;
13   In peace that only thou canst give,
14   With thee, O Master, let me live.
15
16 LEADER 5:   We will have a few moments of silent, directed
17   prayer. Please bow your heads and pray silently as prayer
18   suggestions are made. *(Brief silence)* Let us thank God for
19   our family and friends. Think of someone who means a lot
20   to you, and thank God for that person's life and love. Then
21   pray for that person. *(Brief silence)* Think of those you know
22   who have special needs — the sick, the poor, those with
23   family and personal problems that burden them. Pray that
24   their lives will be open to God's love and that you and
25   others will show God's love to people with special needs.
26   *(Brief silence)* Pray for this church. Ask God to bless the
27   work of the minister, other church leaders, and the entire
28   congregation. *(Brief silence)* Think of the special talents and
29   abilities in his service. Ask for guidance in finding new ways
30   to serve God through serving his children. *(Brief silence)*
31   Hear our prayers, Lord. We make them in the name of thy
32   Son, Jesus Christ. Amen.
33 LEADER 6:   Our next hymn tells us that to worship rightly is to
34   love each other and to serve those in need. It expresses the
35   thought that our smiles can be hymns and our deeds,

prayers. The hymn reminds us to follow the example of Christ, whose work was doing good. As we prepare ourselves for rededication through the commemoration of foot-washing and the Last Supper, let us take to heart the words of the hymn. May we join in singing hymn number ____, "O Brother Man."

O brother man, fold to thy heart thy brother!
Where pity dwells, the peace of God is there;
To worship rightly is to love each other,
Each smile a hymn, each kindly deed a prayer.

For he whom Jesus loved hath truly spoken:
The holier worship which he deigns to bless
Restores the lost, and binds the spirit broken,
And feeds the widow and the fatherless.

Follow with reverent steps the great example
Of him whose holy work was doing good;
So shall the wide earth seem our Father's temple,
Each loving life a psalm of gratitude.

Then shall all shackles fall; the stormy clangor
Of wild war music o'er the earth shall cease;
Love shall tread out the baleful fire of anger,
And in its ashes plant the tree of peace.
Amen.

LEADER 7: In the book of Matthew, we read Jesus' words, "The Son of Man did not come to be served, but to serve ..." *(Matt. 20:28, NIV)*. In Luke, Jesus tells his disciples, "I am among you as one who serves" *(Luke 22:27, NIV)*. But the Master Teacher made his point more vividly in an acted parable, which is recorded in John 13, when he washed the disciples' feet. It was the custom during Jesus' day for

1   guests at the dinner table to have their feet washed by the
2   host's servant.

3   One supposes that in the absence of a servant, it was the
4   practice of the disciples, when they had reached their
5   destination, to take turns washing off the dust of the road
6   from one another's feet. But on the night they were to eat
7   the Passover meal together, there was an argument among
8   the Twelve. The disciples had fallen into a dispute about
9   which of them would be the greatest in what they still
10   assumed would be an earthly kingdom. There were, no
11   doubt, sore feelings when they entered the upper room,
12   and Jesus could feel the tension in the air.

13   Imagine how Jesus felt when, after three years of
14   teaching and working with his disciples, they did not
15   comprehend the nature of his mission and kingdom. They
16   had failed to realize the meaning of humility, sacrifice, and
17   self-giving that Jesus taught. Even at the end of Jesus'
18   ministry, those closest to him argued about their own
19   status. The ruffled tempers, competitiveness, and self-
20   interest of the disciples is sharply contrasted by the actions
21   of Jesus in the upper room. When none of the Twelve
22   showed a willingness to do the customary courtesy of
23   washing one another's feet, Jesus willingly rose from the
24   table and performed the menial task.

25   As Jesus removed his outer garment, he also laid aside
26   any demand for power or self-glorification. In wrapping a
27   towel around himself and taking up the pitcher and basin,
28   the Master took on the dress and duty of a servant. The act
29   not only showed the Lord's unfailing, kindly consideration
30   for others, it served as an example to the disciples and to
31   us of the importance Christ places on service to our fellow
32   human beings. But perhaps more importantly, this
33   dramatic action foreshadows the total self-sacrifice and
34   humiliation to which Christ was willing to submit himself on
35   behalf of all people. It prefigures the supreme act of self-

1   **giving that would come with the cross.**

2   **LEADER 8:** *(Vocal solo. Choose from one of the following hymns or*
3   *other appropriate selections concerning the love of Christ:*
4   *"When I Survey the Wondrous Cross," "What Wondrous Love Is*
5   *This," "Amazing Grace.")*

6

7   *(The section that follows may be used as a lead-in to a*
8   *Communion service in which the entire congregation participates.*
9   *This precedes the foot-washing ceremony.)*

10

11   **LEADER 9: Let us hear God's word as recorded in Luke 22:14-27**
12   **and John 13:4-17: "Then Jesus and the others arrived, and**
13   **at the proper time all sat down together at the table; and he**
14   **said, 'I have looked forward to this hour with deep longing,**
15   **anxious to eat this Passover meal with you before my**
16   **suffering begins. For I tell you now that I won't eat it again**
17   **until what it represents has occurred in the Kingdom of God.'**
18   **"Then he took a glass of wine, and when he had given**
19   **thanks for it, he said, 'Take this and share it among**
20   **yourselves. For I will not drink wine again until the**
21   **Kingdom of God has come.'**
22   **"Then he took a loaf of bread; and when he had thanked**
23   **God for it, he broke it apart and gave it to them, saying, 'This**
24   **is my body, given for you. Eat it in remembrance of me.'**
25   **"After supper he gave them another glass of wine,**
26   **saying, 'This wine is the token of God's new agreement to**
27   **save you — an agreement sealed with the blood I shall pour**
28   **out to purchase back your souls. But here at this table,**
29   **sitting among us as a friend, is the man who will betray me.**
30   **I must die. It is part of God's plan. But, oh, the horror of**
31   **awaiting that man who betrays me.'**
32   **"Then the disciples wondered among themselves which**
33   **of them would ever do such a thing.**
34   **"And they began to argue among themselves as to who**
35   **would have the highest rank [in the coming Kingdom].**

1   "Jesus told them, 'In this world the kings and great men
2   order their slaves around, and the slaves have no choice
3   but to like it! But among you, the one who serves you best
4   will be your leader. Out in the world the master sits at the
5   table and is served by his servants. But not here! For I am
6   your servant.'

7   "So he got up from the supper table, took off his robe,
8   wrapped a towel around his loins, poured water into a
9   basin, and began to wash the disciples' feet and to wipe
10   them with the towel he had around him.

11   "When he came to Simon Peter, Peter said to him,
12   'Master, you shouldn't be washing our feet like this!'

13   "Jesus replied, 'You don't understand now why I am
14   doing it; someday you will.'

15   " 'No,' Peter protested, 'you shall never wash my feet!'

16   " 'But if I don't, you can't be my partner,' Jesus replied.

17   "Simon Peter exclaimed, 'Then wash my hands and head
18   as well — not just my feet!'

19   "Jesus replied, 'One who has bathed all over needs only
20   to have his feet washed to be entirely clean. Now you are
21   clean — but that isn't true of everyone here.' For Jesus
22   knew who would betray him. That is what he meant when
23   he said, 'Not all of you are clean.'

24   "After washing their feet he put on his robe again and sat
25   down and asked, 'Do you understand what I was doing?
26   You call me "Master" and "Lord," and you do well to say it,
27   for it is true. And since I, the Lord and Teacher, have
28   washed your feet, you ought to wash each other's feet. I
29   have given you an example to follow: do as I have done to
30   you. How true it is that a servant is not greater than his
31   master. Nor is the messenger more important than the one
32   who sends him. You know these things — now do them!
33   That is the path of blessing.' "

34 LEADER 10:   Perhaps the disciples were embarrassed and
35   ashamed of themselves for their stubborn self-pride in

refusing to perform the simple, customary courtesy of bathing one another's feet. As they watched Jesus kneel to handle the duty, there was probably an awkward silence, an uneasiness with the situation. But Peter, always impulsive and outspoken, blurted out, "Lord, surely you don't intend to wash my feet!"

Very gently Jesus replied to Peter, just as he often replies to us today, "I know you don't understand what I am doing now, but someday, you will understand."

Peter was a great deal like each of us. In his humanness, he reacted as we usually do when we face the perplexities and pains of life. He, like us, had not learned to fully accept matters that seem incomprehensible when viewed from our own personal angle. Peter probably thought, "This is not going to be. I cannot bear it." He replied stubbornly, "You'll never wash *my* feet!"

Then Jesus gently but gravely told Peter, "If I don't wash your feet, you have no part in me." Jesus was saying that unless Peter understood that Christ's lordship was most truly expressed in his role as *servant*, then Peter did not share in his Lord's mind and work.

No doubt Peter was shocked at the thought that he might not belong to Christ. Panic-stricken at the idea, he swung to the other extreme and immediately said, "In that case, Lord, wash not only my feet, but my hands and head as well." But Jesus explained to Peter that total cleansing over and over again is unnecessary. Once we have made our basic commitment to Christ, our sins are forgiven, and we need only to be cleansed of the dust of the road — that uncleanness that every day mars our lives as we travel through the experiences and temptations of this world.

LEADER 11: We are commemorating not only the washing of the disciples' feet by Jesus, but the breaking of bread and drinking of wine that they shared during their last meal together before the Crucifixion. As we humbly and

1 reverently prepare to come to our Lord's table to partake
2 of the elements in remembrance of his life, death, and
3 resurrection, we will sing the hymn "Let Us Break Bread
4 Together," which is found on page _____.
5
6 　　　Let us break bread together on our knees;
7 　　　Let us break bread together on our knees.
8 　　　When I fall on my knees,
9 　　　　　with my face to the rising sun,
10 　　　O Lord, have mercy on me.
11
12 　　　Let us drink wine together on our knees;
13 　　　Let us drink wine together on our knees.
14 　　　When I fall on my knees,
15 　　　　　with my face to the rising sun,
16 　　　O Lord, have mercy on me.
17
18 　　　Let us praise God together on our knees;
19 　　　Let us praise God together on our knees.
20 　　　When I fall on my knees,
21 　　　　　with my face to the rising sun,
22 　　　O Lord, have mercy on me.
23 　　　Amen.
24
25 MINISTER (LEADER 12): All who wish to participate are invited
26 　　to take part in Holy Communion and foot-washing. This
27 　　service is symbolic of our participation in the life of Christ
28 　　and our willingness to humble ourselves in loving service to
29 　　our fellow human beings. Because it is symbolic, we will not
30 　　wash feet in the exact way in which Christ washed his
31 　　disciples' feet, but we will sprinkle a small amount of water
32 　　on one foot of a brother or sister in Christ.
33 　　　As minister and chief servant of the congregation, I will
34 　　first wash the feet of and serve the elements to those now
35 　　with me at the table. As each one takes a piece of bread

1 from the plate, he or she will dip the bread into the cup
2 before partaking of it. After being served, the first twelve
3 will wait by their chairs while twelve more members of the
4 congregation come forward and take seats at the table.
5 Then the first twelve will serve that group. The second
6 group of twelve will serve a third group of twelve until all
7 who desire to do so have participated. Let us come before
8 our Lord's table silently, reverently, humbly, and with
9 thanksgiving.

10 *(Quiet, worshipful music should be played at this time. The*
11 *MINISTER will kneel before someone seated at the table, remove*
12 *that person's shoe, take the bowl of water from the table, and*
13 *with his/her fingers, sprinkle a few drops of water on the person's*
14 *foot. With the towel, the MINISTER will dry the foot, and then*
15 *he will replace the person's shoe. The water may be sprinkled*
16 *through women's hose. Next, the MINISTER will offer the bread*
17 *to the person, who will take a piece of it, dip it into the cup of*
18 *wine, and place it in his/her own mouth. After the MINISTER has*
19 *served the other eleven seated at the table, one of them — this*
20 *should be pre-arranged — will serve the MINISTER. Then all*
21 *twelve at the table will rise and stand by their chairs while the*
22 *ushers direct twelve more people to the table. When the second*
23 *group of twelve has been seated, the first twelve will kneel and*
24 *serve the second group of twelve with foot-washing and Holy*
25 *Communion. This procedure will be repeated until all those*
26 *wishing to participate have been served. Then the MINISTER —*
27 *LEADER 12 — will rise.)*
28 **MINISTER (LEADER 12): Hear God's word from John 13:34-35:**
29 **"And so I am giving a new commandment to you now —**
30 **love each other just as much as I love you. Your strong love**
31 **for each other will prove to the world that you are my**
32 **disciples." Let us close with the hymn "Blest Be the Tie that**
33 **Binds," number _____. May we stand to sing.**
34
35

1	Blest be the tie that binds
2	Our hearts in Christian love:
3	The fellowship of kindred minds
4	Is like to that above.
5	
6	Before our Father's throne
7	We pour our ardent prayers;
8	Our fears, our hopes, our aims are one,
9	Our comforts and our cares.
10	
11	We share each other's woes,
12	Our mutual burdens bear,
13	And often for each other flows
14	The sympathizing tear.
15	
16	When we asunder part,
17	It gives us inward pain;
18	But we shall still be joined in heart,
19	And hope to meet again.
20	Amen.
21	

22 MINISTER (LEADER 12): The peace of God, which passeth all
23   understanding, keep your hearts and minds in the
24   knowledge and love of God, and of his Son Jesus Christ our
25   Lord; and the blessing of God Almighty, the Father, the
26   Son, and the Holy Spirit, be among you, and remain with
27   you always. Amen.

28
29
30
31
32
33
34
35

Good Friday

The Carpenter and the Cross

A one-act play for Good Friday
by Nancy Thum

CAST

Amos
A carpenter

Rachel
His wife

Elihu
Their ten-year-old son

Ruth
Their six-year-old daughter

David and Jedidiah
Amos's brothers

Martha and Mary
Friends from Bethany

2 Roman Soldiers

A small crowd for the final scene

(To include more participants, the number of soldiers
and the size of the crowd may be increased.)

PRODUCTION NOTES

Overview: Amos's joy at finding new timbers for his work is short-lived. The Roman soldiers ordered that he construct the cross upon which Jesus will be crucified. This shocking command brings deep sadness to Amos and his family. They have many reasons to believe that Jesus is the Messiah for whom they have waited. When the moment of the Crucifixion comes, it is Amos who helps Jesus carry the cross. Despite his weariness, Jesus speaks in gratitude to Amos, saying, "I am a carpenter, too."

Set: A stone wall outlines the acting area of the stage. Entrances are gateposts at the right and left. A low stone bench runs along the left side wall. An olive tree decorates the Upstage Center wall.

Props: Cross — cardboard, 1 foot square pieces, 8-10 feet tall (See diagram on the next page.); two or three timbers — approximately 1 foot square shows up well from a distance. These, too, can be made from cardboard boxes; saw, plane, and chisel for pantomime by men working on wood; small bench for table, later for seat; bowls for wash basin, for serving meal, and for water at end of play; tablecloth; six wooden bowls for meal; sewing fabric.

Lights: Although special lighting is not crucial to the script, if you have access to theatrical lighting, you may use it as indicated in the script to enhance the action.

Costumes: Men: ankle-length tunic
Women: floor-length tunics
Children: short tunics with sashes
Soldiers: helmets with plumes, short capes, skirts with leather (cardboard) strips hanging from belt, sandals, and a spear for one and whip for the other
Sandals for all (or children may go barefoot)
Headcloths for women during the street scene

Playing Time: 20 minutes.

Cross-Making Diagram

Materials: Heavy corrugated cardboard from large boxes
Duct tape for making joints and covering raw edges
Linoleum knife for scoring and cutting
Dark brown spray paint

Down the center of the long upright, build an inner core of cardboard for strength. The cross arms are one piece with a center hole, so they slip down over the center core. The shorter part of the upright then fits on top of the core.

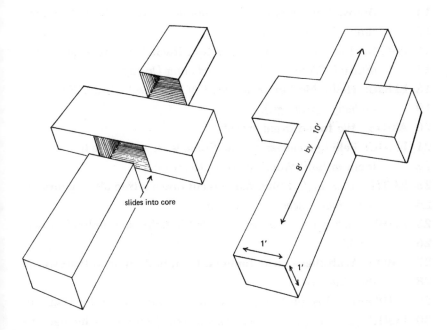

1   *(The scene is early Friday morning in the walled yard of the*
2   *home. RUTH bounces in from Downstage Right, skipping across*
3   *the stage diagonally. AMOS enters Upstage Left just as RUTH is*
4   *partly across to meet him.)*
5   **RUTH:** *(Joyous excitement in her voice)* **Father, you're home!** *(Turns*
6   *and calls back toward the house.)* **Mother! Mother, they're**
7   **back!**
8   **AMOS: Good morning, little daughter. You grew prettier while**
9   **we were gone.** *(Hugs her.)*
10   **RUTH: Where's Elihu?**
11   **AMOS: Your brother will be here in a minute. He and your**
12   **uncles are bringing the timber.**
13   **RACHEL:** *(Enters rapidly from Right as he is finishing last sentence.)*
14   **Amos, I'm so glad you're home. Your work took a long**
15   **time.** *(They embrace.)*
16   **AMOS: I'm happy to be home too, Rachel. It was a long trip.**
17   *(ELIHU, DAVID, and JEDIDIAH enter Upstage Left.)*
18   **ELIHU: Hello, Mother.** *(Hugs her. RACHEL, DAVID, and JEDIDIAH*
19   *exchange greetings.)*
20   **AMOS: We found great trees!**
21   **ELIHU: Felling trees isn't easy. Some were so big we had to split**
22   **them in half! Watch us drag them in!**
23   **RUTH:** *(Tauntingly)* **Elihu, did you cut down a tree all by yourself?**
24   *(They make faces at one another.)*
25   **ELIHU:** *(Disgusted look at RUTH)* **I'll help you unload, Uncle**
26   **David.**
27   **AMOS: With these large timbers, I can build that watchtower in**
28   **the vineyard.**
29   **JEDIDIAH: Joseph the grower promised good pay for that job.**
30   **ELIHU:** *(Eagerly, from where he's working)* **Father, if he pays us**
31   **enough, may I have my own carpenter's tools?**
32   **AMOS:** *(With laughter in his voice)* **That's a good idea, Son.** *(RUTH*
33   *is playing in and out the gate as the men unload the timbers. As*
34   *MARTHA enters, RUTH leans out to look for MARY. Lights rise*
35   *almost imperceptibly, as day is progressing.)*

1 **MARTHA:** *(Smiling happily)* **Greetings, Rachel. We've not seen**
2   **you for months.**
3 **RACHEL: Martha, what a surprise. Is — ?** *(Starts to ask if MARY*
4   *is with her, but she is interrupted by RUTH.)*
5 **RUTH:** *(Interrupting her mother and leading MARY in)* **Mother,**
6   **here's Mary, too!**
7 **AMOS: Welcome. Welcome. Come in. Refresh yourselves.**
8 **MARY: Thank you, Amos. We're on our way into Jerusalem. For**
9   **Passover.**
10 **MARTHA: Jesus is here. We came to celebrate the Feast with him.**
11 **MARY: We owe him so much.**
12 **RACHEL: What do you mean?**
13 **MARY: Lazarus. Oh ...** *(Long pause)* **... Lazarus was dead, and ...**
14 **AMOS: What?! Your brother ... was dead?** *(MEN stop working and*
15   *pay attention.)*
16 **MARTHA: He was dead, but Jesus raised him.**
17 **ELIHU:** *(With a snort of disbelief)* **How could he do that? I don't**
18   **believe it!**
19 **MARY: By a strange power.**
20 **ELIHU: Is he a sorcerer?**
21 **MARTHA: He's a healer.**
22 **MARY: We think he's the Son of God.** *(MARTHA nods in agreement.)*
23 **ELIHU: I don't understand. Rabbi hasn't taught me that!**
24 **RACHEL:** *(Amazed)* **A fantastic story!**
25 **AMOS:** *(Spreads his arms, palms upward, shrugs.)* **I've heard**
26   **rumors, but ...** *(Looks to his BROTHERS for agreement;*
27   *nodding and skeptical looks among them.)*
28 **MARTHA:** *(Strong voice; raises one hand as if commanding.)* **Come**
29   **to the temple. You see him. You hear him. Then you'll**
30   **know.** *(Sudden knocking at the gate, Upstage Left. Two*
31   *SOLDIERS step inside. FAMILY moves back a bit.)*
32 **FIRST SOLDIER:** *(Brusquely)* **Which of you is Amos the carpenter?**
33 **AMOS: I am.**
34 **FIRST SOLDIER: This is your wood?**
35 **AMOS: Yes.**

1   **FIRST SOLDIER:** Caesar needs it.

2   **AMOS:** But my contracts! There's no wood here to spare!

3   **FIRST SOLDIER:** This is not a contract; this is a command.

4   You're to build a cross — now. We've got a public execution

5   scheduled. A trouble-making Jew.

6   **SECOND SOLDIER:** *(Sneering)* **The one whose followers have**

7   **been calling him "King of the Jews."** *(MARY and MARTHA*

8   *glance quickly at each other. MARY bites her lip. MARTHA*

9   *clasps her hands together.)*

10 **FIRST SOLDIER:** He looks about four and a half cubits. Build it tall.

11 **SECOND SOLDIER:** We'll be back for it in a couple of hours.

12   *(The SOLDIERS exit Upstage Left. DAVID and JEDIDIAH purse*

13   *their lips in disgust. DAVID shakes his head sadly. JEDIDIAH*

14   *lowers his head and puts an arm around AMOS's shoulders.*

15   *AMOS rubs his brow slowly, head lowered. DAVID steps toward*

16   *the gate and shakes his fist after the SOLDIERS.)*

17 **MARY:** *(Trembling voice)* **No! Oh, not Jesus! Not Jesus!**

18 **MARTHA:** We'd better go. Oh, what can we do to stop them?

19 **MARY:** Let's hurry. *(Looks up, pained.)* **God! This can't be!**

20 **RACHEL:** Farewell. *(FAMILY, stunned and bewildered, waves good-bye.)*

21 **AMOS:** *(Dazed, slowly raises his head and speaks bitterly.)* **There go**

22   **your tools, Elihu. A week's work on those trees. Two profitable**

23   **contracts. And now this ... How will we even buy food?**

24 **RACHEL:** Oh, Amos! What useless work. *(Pause)* **Elihu, fill the**

25   **basin. Wash off the dust. I'll prepare some food.** *(ELIHU*

26   *brings the basin to Downstage Right. DAVID and JEDIDIAH*

27   *kneel to wash themselves. They then go to Upstage Center and*

28   *begin pantomiming the necessary measuring and planning.*

29   *ELIHU removes the basin after he and AMOS have washed.*

30   *AMOS joins the woodworkers. ELIHU goes to eat. As the MEN*

31   *were washing, RACHEL and RUTH spread a tablecloth on the*

32   *low projection [or a bench] Downstage Left. They bring a wooden*

33   *serving bowl and spoon and small bowls for eating. ELIHU*

34   *carries a bowl to AMOS, as RACHEL is beginning her speech*

35   *"Now I remember ..." [See line 12, next page]. AMOS, DAVID,*

1   *and JEDIDIAH rise or raise their heads when they speak, so their*
2   *voices carry over the wood to the audience.)*
3   **ELIHU: Father, I don't understand ... who is this man? Why are**
4   **they crucifying him?**
5   **AMOS: I don't know much about Jesus.**
6   **DAVID: Remember the shepherd who was here about a year ago**
7   **talking about Jesus?**
8   **AMOS: Yes. He was ordering a staff. He broke his old one in a**
9   **fracas with a Pharisee.**
10   **JEDIDIAH: Some argument about Jesus and miraculous healing,**
11   **I think.**
12   **RACHEL: Now I remember. Jesus did come to Jerusalem last year**
13   **to the Passover. He stopped at the well just outside town.**
14   **DAVID: There was a cripple there. They say Jesus healed him.**
15   **AMOS: That caused a fight between the men of the synagogue**
16   **and the people traveling with Jesus.**
17   **DAVID: That shepherd believed Jesus had special powers from**
18   **God.**
19   **ELIHU: I wish I'd been here when that shepherd came. That**
20   **sounds better than these mean soldiers!**
21   **DAVID: We'd better finish this cross before they return!**
22   **AMOS: What a dreadful job!** *(He hands the empty bowl to ELIHU*
23   *and stretches.)* **That was a good meal, Rachel. I needed some**
24   **refreshment, after being on the road all night.** *(ELIHU brings*
25   *a bowl to JEDIDIAH.)* **Elihu.**
26   **ELIHU: Yes, Father?**
27   **AMOS:** *(Resignedly)* **Help me with this saw.** *(The MEN and BOY*
28   *continue working the wood. RACHEL and RUTH clear the table*
29   *slowly. RUTH brings a bowl to DAVID. He can leave his bowl*
30   *with the tools to reduce back and forth activity, if necessary. On*
31   *the same trip, RUTH brings back the empty bowl from*
32   *JEDIDIAH.)*
33   **ELIHU: Shall I plane it after it's sawed?**
34   **AMOS: Yes. I'll chisel out the notches.**
35   **JEDIDIAH: Save a little block for his feet to rest on.**

1   **ELIHU:** Why are people saying Jesus is our king? Rabbi teaches
2   a messiah will come — someday. Is he the Messiah? How
3   can we tell?

4   **AMOS:** *(Slightly annoyed at the boy's persistence)* **Son, I don't**
5   know. People up north seem to believe he is. A couple of
6   years ago I went to Capernaum, to help Uncle Jedidiah
7   move down here to Jerusalem.

8   **ELIHU:** I remember when you went.

9   **AMOS:** Well, this man was in Capernaum then.

10   **JEDIDIAH:** That's right. So many people wanted to hear him
11   that they almost wrecked a house.

12   **ELIHU:** Your house, Uncle?

13   **JEDIDIAH:** No, but it was nearby.

14   **AMOS:** Some men went up on Jedidiah's roof, carrying a sick
15   fellow. Then they took him across to the roof over Jesus.

16   **ELIHU:** What good did that do?

17   **AMOS:** They chopped a big hole in the roof. Then they tied
18   ropes on the blanket and let him down into the room.

19   **ELIHU:** What happened? Was Jesus angry?

20   **AMOS:** I heard he told the sick man to roll up his blanket. To
21   get up and walk away on his own. That he was well.

22   **ELIHU:** Did you see him?

23   **AMOS:** No. We were busy packing.

24   **ELIHU:** I wish I'd been there. I'd have squeezed in to watch.
25   *(Pause. He holds up a piece of wood.)* **Father, is this shaped**
26   **right?** *(The WOMEN have finished clearing the table. They are*
27   *now sewing. RUTH goes to the outside gate Upstage Left several*
28   *times to look for the SOLDIERS. DAVID and JEDIDIAH*
29   *continue planing wood.)*

30   **AMOS:** Good, Son. Oh, such beautiful wood. But I hate giving
31   it to the Romans.

32   **RACHEL:** Do you think they decided to crucify Jesus on account
33   of Lazarus?

34   **ELIHU:** Were Mary and Martha telling us the truth about
35   Lazarus?

1   **RACHEL:** I think they were. They wouldn't lie.

2   **RUTH:** *(Piping up defensively)* **Mary and Martha would never play**

3   **a trick on us!**

4   **ELIHU: Father, suppose Jesus is the Messiah. How will we know?**

5   **AMOS:** *(Shaking his head slowly)* **I ... don't ... know.** *(Pause)* **All I**

6   **know right now is we'd better finish this job. Bring the**

7   **plumb line; let's be sure it's straight.**

8   **RUTH:** *(Wide-eyed, jumping up and down)* **The soldiers are coming**

9   **down the road, Father.** *(The SOLDIERS enter from Upstage*

10   *Left. RUTH has retreated to the bench with RACHEL. DAVID*

11   *and JEDIDIAH are supporting the cross, having raised it when*

12   *AMOS called for the plumb line.)*

13   **FIRST SOLDIER:** *(Thumping the cross)* **Good job, carpenter! That**

14   **ought to take care of this so-called "King of the Jews."**

15   **He'll have to carry it. That'll be a load.**

16   **SECOND SOLDIER:** *(Gloating voice)* **And it's all uphill from the**

17   **prison to Golgotha!**

18   **FIRST SOLDIER:** *(Gesturing to DAVID and JEDIDIAH)* **You two,**

19   **help us load it up. Let's go.** *(The SOLDIERS and the*

20   *BROTHERS exit Upstage Left. RACHEL moves to Center of*

21   *stage to stand with AMOS. RUTH remains on bench. ELIHU*

22   *leans against the gate at Upstage Right.)*

23   **AMOS:** *(Serious, thoughtful voice)* **Rachel, what's wrong with me?**

24   **I've had to build these crosses before. But this one bothers me.**

25   **RACHEL: Maybe because of Lazarus. I wouldn't have cared if I**

26   **hadn't heard what Mary and Martha said about Jesus.**

27   **AMOS:** *(Looks at her keenly, purses his lips.)* **They're so sure.**

28   **RACHEL: How could we tell if he's the Messiah?**

29   **AMOS:** *(Decisively)* **We must be there this afternoon to see for**

30   **ourselves.**

31   **RACHEL: I hope we'll be able to understand.**

32   **RUTH: May we go too, Mother?**

33   **RACHEL: No. Ruth, you wash the dishes.** *(She points toward the*

34   *Upstage Right exit; RUTH heads that way.)* **Elihu, you feed the**

35   **animals.**

1   **ELIHU: But Mother!**

2   **AMOS: Elihu! We'll tell you what we see and hear. Take care of**

3   **things here at home.** *(He motions ELIHU toward the Upstage*

4   *Left exit. Quiet music will aid in bridging this change of scene.*

5   *Lights are now afternoon bright. Parents move to Downstage*

6   *Right and join SOLDIERS and crowd who enter Downstage Right*

7   *and begin moving toward rear of stage. Jesus is supposedly near*

8   *the wall, so the CROWD blocks the audience's view of him.*

9   *RACHEL and AMOS move to Center Stage as they talk and look*

10   *toward Jesus. During this scene the CROWD moves slowly along*

11   *the wall toward the rear of the stage. The SOLDIERS pantomime*

12   *keeping the CROWD orderly. AMOS and RACHEL stay Center*

13   *and in front of the CROWD.)*

14   **AMOS: The road is so rough and steep.**

15   **RACHEL: Look how weary he is.**

16   **AMOS: Why don't they give him a drink?** *(RACHEL darts into the*

17   *crowd.)* **Rachel, where are you going? Rachel!** *(Pause for her*

18   *to return)* **Rachel, when you ran out there, you scared me to**

19   **death! Those soldiers could turn their whips on you!**

20   **RACHEL: I just had to do something. At least I tried to wipe his**

21   **face. Look! The soldier is making another man drag the**

22   **cross.**

23   **AMOS: Rachel, I have to try to look into his face. I want to**

24   **understand.**

25   **RACHEL: I'll stay with you. Maybe I'll see Mary and Martha as**

26   **we go along. That poor man is stumbling under the cross.**

27   **FIRST SOLDIER: Come on, you. Get going with this cross.**

28   **You're hardly moving.**

29   **SECOND SOLDIER:** *(Pointing)* **Hey, there's the carpenter. The**

30   **one who made it. He can carry it.**

31   **AMOS: Those trees should have been left growing in the valley.**

32   **SECOND SOLDIER: Too late for that. You built it. Now you can**

33   **carry it. Go.** *(MARY and MARTHA emerge from the crowd and*

34   *move to RACHEL's side.)*

35   **MARY: Rachel. Rachel. Walk with us. We've been following Jesus.**

1   **MARTHA: We saw you and Amos, but we couldn't get through**
2   **the crowd.**
3   **RACHEL: I'm so glad to see you. I knew you'd be here.**
4   **MARTHA: They're taking the cross off Amos's shoulder.**
5   **MARY: I'll get water for him, Rachel.** *(Action ends at Upstage Left,*
6   *where AMOS is relieved of the cross. RACHEL and MARTHA*
7   *bring AMOS to sit on the low bench at the front. MARY brings a*
8   *bowl, kneels, and they bathe AMOS's shoulder. CROWD stands*
9   *facing Upstage Left, looking at crucifixion which is occurring Off-*
10   *stage. Lights are dim, with a subtle spot on RACHEL and*
11   *AMOS.)*
12 **RACHEL: Amos, you helped Jesus. He was grateful.**
13 **MARY: Here's water.**
14 **RACHEL: Let me bathe your shoulder; it's bleeding.**
15 **AMOS:** *(Mesmerized expression)* **His eyes were quiet — even**
16   **loving — when I looked into them.**
17 **RACHEL: He's dying. Listen! He asks his Father to forgive the**
18   **people ... he says we don't know what we're doing.**
19 **AMOS: Forgive? Forgive ... Oh, God, it is your Son. On that**
20   **cross I built.**
21 **RACHEL:** *(Choked and weeping)* **Oh, Amos.**
22 **AMOS:** *(Standing, voice sad and breaking)* **Yes. Yes. He knew I built**
23   **it. But his eyes were kind. He just said, "I'm a carpenter,**
24   **too."**
25
26
27
28
29
30
31
32
33
34
35

Tenebrae

This Is My Story

A Holy Week Tenebrae Service
by Jon McCauley Smith

CAST

Mary 1

Mary 2
The mother of John Mark

John

The Slave of the High Priest
Male or female

Peter

Judas

John Mark
Approximately eight years old

Voice of Jesus

NOTE: The voice of Jesus is located out of sight
and is heard over a loudspeaker.

PRODUCTION NOTES

Overview: Several readers portraying biblical characters from Holy Week are seated at a table with seven lit candles. Each character tells the moving story of his or her Holy Week experience with Jesus. Characters include Mary Magdalene, Mary of Bethany, John, the High Priest's Slave, Peter, Judas, and John Mark. As each reader finishes, one candle is extinguished. Following the monologs, the service concludes with Communion.

Set: The six adults should sit in a wide semicircle around a large table facing front. There is one stool in front of the table for the boy, John Mark, who sits with his back to the audience.

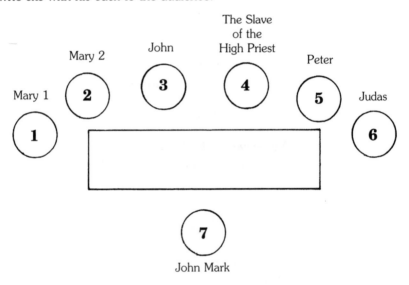

Props: The following should be placed on the table: seven lit candles, a cup, and a plate with a loaf of bread. Suggestive props from the foot-washing ceremony may be added if desired.

Costumes: Biblical robes and sandals for all characters, with the addition of rectangular cloths placed on their heads (secured with cord for the men and left hanging loosely for the women).

Playing Time: 50 minutes.

1   *(The seven On-stage READERS enter during the congregational*
2   *singing of the hymn "Blessed Assurance" [verses 1 and 3] and*
3   *take their seats. After the hymn, JOHN MARK stands, moves to*
4   *a microphone, and begins the story. ALL CHARACTERS read*
5   *their parts from scripts or scrolls.)*
6 **JOHN MARK: Hi. My name is John Mark. That is my mother**
7   **over there.** *(MARY 2 raises her hand and waves.)* **And these**
8   **others ... well, they're friends of mine. I asked them to**
9   **come here to tell you a story. I'm not so good at telling**
10   **stories in front of people. Tonight is the anniversary of the**
11   **Last Supper of Jesus with his disciples. I was there, too,**
12   **but let my friends tell their stories first. I think we'll begin**
13   **with Mary. No ... not you, Mom, the other Mary.** *(JOHN*
14   *MARK goes to his seat and sits down. As the VOICE OF JESUS*
15   *is heard after each of the following speakers, the boy will*
16   *extinguish one of the candles from his stool. Make sure that the*
17   *candles are high enough so that this action is clearly seen by the*
18   *audience. The tallest, central candle should be left for the last.)*
19 **MARY 1: It was on a Wednesday. It's funny ... you remember**
20   **those little things sometimes. Days of the week don't**
21   **usually mean much to me — just another day of struggling**
22   **to get by ... you know how it is. Oh, my name is Mary. I**
23   **hope you don't mind me being in your fine church, me**
24   **being what I am and all. But I am a part of the story of this**
25   **week, and I came with the others to tell you how it was.**
26   **Jesus said people would always tell my part of the story.**
27   **I'm just a common woman, not dressed as grand as some**
28   **of you are, and I know that I may not be the kind you'd**
29   **want hanging around your church. But I came. He** *(Looking*
30   *at JOHN MARK)* **invited me, and I came. I hope that's all**
31   **right. My name is Mary. Oh, did I tell you that already? I'm**
32   **sorry. But I really get nervous speaking to people like you**
33   **... you know, people who usually don't listen much to**
34   **people like me. But here we are.**
35   **It was on a Wednesday, just two days before Jesus died.**

1   I live in the little town of Bethany, just outside of
2   Jerusalem. Jesus had entered the city of Jerusalem on what
3   you call Palm Sunday with quite a bit of fanfare, let me tell
4   you! People waving leaves and shouting "Hosanna" and
5   cheering him, and calling him names like "Son of David"
6   and "King." It was really great. I had come into the city that
7   morning, and I was at the edge of the crowd ... right on the
8   fringe, you know. And there was Jesus. At first, I didn't see
9   anything so special about him. I mean, I see a lot of men,
10 and this one didn't seem any different. Just a man in a dirty
11 robe sitting on a white donkey. But then he turned, and I
12 saw his face ... first just the profile, and then he turned his
13 head and was looking right into my eyes, like I was the only
14 one there. Oh, those eyes. They went right through you.,
15 And something told me he knew everything I had ever done,
16 but it didn't matter. He loved me. When I looked deeper, I
17 saw such a sadness in those eyes. The crowd was cheering
18 wildly, but he was nearly crying. It was as if he had a
19 broken heart. And then I knew, I don't know how, but I
20 suddenly knew that Jesus was crying because he had been
21 misunderstood. I knew how much that hurt ... people not
22 understanding. Later, I found out why he was so sad. He
23 was going into Jerusalem to die, and the people were
24 cheering. They were cheering his coming death on a cross,
25 and Jesus wept. And I wept, too, that day. I wept for those
26 eyes ... those loving, sad eyes of Jesus.
27   On Wednesday, I knew I had to see him again. His look
28 was haunting me. I needed to go and see him and comfort
29 him if I could. I asked in the city and was told that he
30 wouldn't sleep in the city, but went to Bethany to sleep
31 each night. People told me he would be at the home of his
32 friends Lazarus, Martha, and Mary. They were good people.
33 They tried to help me many times. But when I went there,
34 they told me Jesus had gone over to Simon the Leper's
35 house for supper. Oh, it made me sad to think of Jesus

1   there. Simon was such a snooty man ... thought he was too
2   good for everyone.
3   I went over to Simon's and saw Jesus sitting on the floor
4   having supper. I don't know what got into me. I knew I
5   could be whipped or even killed for entering such a grand
6   house as that was, but I just walked in. I had a flask on a
7   chain around my neck. It was an alabaster flask filled with
8   a very costly ointment. It was the nicest thing I owned ...
9   the only thing I owned, really. It was the oil that was
10   supposed to be used on me when I died. It guaranteed me
11   a good funeral. But all that was worth nothing to me now.
12   I saw Jesus, and I broke the flask and poured the lovely
13   smelling oil on his hair. Oh, there were a lot of people there
14   who complained about that awful waste, but Jesus said to
15   let me alone. He took my face in his hands and told me
16   what I did was beautiful. He told them I had done all I could
17   — by preparing his body for burial. No one else would do
18   that. No one else could ever do that for him. And he called
19   what *I* did "beautiful"! No one had ever said that to me
20   before. And that's my story.
21 VOICE OF JESUS: Truly, I say unto you, that wherever the
22   gospel is preached in the whole world, what this woman
23   has done will be told in memory of her *(Mark 14:9)*. *(JOHN*
24   *MARK puts out one candle. JUDAS comes to microphone as*
25   *MARY 1 sits.)*
26 JUDAS: OK, I'll admit it. I was one of those complainers when
27   Mary dumped that alabaster flask and just poured it all over
28   Jesus' hair. Of all the stupid things to do! What a waste!
29   What could have gotten into that girl? I mean, here we
30   were, going all over the countryside trying to help the poor,
31   and this woman wastes three hundred denarii in one fell
32   swoop. That oil could have been sold for a tidy profit to buy
33   food for the poor. But Jesus did what he always did — he
34   stood up for the woman.
35   That really makes me mad! He treats us like we don't

1 have any brains at all ... almost like Romans! Hey, we gave
2 up everything to follow him. We spend three years looking
3 for our next meal and a place to sleep ... and he makes fun
4 of us ... tells us we're thinking too much of worldly things
5 and not what counts. Well ... dang it, Mary — why shouldn't
6 we think about things like that once in a while? After all,
7 those fancy gestures make for great reading, but they don't
8 keep a body alive. They didn't keep him alive!

9 Oh, no — what am I saying? I'm sorry, Mary. I just
10 remember that night and how it was. That was the last
11 straw. Humiliated in front of everyone! But I couldn't help
12 it. I just couldn't!

13 Do you know who I am? I guess everyone does. I was the
14 treasurer of the band of disciples that followed Jesus. Jesus
15 gave me that job; I never asked for it. I'll never know why
16 he didn't pick Matthew. That man was a saint! I mean, he
17 was an honest tax collector. A rare find! For years he
18 worked with money and never took more than what was
19 owed to him. He should have been made the treasurer ...
20 he knew how to handle money. He knew how to be happy
21 with what he had. But Jesus picked me. I was the only
22 disciple who came from money. That's right. My old man
23 was loaded! I got everything I ever wanted! And then I met
24 Jesus and became a disciple, and I gave it all up ...
25 sincerely gave it all up, too. I didn't want to worship the
26 almighty buck anymore. But to make me treasurer — me,
27 who felt the poverty of our new lifestyle more than any
28 other — me, who was used to having pockets full ... now
29 struggling to see the blessing of empty pockets. Why didn't
30 he ask someone else to be the treasurer? Why?

31 That oil could have been sold for three hundred denarii
32 and given to the poor. Three hundred denarii! Gone, just
33 like that. And Jesus jumps on me — right there in front of
34 everyone. I didn't want the money for myself! I wanted the
35 money for the poor! Why did he have to put me down in

public like that, and in front of a woman like Mary? *(Acts sorry.)*

Well, that was all I could take. I went out to the chief priests and asked them if they wanted a stool pigeon. I asked them what they'd give me to betray Jesus to them, and they offered thirty pieces of silver. I took it. I figured I would give the money to the poor. I didn't care about the money. I just wanted Jesus to be humiliated a little in public, just like I was. But I never thought anything this bad would happen to him; you gotta believe me! I never figured on this!

The funny thing is that the thirty pieces of silver did go to the poor. I threw it back at the priests when I saw how things were going, and they used it to build a cemetery for the penniless. Ironic, don't you think?

Yes, I am Judas. I was the one who betrayed him. But I was also among those whose feet were washed by Jesus. I was among those who shared the last Passover with him. I was among those for whom he said he died so that I might live. I am Judas. And that is my story.

VOICE OF JESUS: Truly, I say unto you, that one of you who is eating with me will betray me *(Mark 14:18)*. Go and do quickly what you must do *(John 13:27)*. *(JOHN MARK puts out the second candle. MARY 2 comes to the microphone as JUDAS sits.)*

MARY 2: My name is Mary. It was a common name then. Still is, so I'm told. I was in quite a different stratum of society than *this* Mary was, though. I was a householder. That may not mean much to you, but in those days, only a very few people in Jerusalem owned their own homes — and it was an especially tough feat for a woman. But I was the owner of a home. I had servants, too. I was a widow and a mother. John Mark was my son. What a joy to me he was. What a son. By the time he was only nine years old, he was reading from the Holy Word of God. What a joy to a mother's heart,

1   let me tell you! But I am getting off my storyline. Sorry. It's

2   hard for a mother not to brag a little when she has such a

3   nice audience as you are.

4   I was a part of that Last Supper scene so many years

5   ago. Jesus had been watching me since Palm Sunday when

6   he first entered the city on a white donkey. I was there in

7   the crowd, not really very interested in all that was going

8   on, but I saw him. He looked at me, but *(Looking with*

9   *disapproval at MARY 1)* being a woman brought up with the

10   right sense of morals and womanly duty, I looked down and

11   didn't return his gaze. But I did see him that day,

12   nonetheless. Later, I was at the temple buying some doves

13   for my sin-sacrifice, and in comes this man again. This time

14   he wasn't so calm. He was real upset, and he started

15   throwing down the animal cages and overturning the tables

16   in the temple's outer courtyard. I hid behind a tree and

17   watched and listened. Jesus told them they were making his

18   Father's house into a den of thieves. I really didn't

19   understand. Those tables had been set up all my life ... all

20   of my grandparents' lives, too. What was so horrible about

21   selling the temple coins? I didn't understand, but I felt his

22   energy, you know. You can just tell when a person really

23   believes in what he's saying. And this Jesus really felt every

24   word he said! I was astonished! After that, I found myself

25   more and more going to where Jesus was speaking. And by

26   Wednesday, I became a believer — just like you. I knew that

27   Jesus was a king — oh, not a king of this city — a King of

28   heaven itself!

29   You can imagine how I felt when Jesus came up to talk

30   to me Wednesday evening, just before he left to go back to

31   Bethany. "Mary," he said. "I would like to have the

32   Passover meal at your house." Just like that. It was

33   wonderful! We set up a plan so that he and his disciples

34   would know the way. My servant would wait at the gate

35   with a water jug on his head. And when the disciples came

1   to prepare the place for the meal, my servant would lead
2   them to the house.
3   When they arrived, I tried to look calm, but my heart was
4   beating faster than a butterfly's wings. The Master was
5   coming to *my* house! Can you imagine it? The disciples
6   asked where the room was, and I showed them a large,
7   upper room that I had furnished and made ready. There,
8   the disciples set everything out the way they wanted it. And
9   that evening, he came. I opened the door, and he leaned
10   down and brushed my cheek with a kiss of peace. And then
11   I showed him the way ... although he seemed to already
12   know. He asked me for a pitcher, a basin, and some towels,
13   and I went up to get them, leaving Jesus by the stairs. Then
14   he saw my son hiding around the corner. John Mark was
15   only a child, but he seemed to know all about Jesus. As
16   soon as their eyes met, John Mark came running for Jesus,
17   and Jesus just scooped him up in his arms. Together, they
18   went up the steps ... the Lord of all the earth and my son.
19   A lot of other things happened that night, but for a
20   mother, that was the most important one. That was what
21   made this night so special for me. That is what I think of
22   when I share the Communion meal — Jesus enjoying a
23   child. *My* child. And that's my story.
24 VOICE OF JESUS: Truly, truly I say unto you, whosoever does
25   not receive the Kingdom of God like a child shall not enter
26   into it. *(JOHN MARK puts out the third candle. MARY 2 sits,*
27   *and PETER goes to the microphone.)*
28 PETER: My name is Peter. Some people call me the "Big
29   Fisherman." Some people call me the "Rock." You can call
30   me "Peter." I'm not really as great as people try to make
31   me out to be. I had a lot of blind faith — sort of enthusiastic
32   faith, I guess you could say. But I made a lot of mistakes
33   because of that enthusiasm, let me tell you. I couldn't wait
34   to walk on the water like Jesus did, but I forgot to ask
35   Jesus what would happen if I took my eyes off of him and

1   began looking at the world. I know now. You sink! It
2   seemed as if I kept repeating that scene over and over
3   again. Oh well, there's no fool like an old fool, so they say.
4   John Mark, here, asked me to talk about what happened
5   that Thursday. That's real hard to do. If I had just one day
6   to live over in my whole life, it would be that Thursday.
7   Believe me, the Scriptures are kind when they tell the story
8   to you. Oh, don't get me wrong. They tell the truth. But
9   they say it with so much pretty language that you can easily
10   miss what a mess I made of that day — what a mess we all
11   made of that day, I guess. I don't know ... if only I had
12   known then what I know now ... but I guess you've all
13   heard that story before, haven't you? Well, I had better get
14   on with it.

15   It began with the walk into Jerusalem. Every day we
16   walked all the way to Jerusalem in the morning, and back
17   to Bethany at night. Jesus just wouldn't spend the night
18   there. No one liked this arrangement much, but we went
19   along with it. Anyway, this was the fifth day in a row that
20   we were walking to Jerusalem — and those miles were
21   really getting on our nerves. We knew this was the day for
22   the Passover meal, and I guess we all figured we would be
23   staying in Bethany that day; after all, it was a holiday. We
24   felt pretty bad. We were missing our families. We were
25   feeling a little abused, I guess. Wouldn't you have?

26   Anyway, we met up with the mother of James and John,
27   and she got the rest of us hoppin' mad because she tried to
28   trick Jesus into giving her sons the seats of honor — the
29   thrones to the left and to the right of Jesus in his kingdom.
30   Well, we were all put out at that. And we started bickering
31   among ourselves — each trying to look better than the
32   others. I know now, that was silly. It wasn't an earthly
33   kingdom that Jesus was in Jerusalem to claim. Three times
34   Jesus had told us he was going to the city to suffer and to
35   die — all to claim his heavenly throne. It's easy to figure it

all out now when we know the whole story. But it was hard for us to understand then. We really didn't think Jesus was serious. We thought all that death talk was just another one of his parables. Oh, how I wish we had believed him!

Finally, at the end of the day, Jesus surprised us by taking us to the upper room so we could celebrate the Passover. He put a towel around himself and washed our feet. I pretended to be holier than all the others and wouldn't let him at first, but he saw right through that. Then he began the meal with a prayer, and then he lifted up the common loaf of bread and reminded us that it was broken for us. We really didn't understand, but we ate and laughed.

Then things got tense again. We began grumbling. There wasn't a lamb for the table. That was a Passover tradition. It just wasn't Passover without a sacrificial lamb! But Jesus said to just wait ... be patient. And then he said something strange. He said that someone was going to betray him. I spoke out the loudest and said that though everyone else might, I would never betray him. Everything kinda quieted down. Everyone knew I was just pulling another "holier-than-thou" kind of stunt. And Jesus looked at me real sad and said that I would deny him three times before the morning cock crowed. Of course, I didn't believe him. But he was right. I denied him. And when the morning came, I remembered what he said, and I cried. But it didn't matter. His body, like the loaf of bread, was broken on the cross ... and his blood was spilled for us. *He* was our Passover Lamb. *He* was our way to pass over from death to life. He was the Lamb of God who took away the sin of the world. And I could never say how sorry I was for that night. I didn't deserve his love. Maybe none of us do. Well, that's my story.

VOICE OF JESUS: Do you know what I have done to you? If I, your Lord and Master, have washed your feet, you also ought to wash one another's feet. For I have given you an example, that you also should do as I have done unto you.

1   **A servant is not greater than his master. If you know these**

2   **things and do them, blessed you are indeed** *(John 13:12-17).*

3   *(JOHN MARK puts out the fourth candle. JOHN, the disciple,*

4   *goes to the microphone and PETER sits.)*

5   **JOHN: My name is John. I'm the one that Jesus was closest to.**

6   **Maybe because I was the youngest. Maybe because I**

7   **depended on him a little more than the others. I don't know.**

8   **No one was jealous of me in the group until my mother**

9   **asked Jesus if my brother James and I could sit on the**

10   **thrones of honor in his kingdom. But I was not part of that.**

11   **Peter told the story of that day pretty well. I don't have**

12   **much to add to it. But maybe because I was sitting nearer**

13   **to him at the table ... maybe I saw a little bit more of what**

14   **was going on at the Last Supper table. Jesus began with a**

15   **prayer. It was a little longer than usual. I figured it was a**

16   **way to get us quieted down. We had had a hard day — like**

17   **Peter told you — and our feelings were a little raw around**

18   **the edges.**

19   **Anyway, after the prayer, Jesus picked up the loaf of**

20   **bread. There was nothing unusual about that. It was the**

21   **first part of the Passover meal celebration — remembering**

22   **the bread that God gave us in the wilderness. But Jesus did**

23   **something odd. He said: "This is my body. Eat of it." I**

24   **didn't understand. What in the world did Jesus mean by**

25   **that? It was a little unsettling. We knew it had to be another**

26   **one of his famous parables, but what could he mean by it?**

27   **I though he might be talking ... you know, the body of his**

28   **friends and followers. I thought he was concerned about**

29   **the unity of our group, because of our bickering that day. I**

30   **figured he meant that we were splitting up because of our**

31   **lack of love. I made a mental note to be sure to ask him if**

32   **I got it right after the meal, but decided to just enjoy the**

33   **rest of the meal without bringing up that sore subject again.**

34   **After we ate, Jesus picked up the cup and said: "This is**

35   **my blood of the covenant which is poured out for the**

1   many" *(Mark 14:24)*. I didn't really understand that until
2   later, either. But still, I was thinking along the same lines,
3   and figured it was a veiled threat that if we didn't shape up,
4   he could find twelve others who would fit the bill and be
5   better disciples for him. During the meal, Judas, one of our
6   original group, got up to leave. We all figured it was because
7   he was the treasurer and that he was going to have to pay
8   for the meal or something. Honestly, at that point, I don't
9   think we really cared a lot. The wine was good, and we all
10   drank just a little too much. I guess that's why I got so sleepy.
11   We sang a hymn to end the meal, and by the harmony of the
12   others, I think we had all overindulged a little.
13   Anyway, we went out to the Garden to pray, and we
14   really couldn't stay awake. It was late, and we knew we
15   would all have to face that long walk back to Bethany soon.
16   Jesus asked Peter, James, and me to come with him and
17   counsel with him. There was something on his mind ... we
18   could see that.
19   Oh, how I wish I could have helped him through that
20   night. I loved him. He loved me. And on the night he needed
21   me, all I could do was sleep. Three times he woke me up to
22   keep him company ... comfort him ... and three times I
23   slept. Funny, the last time he just stayed with us and let us
24   sleep. It was only when he heard the men coming to arrest
25   him that he woke us up. 'Til the last, Jesus cared for us —
26   he helped us even when we let him down. I feel real bad
27   about that.
28   He had told us what was going to happen next in that
29   Last Supper meal, but we just didn't listen closely enough,
30   I guess. I'm glad we remembered it all so well, though. We
31   all share in a part of the memory of that day through this
32   meal. It's awfully important, you know. Awful important.
33   Because in it, he lets us know that he is still caring for us
34   all. Well, that's about all I can add to the story.
35 VOICE OF JESUS: Watch and pray with me. Pray that you will

1   not enter into temptation. The spirit is indeed willing, but
2   the flesh is weak *(Mark 14:38).* I pray for you and for all who
3   come to believe through your word as well *(John 17:20).*
4   *(JOHN MARK puts out the fifth candle. JOHN sits. The SLAVE*
5   *OF THE HIGH PRIEST comes to the microphone.)*
6   SLAVE OF THE HIGH PRIEST: I wasn't in that upper room that
7   night at all. I was at the temple with a whole crowd of other
8   Jews. I guess John Mark just asked me to tell my story so
9   you could see what the rest of Jerusalem was doing while
10 Jesus was lifting that Bread of Sacrifice and sharing that
11 Cup of Life for the first time.
12   I was bored to death that night. It's true. Oh, I know
13 Passover is a big celebration, but since the early evening my
14 master, the high priest, and a bunch of others were gathered
15 in the temple, waiting for a man to come to tell them when
16 it was time to go and be a lynching mob against Jesus.
17 Everyone there was so uptight about Jesus. I really didn't
18 see any harm in him, but I sure didn't go around expressing
19 that opinion. As the slave of the high priest, it wouldn't have
20 been very healthy for me if I had. Who my master hates, I'm
21 supposed to hate, too. I was pretty lucky, being the favorite
22 slave of such a great man. The high priest was the closest
23 thing to God on earth to the Jews. Of course, we didn't
24 know that the real God on earth was walking around all the
25 time. Just think ... Jesus was God here with us, and most of
26 us didn't know God as well as we thought we did.
27   Anyway, we were there, waiting. One of the disciples,
28 Judas, was coming when the coast was clear. You see, my
29 master was having trouble getting rid of this Jesus. Every
30 time Jesus came into town, he was surrounded by a big
31 crowd of people. My master was afraid that he might not get
32 the right man arrested, or else the crowds might rise up
33 against him if they knew he was arresting their hero. Judas
34 came to us on a Wednesday night and said that for thirty
35 pieces of silver, he would let my master know where Jesus

1 would be on Thursday night. Of course, my master agreed
2 to his terms, though it seemed pretty cheap, if you ask me.
3 Judas could have gotten a lot more if he had held out a little.
4   Well, as soon as it turned dark, the temple was filled with
5 elders, scribes, and Pharisees. All of them wanting to be in
6 on the big arrest; all of them waiting for Judas to give them
7 the word to come. Well, it was nearly midnight when Judas
8 came, and we went to the Garden of Gethsemane where
9 Jesus was praying. Judas just sallied up to him and gave
10 him a kiss on the cheek to identify him. There weren't many
11 of us slaves there in the crowd that night. But my master
12 told me I could go. He said it would be safe enough because
13 neither Jesus nor his disciples ever had any weapons on
14 them. But when the crowds started closing in on Jesus,
15 suddenly a sword slashing wildly hit me. It cut off my ear!
16 Oh, what awful pain! I don't even know for sure who held
17 the sword. Maybe one of the disciples grabbed it off
18 someone in the crowd. Maybe there was a secret
19 sympathizer there who just couldn't stand it anymore. I
20 don't know. But whoever it was, I was the one hurting! But
21 then something awful happened ... something wonderful
22 happened. Jesus spoke just a little word, and all the crowd
23 calmed down. He reached out his hand to me and touched
24 me where my ear had been, and suddenly, there it was
25 again ... as good as new! No more pain, no more blood. He
26 healed me right there in front of everyone. He really was
27 something special! He really was who he said he was!
28   Surely they wouldn't arrest him now! He faced the angry
29 crowd and asked, "Have you come out with clubs and
30 swords as against a robber?" And then he reached out his
31 arms. "But let the scriptures be fulfilled," he said *(Mark*
32 *14:48-49)*. And he let them take him.
33   I couldn't go with them, I just couldn't! I turned, ran, and
34 cried and cried and cried. How could they arrest the Lord?
35 How could they doubt him now? In my distress I didn't look

1   where I was going. I tripped over a little boy watching from

2   the bushes. Maybe that boy ought to tell his story now. I'm

3   done with mine.

4   VOICE OF JESUS: Put down your swords. Those who live by

5   the sword shall die by the sword. Do you not think I could

6   appeal to my Father who would at once send me more than

7   twelve legions of angels? But then how would the

8   scriptures be fulfilled? Let it be so for the moment *(Matt.*

9   *26:52-54). (JOHN MARK puts out the sixth candle. He goes to*

10   *microphone as SLAVE sits.)*

11   JOHN MARK: I was that boy in the bushes. I had seen the Last

12   Supper and I understood most everything Jesus was saying,

13   even if the big people didn't. I guess it is easier for a child

14   to believe. I snuck out of bed that night when my mother

15   wasn't looking, and I followed them to the Garden. I

16   watched as the disciples slept. I was with Jesus while he was

17   praying that night, and I was the only one who heard those

18   words: "Father, let this cup pass from me, but if you won't,

19   your will be done" *(Mark 14:36)*. I comforted Jesus at the last

20   while the disciples slept. But when the slave of the high

21   priest showed everybody where Jesus had told me to go to

22   hide, I ran away. The guard grabbed my nightshirt, but I just

23   slipped out of it. I guess you might say I was the first

24   streaker in history, because I ran home naked that night!

25   When I grew up, I wrote it all down just as I remembered it,

26   and just as it was told to me. And that was the first gospel

27   — the one you call the gospel according to Mark. That's me

28   ... John Mark. And that Gospel is my story.

29   VOICE OF JESUS: This is the one who is bearing witness to

30   these things, and who has written these things. And you

31   should know that his testimony is true *(John 21:24)*. *(JOHN*

32   *MARK puts out the seventh candle. Organ plays chorus of*

33   *"Blessed Assurance.")*

34   CHOIR ANTHEM

35   **THE LORD'S SUPPER:** *(The characters rise and take a piece of*

1   *bread and dip it into the cup. As they finish, they leave the*
2   *chancel area. Then the choir comes down and takes the Eucharist*
3   *in the same way. Then the pastor comes to the table and*
4   *partakes, turns, and invites the congregation to come forward to*
5   *partake. The deacons usher them forward in a way that is*
6   *convenient for the church. When all have partaken, then the*
7   *organ music playing in the background stops. In silence, the*
8   *pastor drapes the table and the other crosses in the area with a*
9   *black cloth.)*

10 DRAPING OF THE CROSSES

11 **CHOIR OR CONGREGATION:** *(Sings "When I Survey the*
12   *Wondrous Cross.")*

13   *NOTE: At the end of the hymn, the choir begins its recessional.*
14   *The organist plays a sorrowful postlude and recessional, perhaps*
15   *"Tis Midnight and on Olive's Brow." After the choir, the pastor*
16   *exits, followed by the congregation.*

17
18
19
20
21
22
23
24
25
26
27
28
29
30
31
32
33
34
35

Passion Play

Passion Play

Christus

A Passion play in eight brief scenes
by Alison Spitz

CAST

Jesus

Two Chief Priests

Judas

Three Men*
Who go to Gethsemane with Judas and Chief Priests

Three Disciples*
Peter, James and John

Captain of the Roman Guard

Roman Soldier

Roman Soldier*

Pilate

Four Voices *(from the crowd)*

Barabbas*

Woman*
Who brings bowl to Pilate

Three Women of Jerusalem*

Simon of Cyrene

The Crowd

Men and women — thirty or adjustable

Narrator

* Nonspeaking roles

SCENES

Scene 1 — The Betrayal

Scene 2 — Gethsemane

Scene 3 — The Trial

Scene 4 — The Despair of Judas

Scene 5 — The Sentence

Scene 6 — The Women of Jerusalem

Scene 7 — Simon of Cyrene

Scene 8 — Calvary

PRODUCTION NOTES

Overview: This easy-to-stage play presents the events of Christ's Passion, beginning with the betrayal and ending with his crucifixion at Golgotha. The spirit of the drama is a "pageant with words" rather than a dramatic play in the usual sense. Most parts are short and easy to memorize. A choir, youth, or adult group can stage the entire play.

Set: This Passion play may be presented in the chancel area of a church or on a stage with a curtain. It is easily adaptable to either situation.

Props: Money bag, rope (to bind Jesus' hands), sword for Peter, bowl of water and towel (for Pilate), whip (for sound of lash), purple robe, crown of thorns, reed, cross, cross on platform, small candles or other lights for the entire cast.

Lights: If a curtain is not available, the transition between the scenes may be accomplished with lighting. Most church lighting systems have the capacity to fade up or down. If this is not available, the lights may simply be turned off and on when the actors freeze at the beginning and ending of each scene.

Costumes: All the characters wear biblical robes and sandals, with rectangular cloths placed on their heads (secured with cord for the men and left hanging loosely for the women). Jesus' robe should be torn in the back, revealing "lash marks" (created with theatrical makeup). The robes should vary in quality somewhat, depending on the character's position and lifestyle. For example, Jesus' garment should be plain, but Pilate's should be richly colored and well-made, befitting his position of power. If costuming is a problem owing to the number of participants, the play may be staged in modern dress except for Jesus, who should remain in the characteristic biblical costume. Because Jesus is the Lord, as well as a man, this anomaly will be within the bounds of theatrical license.

Music: "Stabat Mater" (Rossini), "Hallelujah Chorus" (Handel). Suggestions for music before the play begins are "Gregorian Chant" (The Monks of St. Thomas Abbey) and "Holy Art Thou" (Xerxes) — Handel.

Sound effects: Thunderstorm, whip.

Playing Time: 15-20 minutes.

1   **Scene 1 — The Betrayal**

2

3   *(Lights fade up on staging area. TWO CHIEF PRIESTS enter*

4   *from Stage Right and go to Center Stage.)*

5   **CHIEF PRIEST 1:** You said he would be waiting for us.

6   **CHIEF PRIEST 2:** He will be here.

7   **CHIEF PRIEST 1:** What is it that makes you so sure?

8   **CHIEF PRIEST 2:** Judas Iscariot is greedy!

9   **CHIEF PRIEST 1:** Judas Iscariot is a fool!

10 **CHIEF PRIEST 2:** He is that, too! But because he is greedy, he

11   will be here for this! *(He holds up a small money bag.)*

12 **CHIEF PRIEST 1:** What of the rest of the followers of this

13   Jesus?

14 **CHIEF PRIEST 2:** Wholly and completely swayed by the Nazarene!

15 **CHIEF PRIEST 1:** What manner of man is he, that he holds this

16   power over them?

17 **CHIEF PRIEST 2:** *(Slowly)* I don't know. I know only that many

18   of our people are following him, and that this philosophy of

19   forgiveness and equality makes the people troublesome.

20 **CHIEF PRIEST 1:** They say he claims to be the Messiah.

21 **CHIEF PRIEST 2:** Messiah! What good ever came out of Nazareth?

22   *(JUDAS appears, Stage Left. He looks behind him and hesitates.)*

23 **CHIEF PRIEST 1:** Judas comes!

24 **CHIEF PRIEST 2:** You keep us waiting, Judas Iscariot.

25 **JUDAS:** *(Approaching them)* You have the money?

26 **CHIEF PRIEST 2:** We have the money — thirty pieces of silver,

27   but it is not yours yet. Where will we find this Nazarene?

28 **JUDAS:** A place called Gethsemane, not far from here. He goes

29   there to pray.

30 **CHIEF PRIEST 1:** How many will be with him?

31 **JUDAS:** Not more than three — now the money. *(He reaches*

32   *forward greedily.)*

33 **CHIEF PRIEST 2:** Not yet, Judas Iscariot! You must come with

34   us. How else shall we know which is he?

35 **CHIEF PRIEST 1:** Give us a sign when we get there.

1 JUDAS: The one I shall kiss is the man.

2 CHIEF PRIEST 2: *(Handing him the money)* **Come, we must hurry.**

3   **This time we shall not lose him!** *(The THREE hurry off Stage*

4   *Right. Lights fade and soft music is heard. After a pause, the*

5   *spotlight fades up again on NARRATOR.)*

6

7   **Scene 2 — Gethsemane**

8

9   *(General lights also fade up slightly to reveal the figure of JESUS*

10   *seen kneeling in prayer — back to the audience. He is Upstage*

11   *Center. PETER, JAMES, and JOHN recline near him, asleep.)*

12 NARRATOR: **And they went to a place called Gethsemane, and**

13   **Jesus said to his disciples, "Sit here, while I go yonder and**

14   **pray." And taking with him Peter and the two sons of**

15   **Zebedee, he began to be sorrowful and troubled. Then he**

16   **said to them** *(Matt. 26:36-38)*:

17 JESUS: **My soul is very sorrowful, even to death; remain here,**

18   **and watch with me** *(Matt. 26:38).*

19 NARRATOR: **And going a little farther, he prayed:**

20 JESUS: **My Father, if it be possible, let this cup pass from me;**

21   **nevertheless, not as I will, but as thou wilt** *(Matt. 26:39).*

22 NARRATOR: **And he came to the disciples and found them**

23   **sleeping; and he said to Peter** *(Matt. 26:40),*

24 JESUS: **So, could you not watch with me one hour? Watch and**

25   **pray that you may not enter into temptation; the spirit**

26   **indeed is willing, but the flesh is weak** *(Matt. 26:40-41).*

27 NARRATOR: **Again, for the second time, he went away and**

28   **prayed** *(Matt. 26:42)*:

29 JESUS: **My Father, if this cannot pass unless I drink it, thy will**

30   **be done** *(Matt. 26:42).*

31 NARRATOR: **And again he came and found them sleeping, for**

32   **their eyes were heavy. So, leaving them again, he went**

33   **away and prayed for the third time, saying the same words**

34   *(Matt. 26:43-44).* **Then he came to the disciples and he**

35   **roused them.** *(JESUS rises and goes to PETER and gently*

1   *touches him.)* **And Jesus said:**
2   **JESUS: Are you still sleeping and taking your rest? Behold, the**
3   **hour is at hand, and the Son of Man is betrayed into the**
4   **hands of sinners. Rise, let us be going.** *(The THREE*
5   *DISCIPLES get slowly to their feet.)* **See, my betrayer is at**
6   **hand** *(Matt. 26:45-46).* *(JESUS and the THREE DISCIPLES look*
7   *to upper Stage Right, where JUDAS, the TWO CHIEF PRIESTS,*
8   *and THREE MEN have come On-stage and stand watching*
9   *them. The DISCIPLES spring to their feet and group themselves*
10   *about JESUS.)*
11   **NARRATOR: And while he was still speaking, Judas came, and with**
12   **him some of the chief priests and elders of the people. Now the**
13   **betrayer had given them a sign, saying** *(Matt. 26:47-48):*
14   **JUDAS: The one I shall kiss is the man** *(Matt. 26:48).* *(He moves*
15   *toward JESUS with the TWO MEN behind him.)* **Hail, Master!**
16   *(JUDAS kisses CHRIST.)*
17   **NARRATOR: Then they came up and seized Jesus.** *(The group of*
18   *MEN seize JESUS.)* **And behold, one of those who was with**
19   **Jesus drew his sword and struck one of them.** *(PETER swishes*
20   *by one of the MEN with his sword.)* **Then Jesus said to him:**
21   **JESUS: Put your sword back into its place; for all who take the**
22   **sword will perish by the sword** *(Matt. 26:52).*
23   **NARRATOR: And then many came and crowded around Jesus,**
24   **and he was taken away.** *(The CROWD now comes On-stage,*
25   *entering from both wings and hiding JESUS and his DISCIPLES.*
26   *They talk as they come. They stand in groups as people would —*
27   *some with their backs to the audience, some profile, etc. Then*
28   *some voices are raised above the talk.)*
29   **VOICE 1: He said he could destroy the temple and build it in**
30   **three days!**
31   **VOICE 2: Let us see him save himself then!** *(The CROWD laughs.)*
32   **VOICE 1: He blasphemes! He deserves death!** *(This last line is the*
33   *cue for the CROWD to freeze. They become absolutely still and*
34   *silent, but stand in attitudes of conversing. Lights fade to black.*
35   *After a pause, they fade up again to reveal the next scene.)*

1
2 **Scene 3 — The Trial**
3
4 **NARRATOR:** Then those who had seized Jesus led him to
5   Caiaphas, the high priest, where the scribes and the elders
6   had gathered. Now the chief priests and the whole council
7   sought false testimony against Jesus that they might put
8   him to death, but they found none, though many false
9   witnesses came forward ... and said, "This man said, 'I am
10   able to destroy the temple of God, and to build it up in
11   three days'" *(Matt. 26:59-61)*.
12   And the high priest stood up and said, "Have you no
13   answer to make? What is it that these men testify against
14   you?" But Jesus was silent. And the high priest said to him,
15   "I adjure you by the living God, tell us if you are the Christ,
16   the Son of God." Jesus said to him, "You have said so. But
17   I tell you, hereafter you will see the Son of man seated at
18   the right hand of Power, and coming on the clouds of
19   heaven" *(Matt. 26:62-64)*. Then the high priest tore his robes
20   and said, "He has uttered blasphemy. Why do we still need
21   witnesses? You have now heard his blasphemy. What is
22   your judgment?"
23   They answered, "He deserves death!" Then they spat in
24   his face, and struck him ... saying, "Prophesy to us, you
25   Christ! Who is it that struck you?" Then when morning
26   came, all the chief priests and the elders of the people took
27   counsel against Jesus to put him to death; and they bound
28   him and led him away and delivered him to Pilate the
29   governor *(Matt. 26:65-68, 27:1-2)*. *(From Stage Left a CAPTAIN*
30   *of the Roman guard comes striding in. He is followed by TWO*
31   *ROMAN SOLDIERS. They begin to move the crowd.)*
32 **CAPTAIN:** Make way! Make way! Move back if you want to see
33   your Nazarene! *(The CAPTAIN and the TWO SOLDIERS push*
34   *the crowd back toward Stage Left and Right, clearing a path and*
35   *making a clear view of the scene for the audience. JESUS stands*

1   *with his hands tied at Upstage Right Center. The ROMAN*
2   *SOLDIERS take positions on each side of him. The CAPTAIN*
3   *stands Upstage Left Center. The CROWD is noisy and jeering.)*
4 **VOICE 1:** *(Above the noise)* **Let us bow to the King of the Jews!**
5   *(The CROWD laughs and makes mock bows.)*
6 **VOICE 2: Show us how you can tear down the temple and put**
7   **it together again!** *(More laughter)*
8 **VOICE 1: One of my sheep is ailing; heal it!** *(Laughter)*
9 **VOICE 2: Pilate comes!** *(The CAPTAIN and the TWO ROMAN*
10   *SOLDIERS snap to attention, and the CROWD becomes silent.*
11   *PILATE enters with a swishing of robes from Upstage Left. He*
12   *strides Downstage Center.)*
13 **PILATE:** *(Standing and looking at the CROWD with his hands*
14   *arrogantly on his hips)* **This man has made no attempt to**
15   **defend himself. I find no evil in him.** *(The CROWD shouts*
16   *"Guilty! Guilty!" PILATE turns to JESUS.)* **You heard the**
17   **charges made against you. Why is it you make no answer?**
18   *(JESUS is silent. PILATE makes a hopeless gesture, then turns to*
19   *the CROWD again.)* **I am empowered on this day to release**
20   **one prisoner. Would you have me free this Nazarene?**
21 **CROWD: Guilty! Guilty!**
22 **PILATE: Then whom would you have me release to you?**
23 **CROWD: Barabbas! Give us Barabbas!**
24 **PILATE: Then what shall I do with Jesus who is called Christ?**
25   *(Matt. 27:22).*
26 **CROWD: Crucify him! Crucify him!**
27 **PILATE: Why? What evil has he done?**
28 **CROWD:** *(Louder)* **Crucify him! Crucify him!**
29 **PILATE:** *(Signals to Stage Left. A WOMAN comes forward with a bowl*
30   *of water, which she holds for him. He washes his hands before the*
31   *CROWD as he cries out.)* **I am innocent of this righteous**
32   **man's blood; see to it yourselves!** *(Matt. 27:24).*
33 **CROWD: His blood be on us and on our children!** *(Matt. 27:25).*
34 **PILATE:** *(Signals to Stage Right.)* **Let them have Barabbas!** *(The*
35   *CROWD cheers and calls, "Barabbas! Barabbas!" as BARABBAS, a*

1   *big, boisterous man, comes rushing Downstage Center. The CROWD*
2   *closes in to hide JESUS and PILATE. BARABBAS is jostled out*
3   *of sight of the audience, and the CROWD resumes, as much as*
4   *possible, its original position along the front of the stage.)*
5 **VOICE 1:** *(Loudly above the crowd)* **What now for the King of the**
6   **Jews?** *(This line is the cue for the CROWD to freeze as the lights*
7   *fade to black. A pause. Fade lights up again to reveal the next*
8   *scene.)*
9
10   **Scene 4 — The Despair of Judas**
11
12   *(JUDAS appears from Stage Left. He walks hesitantly to the*
13   *extreme Front Center of the stage. As he does so, the TWO*
14   *CHIEF PRIESTS who bargained with JUDAS detach themselves*
15   *from the CROWD and walk to meet him.)*
16 **JUDAS: I must speak with you!**
17 **CHIEF PRIEST 1: Of what? Our business is finished.**
18 **JUDAS:** *(Holding up the money bag)* **I have brought the money**
19   **back. I want no part of it.**
20 **CHIEF PRIEST 2: Do you seek to ease your conscience, Judas**
21   **Iscariot?**
22 **JUDAS: I have sinned in that I have betrayed innocent blood.**
23   **Take the money!**
24 **CHIEF PRIEST 1: We cannot accept blood money.**
25 **JUDAS: Take it!** *(He flings down the money and rushes Off-stage Left.)*
26 **CHIEF PRIEST 2: We must take counsel.** *(The two move back to*
27   *the CROWD.)*
28 **NARRATOR: So they took counsel, and used the money to buy**
29   **the potter's field — a burying place for strangers.**
30   **Therefore, that field has been called the Field of Blood to**
31   **this day. Then was fulfilled what had been spoken by the**
32   **prophet Jeremiah, saying, "And they took the thirty pieces**
33   **of silver, the price of him on whom a price had been set by**
34   **some of the sons of Israel, and they gave them for the**
35   **potter's field." The despairing Judas, after throwing the**

1   **money at the feet of the chief priests, went out and hanged**
2   **himself** *(Matt. 27:7-10). (Spotlight on NARRATOR fades to*
3   *black. Pause, then general lights fade up to reveal the next*
4   *scene.)*
5
6   **Scene 5 — The Sentence**
7
8   *(There is no sound in the auditorium except the sound of the*
9   *whip as it strikes, "One, two, three, four, five!" The sound of the*
10   *whip continues as the NARRATOR's voice breaks in upon it.)*
11 **NARRATOR: And the soldiers led Jesus away to the courtyard,**
12   **and there they scourged him, and mocked him, and jeered**
13   **at Jesus, the Christ. And placing a purple robe upon him,**
14   **they cried out, "Hail, King of the Jews!" They plaited a**
15   **crown of thorns for his head and placed a reed in his right**
16   **hand. And kneeling before him, they mocked him and spat**
17   **upon him.**
18 **VOICE 1: Come, let us pay homage to the King of the Jews!**
19   *(This is a cue for the CROWD to move back into action —*
20   *talking, laughing, jeering, they fall back to the diagonal*
21   *formation to allow the audience full view of the scene. JESUS is*
22   *in kneeling position with arms and head hanging down. There is*
23   *a tear in the back of his garment to reveal lash marks on his*
24   *shoulders. The CROWD is still noisy as the TWO ROMAN*
25   *SOLDIERS stride over and drag him to his feet. One picks up a*
26   *purple robe that is lying on the stage and roughly puts it on*
27   *JESUS. He steps back and cries:)*
28 **SOLDIER: Hail, King of the Jews!**
29 **CROWD:** *(Echoing)* **Hail, King of the Jews!** *(Another SOLDIER*
30   *picks up a crown of thorns from the stage and puts it on JESUS.*
31   *He steps back and the SOLDIER cries out:)*
32 **SOLDIER: Hail, King of the Jews!**
33 **CROWD:** *(Echoing)* **Hail, King of the Jews!** *(The CROWD laughs*
34   *and makes mock bows. ONE OF THE CROWD runs up and*
35   *places a reed in JESUS' hand and shouts:)*

1   **VOICE 1: Show your power now, Jesus of Nazareth!**

2   **VOICE 2: Let him be crucified!** *(The CROWD takes up the chant.)*

3   **CROWD: Let him be crucified! Let him be crucified!** *(The*

4   *SOLDIERS snatch the purple robe and crown of thorns from*

5   *JESUS and fling them down on the stage. Then they lift the cross*

6   *onto his shoulders. The CROWD closes in, chanting:)* **Crucify**

7   **him! Crucify him!**

8   **VOICE 1: To Calvary! To Calvary with this Jesus of Nazareth!** *(This*

9   *is the cue for the CROWD to freeze as the lights fade again to*

10   *black. After a pause, slowly fade them up to reveal the next scene.)*

11

12   **Scene 6 — The Women of Jerusalem**

13

14   **NARRATOR: And what of these people here — the people of the**

15   **crowd? They persecuted Jesus, they lashed and mocked**

16   **him — and finally crucified him — but was every heart**

17   **spilling over with hate? No, for the people of a crowd**

18   **almost two thousand years ago were much the same as the**

19   **people of a crowd today. There were those who loved him**

20   **and later died for him. There were those who hated and**

21   **feared him, for holiness has a way of disturbing the evil**

22   **heart. There were those who doubted, because they did not**

23   **really believe God can do all things.**

24   **And there were gentle hearts in that crowd, and some of**

25   **the compassionate were women. Down through history,**

26   **man has looked upon the compassionate and gentle heart**

27   **as one of the glories of womanhood — such were the hearts**

28   **of the women of Jerusalem.** *(The CAPTAIN and the TWO*

29   *ROMAN SOLDIERS stride through the center of the CROWD,*

30   *pushing them back to reveal the scene. The CAPTAIN's first*

31   *speech is the cue for the CROWD to break into action.)*

32   **CAPTAIN: Move back! Move back! Make way for your Nazarene!**

33   *(The CROWD moves, talking and jostling, back to Stage Left and*

34   *Right. The SOLDIERS guide the CROWD, making comments*

35   *like:)*

1   **SOLDIERS: Make way for the King of the Jews! Move back!**
2   *(Etc. JESUS stands Center Stage, bowed beneath the weight of*
3   *the cross. The CAPTAIN and the SOLDIERS take up positions*
4   *behind him. Suddenly THREE WOMEN move quickly from the*
5   *CROWD at Stage Left toward JESUS. The CAPTAIN and the*
6   *TWO SOLDIERS move forward to stop them, but a voice comes*
7   *from the CROWD and they hesitate.)*
8   **VOICE 3: Let them be, Romans!**
9   **VOICE 4: What harm do they do?**
10 **VOICE 3: Let them speak with him!** *(Some of the CROWD echoes*
11 *this, and the SOLDIERS look at each other, then the CAPTAIN*
12 *signals them back to their positions behind JESUS. The WOMEN*
13 *move forward and stand in front of JESUS; they stand with*
14 *bowed heads, and their hands cover their faces. The CROWD*
15 *becomes quieter.)*
16 **NARRATOR: And Jesus turned to them and saw their tears.**
17 **Gently he said to them:**
18 **JESUS: Daughters of Jerusalem, do not weep for me, but weep**
19 **for yourselves and for your children** *(Luke 23:28).*
20 **VOICE 1: Enough of this! To Calvary with the Nazarene!**
21 **CROWD: To Calvary! To Calvary!** *(The SOLDIERS push the*
22 *WOMEN back. The CROWD closes in to hide the scene.)*
23 **VOICE 2: Only fools weep for this man!** *(This is the cue for the*
24 *CROWD to freeze as the lights fade to black. After a pause,*
25 *slowly fade the lights up to reveal the next scene.)*
26
27 **Scene 7 — Simon of Cyrene**
28
29 **NARRATOR: And then Jesus was pushed on toward Calvary. He**
30 **fell, and again he fell, for they had put upon him even the**
31 **indignity of carrying his own cross. And he was dragged to**
32 **his feet, until the impatient soldiers compelled one of the**
33 **crowd to help Jesus.**
34 **CAPTAIN:** *(His voice comes from the back of the CROWD.)* **Back!**
35 **Back, all of you! Make room!** *(The CAPTAIN and the TWO*

1   *ROMAN SOLDIERS push their way through the CROWD. The*
2   *CROWD falls back to show the CAPTAIN and the SOLDIERS.*
3   *Behind them is JESUS, standing with averted head — the cross*
4   *upon his shoulders. The CAPTAIN, with the TWO SOLDIERS*
5   *beside him, addresses the CROWD.)* **One of you will have to**
6   **help him!** *(The CROWD jeers. The CAPTAIN speaks above the*
7   *noise)* **If you want to crucify this Nazarene, one of you must**
8   **help him, or he'll not get to Calvary.** *(The CAPTAIN sees*
9   *SIMON OF CYRENE in the crowd at Stage Left.)* **You! Come**
10   **here!**
11 **SIMON:** I had nothing to do with today's happenings!
12 **CAPTAIN:** Come here!
13 **SIMON:** Why should I be the one? I want no part of this. I have
14   done nothing.
15 **CAPTAIN:** *(To his SOLDIERS)* **Bring him here!** *(The TWO*
16   *SOLDIERS take the struggling SIMON to the CAPTAIN. The*
17   *CROWD voices its approval.)* **Help the Nazarene!** *(The*
18   *SOLDIERS let go of SIMON, who strides resentfully to JESUS.*
19   *Then he looks at him and stands still for a few seconds. The*
20   *CROWD grows silent. SIMON then shoulders the greater part of*
21   *the weight of the cross, and the two begin to move slowly toward*
22   *Stage Right. The CROWD closes in, but moves slowly this time,*
23   *with a murmur of voices.)*
24 **VOICE 3:** Simon is taking all the burden.
25 **VOICE 4:** He wants to help him now!
26 **VOICE 2:** *(Roughly)* **He was forced to help him!** *(The CROWD*
27   *closes in completely and becomes noisier.)*
28 **VOICE 1:** Let them pass! The hour grows late!
29 **VOICE 2:** Calvary! To Calvary! *(This is the cue for the CROWD to*
30   *freeze as the lights fade again to black. After a pause, slowly fade*
31   *the lights up to reveal the next scene.)*
32
33   **Scene 8 — Calvary**
34
35 **NARRATOR:** And they took him to a place called Golgotha,

1   which means "the place of a skull." And there, they crucified

2   him and divided his garments among themselves, casting

3   lots for them, to decide what each should take. And it was

4   the third hour when they crucified him. The inscription of

5   the charge against him read, "The King of the Jews."

6   Those who were there derided him, saying, "You who

7   would destroy the temple and build it in three days, save

8   yourself, and come down from the cross!"

9   So also the chief priests mocked him to one another,

10   saying, "He saved others; he cannot save himself. He is the

11   King of Israel; let him come down now from the cross, and

12   we will believe in him" *(Matt. 27:42)*. And when the sixth

13   hour had come, there was darkness over the whole land.

14   *(The lights are slowly lowered until the whole auditorium is in*

15   *complete darkness.)* **And at the ninth hour, Jesus cried out**

16   with a loud voice:

17 JESUS: *(Off-stage)* Eli, Eli, lama sabachthani?

18 NARRATOR: And some of the bystanders who heard it said,

19   "Behold, he is calling Elijah."

20   And one ran and, filling a sponge full of vinegar, put it

21   on a reed and gave it to him to drink, saying, "Wait, let us

22   see whether Elijah will come to take him down!"

23   And Jesus uttered a loud cry and yielded up his spirit.

24   And behold, the curtain of the temple was torn in two, and

25   the earth shook as nature roared its protest. *(Sound effects*

26   *of thunder and storm. Then the lights come up slowly to reveal*

27   *the cross. This may be a large cross if available, or simply a small*

28   *cross made the center of interest with a spotlight or a circle of*

29   *candles. If a large cross is used, many members of the cast may*

30   *kneel at its base. Spotlight fades up on NARRATOR.)*

31 NARRATOR: And so the message of the cross was borne gently

32   on the winds of Jerusalem — a message of love and

33   strength and dignity. And when the heart and soul are

34   quiet, the message can still be heard, for it has come

35   sweeping joyously to us from Calvary. Sometimes the

message is clouded by our own human tendency to distort and rationalize, but it is still there in all its beauty and wisdom, and when it is embraced, it brings a peace and joy that nothing or no one can touch.

Oh, my brothers and sisters, let us love one another! *(Slowly the spotlight fades on NARRATOR and the joyous sound of the "Hallelujah Chorus" from* The Messiah *is heard. The houselights stay out, and the entire CAST [except for JESUS and the NARRATOR] file from the wings into the audience up through the two aisles, each carrying a light. When they all reach the foyer, the houselights go on and the cast greets the people as they go out.)*

Sunrise Services

Death Day — Life Day

A contemporary sunrise service
by George W. Crumley, Jr.

CAST

Worship Leader

Chorus
Teens or adults

Voices 1, 2, 3
Females from the Chorus

Voices 4, 5, 6
Males from the Chorus

Disciples 1, 2, 3

Woman 1, 2, 3

Modern Man 1, 2

Modern Woman

Proclaimer

Angel

Mary

Emmaus Traveler

Prayer Leaders 1, 2
Males

PRODUCTION NOTES

Overview: This sunrise service is a contemporary expression of the death and resurrection of Christ. It begins solemnly, with a processional and a lamentation on the Crucifixion. Then the Good News comes, and there is joy and celebration! Features music and words of today written in blank verse. May be presented by a youth group — there are many opportunities for participation.

Set: A curtain covers the chancel with its Easter decorations. The curtain may be black or brown, with phrases such as "He Is Dead," "Death," "Defeat," "Death Day," "The End," etc., attached to it. The Easter decorations, which are concealed by the curtain but will be revealed later in the program, could include bright banners with sayings such as "He Is Risen," "Victory," "Life," "Life Day," "The Beginning," etc. Two tables are needed — one at the back of the sanctuary and one in the center aisle, by the first three pews — parallel to the aisle. The table in the center aisle should be painted bright yellow, white, or red.

Props: The only prop needed is the "coffin," which is any kind of box or arrangement on a table. When covered with the cloth and/or its "top," it resembles a coffin. When uncovered, it is a table filled with bright flowers — like azaleas.

The "coffin" is made in the following fashion:
1. A base is constructed of plywood and boards, about two feet wide and six or seven feet long. This is covered with aluminum foil.
2. A top piece is made of two solid ends, curved at the tops (the two ends resemble tombstones). Struts are constructed to run the length of the "casket," and they are inset into the end pieces. When finished, the top piece fits down over the base, and is held in place (kept from wobbling) by several headless nails. It is thus an easy matter for the top piece to be lifted straight up and removed from the base piece.
3. A shroud is made, about nine-and-a-half feet long and six feet wide. When laid over the top piece, it comes down a couple of inches below the bottom of the bottom piece. It completely covers all the woodwork.

Costumes: Long black or brown robes for all participants.

Music: The songs referred to are only suggestions. Feel free to substitute from the available selections in your church's music library. Two of the suggested songs may not be familiar. "Jubilee" by James Thiem is published by F.E.L. Church Publications, Chicago, as is "Allelu!" by Ray Repp. All contemporary selections should be accompanied by drums, guitars, and tambourines, as well as by smiles, clapping, and bodily movements of freedom and happiness by the singers.

Acknowledgment: Portions of this playlet are quotes from the book "The Psalms in Modern Speech" translated by Richard S. Hanson. It is published by Fortress Press, 2900 Queen Lane, Philadelphia, Pennsylvania 19129.

Playing Time: Complete one-hour service.

PRESENTATION SEQUENCE

Prelude (Organ)

Processional

Call to Worship

A Song of Sorrow
>*Suggestion: "O Sacred Head, Now Wounded"*

Anthem
>*Suggestion: "Were You There When They Crucified My Lord?"*

A Scripture Presentation
>Mark 15:15-20, 24-30; Matthew 27:40;
>Luke 23:37 (TLB)

Lamentation and Wailing
>The Apostles on Saturday Night
>The Women Early on Sunday Morning
>Some People of Our Time

The Turning Point (The Good News Comes)
>Proclaimer
>An Angel, Mary, An Emmaus Traveler,
>>Group of Disciples
>Leader:
>>*The strife is o'er, the battle done!*
>>*The victory of life is won!*
>>*Now be the song of praise begun: Alleluia!*

A Song of Celebration
>*Suggestion: "Jubilee"*

Words and Shouts of Praise (Congregation and Chorus)

A Song of Joy
>*Suggestion: "Allelu"*

Celebration: Death Day and Life Day

Prayer

A Song of Life
   Suggestion: "Lord of the Dance"

Benediction

1   **PRELUDE**

2   *(Sad Lenten songs should be played on the organ, mournfully*

3   *and slowly. The lights are dim, i.e., only bright enough for the*

4   *congregation to read the hymns from the hymnals. The "coffin"*

5   *is covered with a black shroud and rests on a table at the rear of*

6   *the sanctuary. It is off to the side, but is clearly visible to those*

7   *who enter the church for the service. The members of the Chorus*

8   *are wearing their dark robes and stand in small groups around*

9   *the coffin, in the dim light. They stand motionless and*

10   *speechless, as if in mourning.)*

11

12   **PROCESSIONAL**

13   *(A tolling bell is heard during the whole of the Processional.*

14   *About two-thirds of the members of the Chorus walk down the*

15   *aisle — slowly, as if in mourning, and single file, about ten feet*

16   *apart. Then four "pall bearers" carry the coffin down the center*

17   *aisle and set it on a table in the center aisle, by the first three*

18   *pews — parallel to the aisle. There is room on both sides of it for*

19   *people to pass. The other third of the Chorus members follow the*

20   *coffin up the aisle, walking past the coffin and taking their places*

21   *in the choir loft or on risers, facing the congregation. If using the*

22   *choir loft, each person sits down as he or she reaches his/her*

23   *seat. The Worship Leader enters last and goes to the pulpit to*

24   *begin the Call to Worship.)*

25

26   **CALL TO WORSHIP**

27

28   **WORSHIP LEADER:** *(Reading slowly)* **O come and mourn with me**

29   **a while;**

30   **O come ye to the Savior's side;**

31   **O come, together let us mourn:**

32   **CHORUS:** *(Males only)* **Jesus, our Lord, is crucified!**

33   **WORSHIP LEADER:** **Seven times he spake, seven words of love;**

34   **And all three hours his silence cried for mercy on the souls**

35   **of men:**

1   **CHORUS:** *(Males only)* **Jesus, our Lord, is crucified!**

2   **WORSHIP LEADER: O love of God!**

3   **O sin of man!**

4   **In this dread act your strength is tried,**

5   **And victory remains with love:**

6   **CHORUS:** *(Males only)* **Jesus, our Lord, is crucified!**

7   *A SONG OF SORROW:* Suggestion: "O Sacred Head, Now Wounded"

8   *(Sing the song slowly, but not so slow as to produce anxiety*

9   *because of the slowness. On the second note of each phrase,*

10   *there should be a toll struck on a bell.)*

11   *ANTHEM:* Suggestion: "Were You There When They Crucified My Lord?"

12   *(Accompany by a drum roll on the organ.)*

13

14   **A SCRIPTURE PRESENTATION**

15   **Mark 15:15-20, 24-30; Matthew 27:40; Luke 23:37 (TLB)**

16

17   **WORSHIP LEADER: Then Pilate ... ordered Jesus flogged with**

18   **a leaded whip, and handed him over to be crucified. Then**

19   **the Roman soldiers took him into the barracks of the**

20   **palace, called out the entire palace guard, dressed him in a**

21   **purple robe, and made a crown of long, sharp thorns and**

22   **put it on his head. Then they saluted, yelling,**

23   **VOICES 1, 2, 3, 4:** *(Shouting)* **Hail, King of the Jews!** (KJV)

24   **VOICES 4, 5, 6:** *(Shouting)* **Hail, King of the Jews!**

25   **WORSHIP LEADER: They beat him on the head with a cane,**

26   **and spit on him and went down on their knees to "worship"**

27   **him. When they finally tired of their sport, they took off the**

28   **purple robe and put his own clothes on him again, and led**

29   **him away to be crucified.**

30   **And then they crucified him — and threw dice for his**

31   **clothes. It was about nine o'clock in the morning when the**

32   **crucifixion took place. A signboard was fastened to the**

33   **cross above his head, announcing his crime. It read, "The**

34   **King of the Jews." Two robbers were also crucified that**

35   **morning, their crosses on either side of his. The people**

1 jeered at him as they walked by, and wagged their heads in
2 mockery.
3 VOICE 5: *(Shouting)* Ha! Look at you now! Sure, you can destroy
4 the temple and rebuild it in three days! If you're so
5 wonderful, save yourself and come down from the cross.
6 VOICE 7: *(Shouting)* Come on down from the cross if you are the
7 Son of God.
8 VOICE 6: *(Shouting)* If you are the King of the Jews, save
9 yourself!
10
11 **LAMENTATION AND WAILING**
12
13 *THE APOSTLES ON SATURDAY NIGHT*
14 *(Each group — DISCIPLES, WOMEN, and MODERN MEN and*
15 *WOMAN — will come to the front of the chancel and then return*
16 *when finished. Parts may be read from a music stand, but are*
17 *better memorized [if well remembered].)*
18 DISCIPLE 1: It's all over! He's dead!
19 DISCIPLE 2: We *told* him to stay away from Jerusalem! It was
20 just too dangerous to be caught there by those lousy
21 Roman soldiers.
22 DISCIPLE 3: And *Judas*! We should have known that he was a
23 traitor! Wasn't he always sneaking off someplace, with no
24 explanation?
25 DISCIPLE 1: We should have disobeyed Jesus and armed
26 ourselves with swords and spears. God would have been on
27 *our* side, and we could have protected him. It's *our* fault
28 that he's dead!
29 DISCIPLE 2: And all those people standing by and just
30 *watching* while they nailed him up to that accursed cross!
31 Why didn't we *do* something instead of just stand there?
32 DISCIPLE 3: What a horrible sight. Even though I've watched
33 crucifixion after crucifixion, I never get used to it. The
34 screams, the blood, the tears, and the *sight* of a poor,
35 tortured body!

1 DISCIPLE 1: I know. And to see *Jesus* up there, hanging there,
2   waiting to die! And not a whimper out of him! Not a curse!
3   Nothing but kind words for his mother and forgiveness for
4   his enemies!
5 DISCIPLE 2: And what *faith*! Who could trust in God *that*
6   much? Who could *love* that completely? Who but God's son
7   could die that way?
8 DISCIPLE 3: But now it's all over! He's dead! Our dreams of
9   building the kingdom of God are over!
10 DISCIPLE 1: You're right. It's finished! With the Lord Jesus by
11   our side, God would've been able to *transform* this world.
12   He would've been able to bring in an era of peace and
13   brotherhood and love.
14 DISCIPLE 2: The dream is ended. The great plan is over. It died
15   when Jesus died. It's all over!
16
17 *THE WOMEN EARLY ON SUNDAY MORNING:*
18 WOMAN 1: How sad! How terrible and how sad!
19 WOMEN 2: I wish I could just forget Friday altogether!
20   To remember the Master hanging there, dying so slowly!
21 WOMAN 3: How he loved us! How he loved the disciples!
22   And how he loved everybody he met! Surely he *was* the Son
23   of God!
24 WOMAN 1: The disciples are *so* discouraged now! So sad, and
25   so disheartened! All their confidence is gone. All their
26   hopes have vanished. They know their dreams of bringing
27   in God's kingdom are now destroyed.
28 WOMAN 2: All this talk about the disciples and about God's
29   kingdom! Think about Jesus! How he suffered! What pain he
30   endured. What *terrible things* they did to him before he
31   died! And then to bury him so quickly! To put him in that
32   tomb so fast! We didn't even get the chance to prepare his
33   poor body for burial.
34 WOMAN 3: We have the spices at home. All the ointments are
35   at hand. Why don't we go now to the garden? Why don't we

1   go right away and ask the soldiers if we can get into the
2   tomb to do the decent thing to his body? They'll have mercy
3   on us. Those Roman soldiers are human, aren't they? The
4   sabbath is over now; the sun is just about to come up. Let's
5   go now and prepare his corpse — before it's too late!

6

7   *SOME PEOPLE OF OUR TIME:*

8   **MODERN MAN 1:** *(Speaking to the congregation)* **Let me tell you**
9   **people something about life: It's not *what* you know, it's**
10   **_who_ you know! There's no such thing as putting the other**
11   **fellow first; if you want solid advice that will help you get**
12   **ahead in this world, put number one first! "Number One" is**
13   **you, yourself! If you don't look out for "number one," no**
14   **one else will, that's for sure! Get them before they get you**
15   **— that's my motto! If you want to get to the top of the**
16   **heap, go for the throat first and make your opening**
17   **move a death blow. Show no mercy on your enemy,**
18   **because he sure won't show any mercy on you. Don't be**
19   **afraid to walk on people. Don't fear to hit below the belt.**
20   **Use any weapon you can get your hands on, and keep**
21   **slugging it out until you win! To the victor belong the**
22   **spoils, and don't you ever forget it!**

23   **MODERN MAN 2:** *(To the congregation)* **Yes, and don't think**
24   **anybody will love you, either! Love is for the movies and the**
25   **novels and the TV shows. Love is a bunch of wishy-washy**
26   **mush, fit only for children and old ladies. My mother said**
27   **she loved me, but she sure didn't show it all the time. If**
28   **she'd thought more of me and less of herself, I could've**
29   **gone to an Ivy League college instead of to the state**
30   **university. My old man said he loved me, but he spent so**
31   **much time at his second job that he couldn't be with me the**
32   **way I wanted him to. And my wife! She says she loves me,**
33   **but she sure had a fit when she found out about me and the**
34   **office secretary! Doesn't she know that every man has to**
35   **have his fling once in a while? Love! They say they love *me*,**

1   **but they sure don't let me do what I want to do!**

2   **Don't believe all that bunk about love. Take what you want;**

3   **that's life!**

4 **MODERN WOMAN:** *(To the congregation)* **You're here in church,**

5   **aren't you! You think you've come to worship God, don't**

6   **you! But you are wrong! Yes, you are** *so* **wrong! There isn't**

7   **any God; and if there is a God, he's dead! If there** *is* **a God,**

8   **then why are babies born dead sometimes? And if there is**

9   **a divine power, then why does he allow wars and killing?**

10   **And how come there are things such as cancer, or**

11   **emphysema, or heart disease? If God** *is* **in existence, then**

12   **explain to me why there is so much hate and evil in the**

13   **world! Why didn't God make the world perfect instead of so**

14   **rotten, the way it is? Why didn't your God create a world**

15   **free of spiders and mosquitoes and rats? Why didn't he**

16   **make the universe without earthquakes or tidal waves or**

17   **avalanches? And get this: If there really is a God, then**

18   **why'd he let Jesus get crucified?! Why'd he permit such a**

19   **good man to be tortured to death? I'll tell you why: Because**

20   **there is no God! God is dead!**

21

22   **THE TURNING POINT**

23   **(The Good News comes)**

24

25 *(ANGEL, MARY, EMMAUS TRAVELER, and DISCIPLES say their*

26 *lines from their positions in the CHORUS. They should shout their*

27 *lines with jubilation! During* The Turning Point, *the curtain is*

28 *drawn, the "coffin" top is lifted by pallbearers and lowered to the*

29 *floor, the black and brown cloaks are removed [reversed?], and the*

30 *sanctuary lights are raised to maximum brightness.)*

31 **PROCLAIMER:** *(Shouting from the rear of the sanctuary)* **Good**

32   **news! I have good news!** *(While running down the aisle to the*

33   *front of the sanctuary)* **Hold everything! Don't give up! I've**

34   **heard some really good news!** *(At the front of the sanctuary,*

35   *addressing the congregation)* **Jesus Christ is not dead! He is**

1   *alive!* An angel said this:

2   ANGEL: Why do you look for the living among the dead?

3   He is not here: he has risen!

4   PROCLAIMER: And then Mary told the disciples:

5   MARY: I have seen the Lord!

6   PROCLAIMER: And a man who traveled on the road to Emmaus

7   reported:

8   EMMAUS TRAVELER: The Lord is really risen!

9   PROCLAIMER: And the disciples are saying:

10 DISCIPLES 1, 2, and 3: We have seen the Lord.

11 PROCLAIMER: Christ is raised from the dead! Now God's

12   kingdom can come on this earth, as it is in heaven!

13   Now we know that God is the winner, and not death!

14   Now we know that love *is* the greatest!

15   Christ is alive again! Hooray! Hallelujah!

16   It's now the time for jubilee!

17 WORSHIP LEADER: The strife is o'er, the battle done!

18   The victory of life is won!

19   Now be the song of praise begun: Alleluia!

20 *A SONG OF CELEBRATION:* Suggestion: "Jubilee" *(Any joyful*

21   *contemporary song may be sung.)*

22

23   **WORDS AND SHOUTS OF PRAISE**

24   **(Congregation and Chorus)**

25

26 CHORUS: Let them confess the Lord's kindness

27   and the wonders he does for mere man.

28   He satisfied the desperate soul

29   and filled the hungry with goodness.

30

31   Let them thank the Lord

32   for his steadfast love,

33   for his wonderful works to the sons of men!

34   And let them offer

35   sacrifices of thanksgiving,

1   and tell of his deeds in songs of joy!

2 ALL: Let them glorify him in

3   the congregation of the people,

4   and praise him in

5   the assembly of the elders.

6 CONGREGATION: *(Ps. 107:8-9, 21-22, 32)*

7   I will glorify you, O Lord,

8   for you have raised me up,

9   and you have not let my enemies

10   rejoice over me.

11   O Lord my God, I cried to you for help,

12   and you have healed me.

13   O Lord, you have brought up my soul

14   from death's pit,

15   restored me to life from among those

16   gone down to death.

17 ALL: Sing praises to the Lord, O you his people,

18   And give thanks to his holy name.

19 CHORUS: You turned my wailing to dancing;

20   you took off my sackcloth,

21   and clothed me with gladness.

22   Therefore my heart is now singing;

23   it cannot be silent.

24 ALL: O Lord, my God, I will praise you forever!

25 CONGREGATION: *(Ps. 40:1-4)*

26   I waited patiently for the Lord

27   and he turned and listened to my cry.

28   He lifted me out of death's pit ...

29   He put a new song in my mouth:

30   a hymn to our God ...

31

32   Happy is the one who puts his trust

33   in the Lord ...

34 CHORUS: *(Ps. 85:8-10)*

35   Let me hear what God, the Lord, has to say,

1   for he is speaking of peace ...

2   His help is there for his worshippers

3   that his honor may dwell in our land.

4   Kindness and faithfulness have met;

5   justice and peace have kissed.

6   CONGREGATION: *(Ps. 86:11-13)*

7   Teach me your ways, O Lord:

8   I would walk in your truth.

9   Inspire my mind to worship your name.

10   I would praise you, O Master, my God,

11   with all my heart,

12   and honor your name forever!

13   You have shown great kindness to me.

14   You delivered my life from Deathland below.

15 ALL: Bless the Lord, my soul;

16   every fiber, bless his holy name!

17   Bless the Lord, my soul!

18   Never forget all his goodness.

19 CHORUS: *(Ps. 103:1-5)*

20   It is he who forgives all your sins.

21   It is he who heals every sickness,

22   who saves your life from the grave,

23   who crowns you with love and compassion,

24   who fills you to flowing with goodness,

25   renewing your strength like the eagle's.

26 CONGREGATION: Confess that the Lord is good,

27   that his kindness endures ...

28   In distress I cried,

29   "Lord, give me victory over death!"

30   The Lord is with me: I fear not.

31   What can man do to hurt me? ...

32 ALL: *(Ps. 118:1, 5-6, 22, 24)*

33   The stone which the builders rejected

34   has become the chief stone of the corner ...

35   This is the day the Lord acted.

1   **May it move us to celebrate with joy!**

2   *A **SONG OF JOY**:* Suggestion: "Allelu." *(Any contemporary song*

3   *about the Resurrection may be used.)*

4

5   **CELEBRATION: DEATH DAY AND LIFE DAY**

6

7   **PRAYER:** *(This prayer is in dialog, with two male voices fairly similar*

8   *in volume and tone. Style should be excited and exuberant, with*

9   *a fast pace. The text should be printed in the bulletin as shown*

10   *on page 207-208). The two must practice aloud so as to pray*

11   *"with one voice.")*

12   **PRAYER LEADER 1: O Lord Jesus Christ, you have made this**

13   **day a "Life Day" in our lives.**

14   **PRAYER LEADER 2: O Master Jesus Christ, you are the One**

15   **who was raised from the dead by the power of almighty**

16   **God, thus being the first of the new humanity to experience**

17   **fully the miracle of resurrection.**

18   **PRAYER LEADER 1: O Savior Jesus Christ, you are alive,**

19   **PRAYER LEADER 2: Not dead!**

20   **PRAYER LEADER 1: You are the victor,**

21   **PRAYER LEADER 2: Not the conquered!**

22   **PRAYER LEADER 1: You are the Risen One,**

23   **PRAYER LEADER 2: Not the dead one!**

24   **PRAYER LEADER 1: You are light,**

25   **PRAYER LEADER 2: Not darkness!**

26   **PRAYER LEADER 1: You are the One who brings in the Kingdom,**

27   **PRAYER LEADER 2: Not the one who ends an era!**

28   **PRAYER LEADER 1: You are Love and Forgiveness and Peace,**

29   **PRAYER LEADER 2: Not hate and vindictiveness and discord!**

30   **PRAYER LEADER 1: You are King,**

31   **PRAYER LEADER 2: Not slave;**

32   **PRAYER LEADER 1: You are Friend,**

33   **PRAYER LEADER 2: Not enemy;**

34   **PRAYER LEADER 1: You are Servant,**

35   **PRAYER LEADER 2: Not lackey!**

1   **PRAYER LEADER 1:** O friend Jesus Christ, you suffer when we
2   suffer;
3   **PRAYER LEADER 2:** You rejoice when we rejoice.
4   **PRAYER LEADER 1:** You call us into the unknown future,
5   challenging us when we are timid,
6   **PRAYER LEADER 2:** Advising us when we are impetuous,
7   **PRAYER LEADER 1:** Comforting us when we are wounded,
8   **PRAYER LEADER 2:** Nourishing us when we are weak,
9   **PRAYER LEADER 1:** Guiding us when we are lost,
10 **PRAYER LEADER 2:** Disciplining us when we are chaotic,
11 **PRAYER LEADER 1:** Calming us when we are beside ourselves,
12 **PRAYER LEADER 2:** Exciting us when we are dreary.
13 **PRAYER LEADER 1:** O dear Jesus Christ, you are the One
14   whom we have often shoved out of our lives.
15 **PRAYER LEADER 2:** But you refuse to leave us;
16 **PRAYER LEADER 1:** You decline to be put to death again in us.
17 **PRAYER LEADER 2:** You will not leave us alone for long,
18 **PRAYER LEADER 1:** But you resurrect yourself in us with love,
19   time and time again.
20 **PRAYER LEADER 2:** You give us the whole of creation as a gift;
21 **PRAYER LEADER 1:** You call us to renewal and to new life.
22 **PRAYER LEADER 2:** You free us from self-imposed slaveries;
23 **PRAYER LEADER 1:** You enable us to be the new man and the
24   new woman,
25 **PRAYER LEADER 2:** To be the selves which the Father means
26   us to be.
27 **PRAYER LEADER 1:** O living Jesus Christ, you give us peace,
28   joy, faith, courage, hope, life and love.
29 **PRAYER LEADER 2:** We give ourselves to you, to one another,
30   to our beloved community, and to the world for whom you
31   died and for whom you are alive evermore.
32 **PRAYER LEADER 1:** All praise to you, O Lord Jesus Christ.
33   Alleluia! Amen.
34 *A SONG OF LIFE:* Suggestion: "Lord of the Dance." *(As before, any*
35   *contemporary song may be used.)*

1	**BENEDICTION**
2	
3	
4	*PRAYER:* For reproduction in church bulletin.
5	O Lord Jesus Christ, you have made this day a "Life
6	Day" in our lives.
7	O Master Jesus Christ, you are the One who was raised
8	from the dead by the power of almighty God, thus being the
9	first of the new humanity to experience fully the miracle of
10	resurrection.
11	O Savior Jesus Christ, you are alive, not dead! You are
12	the victor, not the conquered! You are the Risen One, not
13	the dead one! You are light, not darkness! You are the One
14	who brings in the Kingdom, not the one who ends an era!
15	You are Love and Forgiveness and Peace, not hate and
16	vindictiveness and discord! You are King, not slave; you are
17	Friend, not enemy; you are Servant, not lackey!
18	O friend Jesus Christ, you suffer when we suffer; you
19	rejoice when we rejoice. You call us into the unknown
20	future, challenging us when we are timid, advising us when
21	we are impetuous, comforting us when we are wounded,
22	nourishing us when we are weak, guiding us when we are
23	lost, disciplining us when we are chaotic, calming us when
24	we are beside ourselves, exciting us when we are dreary.
25	O dear Jesus Christ, you are the One whom we have
26	often shoved out of our lives. But you refuse to leave us;
27	you decline to be put to death again in us. You will not
28	leave us alone for long, but you resurrect yourself in us
29	with love, time and time again. You give us the whole of
30	creation as a gift; you call us to renewal and to new life.
31	You free us from self-imposed slaveries; you enable us to
32	be the new man and the new woman, to be the selves which
33	the Father means us to be.
34	O living Jesus Christ, you give us peace, joy, faith,
35	courage, hope, life and love. We give ourselves to you, to

1   one another, to our beloved community, and to the world
2   for whom you died and for whom you are alive evermore.
3   All praise to you, O Lord Jesus Christ. Alleluia! Amen.
4
5
6
7
8
9
10
11
12
13
14
15
16
17
18
19
20
21
22
23
24
25
26
27
28
29
30
31
32
33
34
35

The Morning of the Marys

A Resurrection play with an all-women cast
by Nancy G. Westerfield

CAST

(in order of appearance)

Mary Magdalene
Martha
John's Mother
James' Mother
Jesus' Mother
Clopas' Wife
Mary of Jerusalem
(The mother of a thief)

PRODUCTION NOTES

Overview: This script provides a cast of seven women the opportunity to portray the Resurrection story from the unique point of view of the mothers and wives of the key men in the Resurrection event. Several of the women go to the tomb with spices to anoint Jesus' body. When they arrive, they find the tomb empty! They return and tell Jesus' mother Mary that he is risen. Grief-stricken, she listens in disbelief. Gradually the reality of her son's Resurrection fills her heart, and she — though she hasn't seen him — believes.

Set: The scene is a kitchen in John's house, where the women are preparing a meal. There is a table with chairs at Downstage Center. A fireplace is at Upstage Center. There is a door at Stage Left, to the outside, closed. There is also a door at Stage Right, closed; when it is opened, steps are visible going to an upper room.

The play may be presented on an open stage with only a few pieces of furniture. The opening of doors may be suggested by actions only. A literal biblical set is not necessary. The dynamics of the acting will bring reality to this play.

Lights: Low-key lighting will help create the mood of that historic afternoon. The powerful conclusion of the play, when an intense white light illuminates Mary, Jesus' mother, may be accomplished with powerful high-beam flashlights if a spotlight is unavailable.

Props: A loaf of bread — preferably round — and baskets covered by cloths, which serve as Mary of Jerusalem's gifts of food. Also needed: extra food, pottery dishes.

Costumes: Robes are recommended. They need only be suggestive of what women wore during this period of history. Mary Magdalene needs an outer cloak.

Sound Effects: A shout and a crash (like falling furniture).

Playing Time: 15-20 minutes.

1   *(It is the afternoon of the first Easter day. The WOMEN are*
2   *preparing a meal. Three WOMEN are busy at the fireplace:*
3   *MARTHA is stooping to fan the coals, JOHN'S MOTHER is*
4   *stirring a hanging pot, and JAMES' MOTHER is turning meat on*
5   *a spit. MARY, JESUS' MOTHER, and her sister, MARY,*
6   *CLOPAS' WIFE, are seated quietly together at a table. MARY*
7   *MAGDALENE is near the door at Stage Right.)*

8 **MARY MAGDALENE:** *(Loosening her outer cloak)* **I am perishing**
9   **from the heat in this room!**

10 **MARTHA: I, too, am hot, sister. We are all hot from our work.**

11 **JOHN'S MOTHER: I would've gladly laid a fire out of doors and**
12   **prepared the meal in the open air. For myself, I'm not afraid.**
13   **I don't think the Jews will come to harm us women, even**
14   **those who followed with Mary's son all the way from Galilee.**

15 **MARY MAGDALENE: Then open the door a trifle! Let's open it**
16   **just a little to blow the heat out.**

17 **JAMES' MOTHER: Didn't your son John instruct us that today**
18   **his house must show to the street only a closed door and**
19   **no sound?**

20 **JOHN'S MOTHER: He did. He did. It is for him, and for others**
21   **inside with him, that I fear. Both of my sons, and your son,**
22   **and Simon Peter, Philip, Andrew … the Jews will have them**
23   **all out by the hair if they discover them here.**

24 **MARTHA:** *(Lowering her voice)* **And Mary, too. His mother Mary,**
25   **now that she is with you in this house. Who knows what**
26   **harm could come to her while this madness still holds**
27   **Jerusalem?**

28 **MARY MAGDALENE:** *(Listening at the door)* **No sound? You say**
29   **John instructs us not to make a sound? Listen to them! For**
30   **hours in that room. Raised voices. Arguing. Matching wits.**
31   **Planning. What are they planning?**

32 **MARTHA: It must be hotter still inside, behind that inner door.**
33   **Come away, sister. You are listening. Sister! It is improper**
34   **for you to listen to the men at their talk.**

35 **MARY MAGDALENE: They did not listen to me! I have told them**

1   what I have seen. What I have seen! Why will they not go
2   see for themselves?
3 JAMES' MOTHER: Mary, it is not safe for them to go. Even in
4   the dark, it was not safe.
5 MARTHA: Mary, you have been awake since before dawn. And
6   walked far. No wonder you suffer from the heat. So far ...
7   You are over-tired, and you should take some rest.
8 MARY MAGDALENE: They do not believe me. An idle tale, they
9   said. I have brought them tidings of the greatest joy they
10   could ever know, and they say it's *an idle tale*. Risen Lord,
11   show them the truth!
12 MARTHA: Surely it is not as if you were the only one ...
13 JAMES' MOTHER: I, too, was there. I was with her. I was not
14   the first to see, but I saw. It was empty. And what she told
15   was true, that men like none I have ever met were sitting
16   there against the stone that had closed the entrance.
17 JOHN'S MOTHER: I do not know if I dreamed it. My sons say
18   that I have dreamed. I was slow, and the last one. But it is
19   as she said. I saw her ahead, turning to run. I saw the
20   strange creatures of God behind her. And suddenly in the
21   path, as close as you are to me, the Master stood. I heard
22   him speak. This my sons say I have dreamed.
23 JESUS' MOTHER: Can it be? Sister, can it be? But why not to
24   me? Why did he not come to me? My son!
25 CLOPAS' WIFE: *(To JESUS' MOTHER)* Rest your head against
26   me, Mary. Close your eyes against me. Hush your voice
27   against me. *(To the others)* Help me to calm her.
28 JESUS' MOTHER: Give me ashes to cover my head.
29 MARY MAGDALENE: I have brushed the ashes from my hair.
30   Look at me! I have ceased to mourn. Do not mourn, Mary,
31   mother. The day of mourning is over.
32 JESUS' MOTHER: Tell me again how you found it this morning.
33   I cannot believe, but tell me again.
34 CLOPAS' WIFE: Yes, tell her this tale again. Give her the
35   moment of your hope. Help me to calm her.

1 MARY MAGDALENE: Will you be like the eleven of them, those
2   disbelievers? I weary my tongue uselessly.
3 MARTHA: Speak with kindness, sister. It is the Master's mother.
4   Or let the others tell it.
5 MARY MAGDALENE: You ask for a moment of hope; I bring you
6   an eternity of hope. Far beyond our lives in this room,
7   women's lives like ours, there is hope. I have seen the Lord.
8   We watched him die, but I have seen the Lord.
9 JESUS' MOTHER: I watched my son die.
10 CLOPAS' WIFE: I could never watch such a death again. Only
11   for your sake, sister, I waited and watched.
12 JAMES' MOTHER: I couldn't go that near. I stood back.
13 JOHN'S MOTHER: I followed with him from Galilee. I wanted
14   my sons to share the best of what he would have. But I
15   couldn't climb that hill. I thought: What if they were next?!
16   May he forgive me. I know that he forgives me. He spoke
17   to me in the garden path.
18 MARY MAGDALENE: He forgives us all. He knows what we are
19   like, needing to be forgiven over and over. He forgave me
20   from the first, all that I was then. And he came back to me
21   the first.
22 JESUS' MOTHER: I do not understand it. Perhaps if I go there
23   now, I will have the same vision. What was the path you took?
24 MARY MAGDALENE: Very early in the morning, while it was still
25   dark, I rose and took the spices which we had prepared. You,
26   with your own hands, Mary, mother. I set out on the western
27   path. We set out together, the three of us. I remember we
28   were saying to each other, "Who will roll away the stone for
29   us?" Such a great stone. We could never manage.
30 MARTHA: I told her to take what money we had.
31 MARY MAGDALENE: To bribe the guards, if they still were
32   there. Talk to a Roman soldier with money in your palm.
33   That's been my experience with those pigs. But I was
34   walking very fast. In minutes, I left the others behind. Then
35   I could see ahead. I could see just enough to tell that the

1   stone was out of place. I could never have moved it. But

2   who could have moved it? Someone must have been there

3   before me.

4 JAMES' MOTHER: Up ahead, I saw her stop as if she were

5   frightened. Right there, I dropped the spices I was carrying.

6   If you went that way now, you would find them by the big

7   cedar at the bend of the path.

8 JESUS' MOTHER: If I went that way now. ... Tell me again how

9   you saw him.

10 MARY MAGDALENE: I was frightened by the winged spirits with

11   the eyes shining in the dark behind the stone. They asked

12   what I sought. And I said I came to touch his body, but it

13   was gone. Then to the rich man's gardener, I said it: "Tell

14   me where you have laid him. I have money."

15   And he said my name: "Mary." He held out his hand.

16   When I saw his hand, I knew him. I threw myself at his feet.

17   My mouth kissed his feet that walk again.

18 MARTHA: Thomas doubts this, more than any. He believes that

19   your demon has come back and possessed you again. Oh,

20   he grieved me when he taunted you and said you tell an idle

21   woman's tale.

22 MARY MAGDALENE: Idle, are we? Good enough to toil and serve

23   them, but not to prophesy! I tell you, holy women before us

24   have prophesied in their day. I read in the Scriptures the

25   writing of the holy Joanna, for one. And the holy —

26 MARTHA: *(Interrupting)* But we are not holy women, sister. And I

27   fear they will not last, those Scriptures of the women — not

28   like Moses and the prophets. Thomas says so, though I grieve

29   to hear him. Now I wish that he had not left us here today.

30 MARY MAGDALENE: I heard you bid him a close farewell at the

31   door. Where has he gone?

32 MARTHA: He said there was a need to confer with Lazarus. But

33   Lazarus had left to go to Emmaus with another, more than

34   an hour before. They have walked many miles on that road

35   by now. So Thomas said he would take counsel with Clopas.

1 CLOPAS' WIFE: I sent Clopas a wife's respectful love and the
2   promise of a basket of food to be brought by evening.
3 JOHN'S MOTHER: Did Thomas taste of the pot, Martha? I
4   heard him say that if the Jews ever sampled our fare, they
5   would have the lot of us out by the hair.
6 MARTHA: He knows I do not cook by the Law. When the Master
7   came as a guest to my brother's house in Bethany, he
8   taught us there that the laws are of little importance
9   compared to his command to love God and one another.
10   Believe me, my sister reinforced his teaching. "Thomas," I
11   said, "his own mother does not cook by the Law."
12 JESUS' MOTHER: *(Half smiling)* No, I long ago ceased to use the
13   Books of the Law to cook by. And when my son came home,
14   he ate with pleasure. But, Martha, I am afraid for Thomas
15   now. Is it safe for him to venture into the streets? Here we
16   are, having to keep the doors fast, as John commands.
17 MARTHA: I had his reassurance. He is not afraid. He has always
18   kept a friend or two among the soldiers. That's his practical
19   side. And he will keep to the byways and return by dark.
20 MARY MAGDALENE: "Walk only on the byways," was my advice.
21   "Cover your head and bend yourself; walk as a slave. But
22   walk in faith, Thomas, and you may see the Lord."
23 MARTHA: Sister, before he left, he asked for my permission to
24   speak to Lazarus about me. For the two of us, together. If
25   it is the end of the world, Thomas says, and more of us
26   must die, at least here we ought to comfort one another as
27   best we can. So I did give Thomas my permission, sister.
28 MARY MAGDALENE: Well, you shall have him for your own,
29   little sister. But the end of the world, did he say? It's the
30   beginning of the world. Of course, we must certainly die.
31   Some of us will die in who knows what misery. But we shall
32   also live.
33 JESUS' MOTHER: If I rejoice, I rejoice that Joseph, my beloved
34   Joseph, fell asleep before this week of my travail began.
35 JAMES' MOTHER: All in one week! I hardly dare to think back.

1   It seemed like such a victory. The first day of the week was
2   glorious. This was what we had come for. Didn't you think
3   so? His triumph.

4 JOHN'S MOTHER: I was so proud of my sons. They walked like
5   princes beside him. Every mother among us the mother of
6   a prince. And your son, Mary, like a king.

7 JESUS' MOTHER: He was never meant to be a king. He was not
8   born a king.

9 MARY MAGDALENE: I never thought of him as a king. Master,
10   yes, teacher, brother, friend. Even now, I cannot think of
11   him as king.

12 MARTHA: King is a word for a heavy hand. He had gentle hands.

13 CLOPAS' WIFE: I did not think he had the mark of a king. He
14   did not go about it in the right way. There were times this
15   week when I thought: If he would just seize the
16   opportunity! Seize the power! This is what everyone
17   expected. He let it pass him by, when he could have had it.
18   Not the mark of a king.

19 MARTHA: *(Lifting a loaf of bread from the hearth)* **The bread is**
20   **done. Sister, will you knock and give them the fresh loaf to**
21   **break together?** *(MARY MAGDALENE knocks on the door at*
22   *Stage Right and delivers the bread.)*

23 CLOPAS' WIFE: I suppose I shouldn't have expected differently.
24   Knowing him so well from the beginning, because he was
25   my sister's son, I could see his good points and his
26   limitations.

27 JESUS' MOTHER: He was never really mine.

28 JOHN'S MOTHER: Oh, Mary, you should not say so hard a
29   thing. He loved you to the end.

30 MARY MAGDALENE: There is no end to his love. He loves you now.

31 JESUS' MOTHER: If he loved me and came again, he would
32   surely come to me. All the hours of this Sabbath past, I
33   have remembered the hurts of my life. Oh, yes, I prayed; I
34   remembered my Sabbath prayers to the Lord God of our
35   fathers, who brought us out of bondage.

1 JAMES' MOTHER: Praise God in his sanctuary. Praise his name
2   forever and ever.
3 JESUS' MOTHER; But it is also written that David prayed, "Out
4   of the depths, I have called unto thee" *(Ps. 130:1, author's*
5   *paraphrase).* Today I call out of the depths. Where is my
6   God? Who is my God? I have pondered in my heart lifelong
7   the hard things said to me. Blessed among women. A sword
8   will pierce through my own heart. This week my heart has
9   been pierced through, and still it beats.
10 CLOPAS' WIFE: Sister, if anything I have said has hurt you,
11   forgive me. This week we have all hurt each other with
12   things said and the things done.
13 JESUS' MOTHER: You tell me clearly who I am. Not blessed,
14   but an ordinary woman. The woman in John's house taken
15   in by friends because her only son is dead. He died an
16   ordinary death, but he was not an ordinary man.
17 MARY MAGDALENE: Mary, mother, there is more than that. He
18   did not leave us forever. We have each other, and yet we
19   have him, too. *(A soft knock at the outer door)*
20 JOHN'S MOTHER: Shall I open it, or not?
21 MARTHA: Perhaps it is Thomas returning.
22 JAMES' MOTHER: That was not a soldier's blow. I hear the
23   voices of women.
24 JOHN'S MOTHER: Shall I call John?
25 MARY MAGDALENE: They are disputing even louder in there.
26   Let that comer speak through the door.
27 JOHN'S MOTHER: They say they are women of Jerusalem. *(She*
28   *opens the door slightly.)*
29 MARY OF JERUSALEM: Pray do not be afraid. I bring you these
30   gifts of food, to feed yourselves and others, if they are here.
31   We are no friends of Romans. We weep for ourselves and
32   for our children. I myself am a woman who mourns.
33 JOHN'S MOTHER: We thank you for your gifts. You see only
34   women here.
35 MARY OF JERUSALEM: Is one among you the mother of the

1   man called King of the Jews?

2 JESUS' MOTHER: I am Mary of Nazareth. My son was Jesus the

3   Nazarene. He never called himself a king.

4 MARY OF JERUSALEM: They put the writing over his head. I

5   could not read it, but others told me. Once I was at the

6   front of a crowd when he spoke. He walked among men like

7   a prophet.

8 MARY MAGDALENE: Yes, we followed him from Galilee to be

9   his maidservants. He honored me by letting me serve him.

10   But he was not our king. His mother spoke rightly. He was

11   the Chosen One of Israel.

12 MARY OF JERUSALEM: Then blessed are you among women,

13   Mary of Nazareth. I am the mother of a sinful man. My son

14   died after his legs were broken, at the right hand of your son.

15   He was my only son, and he was not always a wrongdoer.

16 JESUS' MOTHER: I grieve for you, sister, in your sorrow.

17 MARY OF JERUSALEM: But your own son spoke to him before

18   he gave up his spirit. My son repented of the wrong. And

19   your son made him a promise, there as they hung to die.

20 CLOPAS' WIFE: I was beside my sister. I heard this said.

21 MARY OF JERUSALEM: Now there is talk everywhere on the

22   streets. The women say that your son did not die on the day

23   of preparation.

24 JAMES' MOTHER: He died. We saw him laid that day in a tomb.

25 MARY OF JERUSALEM: Or that he lives again. How this can be,

26   I do not understand. They say that one among you, several

27   among you, have spoken with him.

28 MARY MAGDALENE: I was the first. Truly, he spoke to me. Also

29   to these others. We have seen the tomb empty, the burial

30   cloths thrown aside. He walked toward us. We have seen

31   the risen Lord.

32 MARY OF JERUSALEM: O, sisters, I come to ask: Did you see

33   my own son as well?

34 JAMES' MOTHER: We believe that we also saw the winged

35   messengers of God.

1   **MARY MAGDALENE:** We were together, but each saw differently.
2   There is a confusion. We know that we saw the Lord Jesus,
3   and two more. Who they are, we cannot tell. Sister, my heart
4   says this may well be.
5   **MARY OF JERUSALEM:** Did you, his mother, see this wonder?
6   **JESUS' MOTHER:** I did not walk with them. I stayed in this
7   house. No, I did not see.
8   **MARY OF JERUSALEM:** But do you, his mother, even though he
9   did not come to you, do you believe this? *(A pause. The*
10   *answer, when it comes finally, is firm.)*
11 **JESUS' MOTHER:** I believe. *(A shout and a crash like falling*
12   *furniture from the inner room. Hastily, MARY OF JERUSALEM*
13   *covers her head.)*
14 **MARY OF JERUSALEM:** I must not know more. May the God of
15   Abraham guard you all. Blessed are you, Mary of Nazareth.
16   Though you did not see, you believe. Because of you, I,
17   too, can believe. I believe the promise was kept: Where
18   your son abides, my son abides with him. Peace be to your
19   house. Farewell, sisters. We will come together for the
20   breaking of bread and the prayers. *(JOHN'S MOTHER opens*
21   *the door for her.)*
22 **MARY MAGDALENE:** What can have happened within?
23 **MARTHA:** If they are quarreling among themselves, I rejoice
24   that Thomas is gone.
25 **JOHN'S MOTHER:** Why would they quarrel?
26 **MARY MAGDALENE:** Men quarrel. I am listening despite you,
27   Martha. There is no sound, as if all were gone. No, now
28   they murmur. They murmur. I cannot make out the voices.
29 **MARTHA:** Let us serve the meal. They will have to open the
30   door to be served. Sister, help me. *(The final preparations are*
31   *hastily made. MARTHA and MARY MAGDALENE carry dishes*
32   *through the door. Their voices cry out inside, and they retreat,*
33   *still bearing food.)*
34 **MARY MAGDALENE:** Mary, mother! Sisters all! They have seen
35   the Lord.

1 JAMES' MOTHER: But the door was never open. No one has
2   come.
3 MARY MAGDALENE: Even while the door was closed, he stood
4   among them.
5 JOHN'S MOTHER: When did this happen?
6 MARY MAGDALENE: This very moment past. It is over; he is
7   gone. I was too late. But he spoke the word of peace to
8   them. You did not see him, then? He didn't pass this way
9   before you to come out?
10 JESUS' MOTHER: No, none of us saw. Not one of us.
11 MARTHA: Thomas will never believe them. If only he had stayed!
12 MARY MAGDALENE: All ten of them have witnessed it. He
13   breathed upon them. John says he breathed like any one of us.
14   He spoke, as any one of us can speak. A scrap of food, he ate
15   it before them. Throw open the door to the evening, sisters.
16 JOHN'S MOTHER: Oh, no, John says, for fear of the Jews —
17 MARTHA: I am not afraid. I can never fear again. He is with us
18   wherever we are.
19 JESUS' MOTHER: He has passed again beside me, within this
20   very room. But not a touch or word.
21 MARTHA: We will go to Galilee with John — you said we must
22   go to Galilee, sister Mary — and there we will see the Lord
23   again. He is alive and will come to us all, through doors and
24   through the darkness of any night.
25 MARY MAGDALENE: It was very early in the morning of this same
26   day, and I, Mary of Magdala, was chosen to be the first ...
27 MARTHA: We are only the first. After us, others may see.
28 CLOPAS' WIFE: I have not seen, yet I believe.
29 MARY MAGDALENE: Mary, dear to us as our own mothers, will
30   you also go with us to Galilee, there to see him?
31 JESUS' MOTHER: What power have I to stay? What power have
32   I to go? But let it be done to me always according to the
33   will of your Lord. *(The door slowly opens; from it, an intense*
34   *white light illuminates MARY, JESUS' MOTHER, who opens her*
35   *arms to it.)* **My Lord. My son. I believe.**

Easter

Jesus Our Brother Is Alive!

A one-act play for Easter
by William D. Blake and Cynthia H. Blake

CAST

James
Jesus' oldest younger brother

James, age 27-29, is the mature, "older" brother among Jesus' younger siblings. Grief-stricken at Jesus' death, James is nevertheless composed and articulate, and remains a conscious peacemaker among the other three brothers.

Martha
The four brothers' hostess in Bethany

Martha is a curious combination of domestic industry and spiritual opaqueness. She is fully aware of the brothers' grief over Jesus' death, but would rather stay busy caring for the brothers than offer spiritual counsel in the face of their recent tragedy.

Joses
Jesus' second younger brother

Joses, age 24-26, is more of a dreamer and romantic than James. Joses gives freer expression to his emotions and longings than does his older brother.

Jude
Jesus' third younger brother

Jude, age 21-23, is a flat-out hothead! He acts first, then thinks about it later. His grief over Jesus' death vents itself in a seething rage and open verbal attacks. The two older brothers are repeatedly having to defuse, distract, or otherwise re-channel Jude's high-octane temper.

Simon
Youngest of Jesus' four brothers

Simon, age 18-20, is the quintessential "little brother." He knows instinctively that he can't compete with his older siblings' level of maturity, so Simon remains emotionally and rationally not yet fully developed. His opinions are thus not yet ready for prime-time theology. Jesus could do no wrong in Simon's eyes — not because Jesus was God, but because Jesus was Simon's older brother. In Simon's reasoning, "If that's not God, it's close enough for me."

Mary #1
The brothers' (and Jesus') mother
Their mother has already arisen before the sun, and the four boys, are up. Returning from the tomb even as they grieve, she will soon burst forth to report to the four brothers Jesus' absence from the grave.

Mary #2
Magdalene
One of the first witnesses of Jesus after his resurrection, Mary Magdalene accompanies Mary, the four boys' mother, from the tomb to Bethany, to share her own witness of the event-in-question.

PRODUCTION NOTES

Overview: This stirring, easily staged drama is set in Bethany, a small town two miles southeast of Jerusalem. The setting is the dining room of the home of Mary and Martha, whose family was close to Jesus during his time on earth (John 11:44). The time is early Sunday morning, the third day following Jesus' crucifixion. The action revolves around Jesus' four brothers as named in Mark 6:3: James, Joses, Jude, and Simon, on the morning after the Crucifixion. Although not full believers in Jesus during his earthly ministry (according to John 7:5), his brothers are nonetheless genuinely grief-stricken over his seemingly senseless death. Around the breakfast table, they engage in searching dialog, attempting to make some sense of their shared loss. The play's triumphant conclusion brings the joy of that first Easter vividly alive!

Set: The stage area is completely empty, except for a table and four chairs. Three exits — A, B, and C — lead to: (A) Martha's kitchen, (B) the bedrooms, and (C) the outside. If this drama is performed in a church sanctuary, Exit A is located off the back of Center Stage, Exit B is located off Stage Left, and Exit C, off Stage Right.

Props: A serving tray containing a kettle and four cups, a basket of bread rolls, and a dish towel. The kettle may contain water (i.e., "hot tea"), at the discretion of the producer.

Costumes: Bathrobes will serve adequately as costumes for all seven characters. The two Mary's may want to wear additional clothing (e.g., headpieces, cloaks, etc.), to indicate that they've just come in from being outside.

Since the drama portrays an opening mood of bleakness and grief, the actors are reminded to remove any watches or other light-reflecting jewelry while "in costume."

Playing time: About 15 minutes.

1 **JAMES:** *(Sitting alone at the table, he stares ahead, talking to*
2 *himself. His head is cradled in his hands.)* **I can't believe it. I**
3 **still can't believe it. He's dead. He's really dead!**
4 **MARTHA:** *(Entering the room through Exit A, she carries a tray*
5 *holding a kettle and four cups.)* **You look like you've spent**
6 **another sleepless night, James. Are you hungry? Here, let**
7 **me pour you a warm drink.** *(She pours a cup for him.)*
8 **JAMES:** *(Still staring ahead, he takes the cup from MARTHA without*
9 *looking up.)* **Thanks for bothering.** *(He then realizes his*
10 *rudeness and turns toward MARTHA.)* **And thanks, Martha, for**
11 **letting our family stay with you here in Bethany these past**
12 **two nights.** *(Looks off into the distance once more.)* **You and**
13 **Mary and Lazarus were always so good to Jesus whenever**
14 **he came down here to Judea.**
15 **MARTHA:** **You're no bother, James. Your family is always**
16 **welcome here. Besides, your brother gave us far more than**
17 **we could ever give in return. There was one time when he**
18 **came down ...**
19 **JOSES:** *(Entering suddenly through Exit B, he interrupts MARTHA.)*
20 **I can't get over it!** *(Approaching the table)* **Already the rabble**
21 **around here are calling him an imposter! Who do they think**
22 **he was? God?!** *(Noticing MARTHA as she offers him a cup)* **Oh**
23 **— morning, Martha. Thanks.** *(Taking the cup, he seats himself*
24 *across from JAMES, to whom he then speaks.)* **He may not have**
25 **overthrown the Romans according to some warmonger's**
26 **timetable, but that didn't make him any less a man!** *(Staring*
27 *ahead and addressing no one in particular)* **I wish we were back**
28 **in Nazareth — away from here.**
29 **MARTHA:** *(Touching JOSES' shoulder to comfort him)* **It's all right,**
30 **Joses. You'll feel better after you eat something. Besides, it**
31 **was too close to the Sabbath for your family to return to**
32 **Galilee, once Jesus was ...** *(She struggles to find the right*
33 *words)* **I mean, after your brother had ...** *(She finally leaves the*
34 *kettle and cups on the table and turns to exit, half-mumbling.)* **I'll**
35 **go fix something to eat.** *(She goes out Exit A.)*

1 **JAMES: Relax, Joses. You're among friends here. We all loved**
2 **him. No, his strange teachings didn't make him any less a**
3 **man ...**
4 **JUDE:** *(Suddenly appearing at Exit B, where JOSES entered,*
5 *interrupting JAMES)* **... Nor the way he died any less a**
6 **scandal for us!** *(Angrily he takes a seat at the table.)* **Curse the**
7 **Romans for what they did to our brother!** *(He begins pouring*
8 *his own cup and freezes momentarily, eyes tightly closed,*
9 *fighting back the lump in his throat. Then, regaining his*
10 *composure)* **Curse them all!**
11 **JOSES:** *(Passing off his own grief and personal guilt)* **You're one to**
12 **talk, Jude. I didn't know you had a soft spot for him. Wasn't**
13 **it you who taunted him for trying to avoid Jerusalem during**
14 **the Tabernacles Festival? I remember what you said:**
15 *(Speaks in a mocking voice.)* **"Why don't you go down to**
16 **Judea and let your disciples know who you really are? If**
17 **you want to be known openly, don't work in secret!"**
18 **JUDE: What about you, Joses? You were always chiding him**
19 **about acting so different from the rest of us!** *(JOSES and*
20 *JUDE, half-rising, begin to argue.)*
21 **JAMES:** *(Breaking the two younger BROTHERS apart)* **All right, you**
22 **two. Sure, he was different. But he wasn't the kind of rebel**
23 **Rome had to fear. I've never seen a revolutionary who**
24 **wanted so little to do with war and violence. Remember ...**
25 *(Taking on a more nostalgic, distant look)* **remember how he**
26 **loved to play with children? He always loved having the**
27 **little ones around him. And remember how he used to**
28 **promise the worried follower: "Not as the *world* gives**
29 **peace do *I* give peace"** *(John 14:27, author's paraphrase)*. **Or**
30 **what about that woman caught in adultery? Everyone else**
31 **wanted to stone her!** *(Shaking his head)* **Jesus just wanted to**
32 **forgive her ...**
33 **JOSES:** *(Echoing JAMES' turn-of-mood)* **Yeah ... and remember**
34 **how good he was at thinning the crowds whenever they got**
35 **too large?** *(Lowering his voice to a somber tone)* **He'd say: "If**

1   you *really* want to live forever, you'll have to eat my flesh
2   and drink my blood!"

3 **JUDE:** *(Catching the mood)* **Yeah, that would always trim down**
4   **the ranks.**

5 **JOSES:** *(With gritted teeth)* **Well, they all had their chance at his**
6   **flesh three days ago!** *(Softening up)* **How strange life is!**
7   **Those crowds are still alive — and he's dead!**

8 **JUDE: Yeah, he's dead.** *(Turning defensive again)* **But don't make**
9   *me* **out to be the heavy for taunting him any more than you**
10   **two did. What about the time, James, when you took**
11   **Mother with you, trying to pry him away from that one**
12   **crowd? You thought he'd finally gone off the deep end**
13   **when he said: "Who is my** *real* **mother and brother and**
14   **sister?** *(Gesturing toward the audience)* **It's all of** *you* **who do**
15   **the will of God!"** *(Matt. 12:48, 50, author's paraphrase).*

16 **JAMES: Maybe. Maybe we never knew him the way the crowds**
17   **did. He was really** *for* **them. He belonged to them.**
18   *(Shrugging)* **Maybe we just go in the way most of the time.**

19 **JOSES: Still, I'd like to see the crowds collect on** *that* **kind of**
20   **inheritance when his last will and testament is read!** *(The*
21   *three force a strained laugh, interjecting phrases like —* "Some
22   testament!" "Drink my blood!" "What a will!" "Eat my flesh!"
23   "Some inheritance!")

24 **SIMON:** *(Appearing at Exit B, where JOSES and JUDE first entered)*
25   **How can you three laugh at a time like this? What do you**
26   **think today is — a holiday?!** *(The other three BROTHERS*
27   *grow silent.)* **He's dead!** *(Pausing briefly)* **That might make**
28   **him a joke to others, but he was my big brother.**

29 **JAMES:** *(In a more subdued voice)* **If we laugh, Simon, it's not in**
30   **celebration. Some memories crush the spirit till there are**
31   **just no tears left to shed.** *(Looking at SIMON)* **When we**
32   **return to Nazareth, little brother, you'll know what I mean.**
33   **Some things back home will always remind me of him.**

34 **MARTHA:** *(Reappears at Exit A during JAMES' speech. She is*
35   *carrying a basket of rolls.)* **Simon, have a seat with your**

1   **brothers.** *(SIMON sits down in the remaining chair, while*

2   *MARTHA passes the basket to JAMES.)* **A well-fed stomach**

3   **will ease some of your pain.**

4 **JUDE:** *(Takes a roll, then looks toward SIMON.)* **Is Mother up yet?**

5 **SIMON:** **Her bed was empty. The spices are gone, too. She must**

6   **have left for the tomb before sunrise.**

7 **JUDE:** *(Shaking his head)* **I don't know how she can do it. She**

8   **was up so late the last two nights.**

9 **MARTHA:** **When it comes to caring for one's children, some**

10   **mothers don't know when to admit they're tired.**

11 **JAMES:** **She spent enough sleepless nights, I remember,**

12   **nursing us through all our childhood diseases.**

13 **JOSES:** **But, you know, she always treated Jesus differently —**

14   **as if she knew some secret about him that we didn't.**

15 **JAMES:** **I know. I saw it long before the rest of you were born.**

16   **And I've never seen her as broken as she is now — almost**

17   **as if someone had driven a sword through her heart.**

18   *(Sighing, he speaks with a renewed sadness.)* **I wish we could**

19   **have spent more time with him at the end. But Pilate's**

20   **orders were strict.**

21 **JUDE:** **And now the Sabbath is over. What do we have left now,**

22   **except the sickening memory of three days ago?**

23 **SIMON:** **And my oldest brother lying dead in some Pharisee's**

24   **borrowed tomb! If only we had been closer to home, we**

25   **could have at least buried him properly. I feel so numb**

26   **now, like I've lost him twice, like I've lost him forever ...**

27 **MARTHA:** *(Trying to brighten the mood)* **Jerusalem is only two**

28   **miles from here. Maybe after breakfast you boys could visit**

29   **the burial garden. It's on a hillside, overlooking the city.**

30 **JOSES:** *(Beginning to reminisce again)* **Speaking of hillsides,**

31   **remember the unusual speech he gave on that mountain?**

32   **"Blessed are the poor in spirit, for theirs is the kingdom of**

33   **heaven. Blessed are the pure in heart, for they shall see**

34   **God. Blessed are the peacemakers, for they shall be called**

35   **sons of God"** *(Matt. 5:3, 8-9).*

1 **JUDE:** *(Interrupting JOSES, he speaks with gritted teeth.)*
2 **"...Blessed are those who mourn, for they shall be**
3 **comforted"** *(Matt. 5:4).* **Hah! Well, now's God's chance to**
4 **comfort me! Or doesn't it work that way?**
5 **JAMES: You know, Jesus spent a lot of his time comforting**
6 **others. I've never seen a man who could touch someone**
7 **who was hurting, and bring such a calm upon them — such**
8 **healing — as he did.** *(He studies his hands.)* **What I wouldn't**
9 **give at times to have a gift like that!**
10 **SIMON:** *(Also thinking back)* **I remember the hillside where he fed**
11 **a huge crowd with that little boy's lunch.** *(Chuckling, as he*
12 *recalls the details)* **Every time they passed the basket to the**
13 **next bunch, it got fuller instead of emptier.**
14 **JUDE: I don't think his disciples ever did give it all away. Maybe**
15 **that's why the rabble kept hanging around him so much**
16 **afterward.**
17 **JOSES:** *(Changing the mood)* **But — he could drive them away as**
18 **quickly as they gathered. Remember the impossible**
19 **demands he made on overanxious followers** *(Recalling as he*
20 *speaks):* **"If you want to see the kingdom of God, you'll have**
21 **to be born all over again!"** *(John 3:3, author's paraphrase)* **—**
22 **or — "Give away all your possessions, and I will give you**
23 **treasures in heaven!"** *(Matt. 19:21, author's paraphrase)* **— or**
24 **— "Follow me, and let the *dead* bury your dead!"** *(Matt.*
25 *8:22, author's paraphrase).*
26 **MARTHA:** *(Suddenly remembering)* **Once I thought Jesus made a**
27 **bad decision, the time my brother was deathly ill. I**
28 **assumed he delayed coming to us because he didn't think**
29 **he could help Lazarus. Then, suddenly, four days later,**
30 **there he was! Even now I can't understand how Jesus did it**
31 **— how he made Lazarus return from the d—** *(Trying to avoid*
32 *the subject of death, in light of the BROTHERS' loss, MARTHA*
33 *rephrases herself.)* **I mean, how Lazarus was restored to us.**
34 *(MARTHA walks toward Exit A, then turns back for a moment.)*
35 **But I guess when God does a miracle in your life, you're so**

1   **busy saying "Thank you," you don't even think about**
2   **asking "How?"** *(She turns again and exits.)*
3   **JAMES:** *(Calling out after MARTHA)* **I don't know how God**
4   **restored your brother either, Martha ...** *(Turning back to the*
5   *other three BROTHERS)* **but I doubt that** *our brother* **had**
6   **much to do with it. He may have prayed more than the rest**
7   **of us, but only God raises the dead!**
8   **SIMON:** *(Coming to Jesus' defense)* **Maybe, but when we were all**
9   **growing up, Jesus never did to me the kinds of things you**
10   **three used to do. I worshiped him for that. If that's not**
11   **God, it's close enough for me!**
12 **JUDE:** **There's a difference, Simon. Remember how the mob**
13   **gave Jesus a chance to prove he was God, right there on**
14   **Golgotha? It would have been the perfect moment for him**
15   **to deliver himself — and us! — from all that needless**
16   **torture. If Jesus** *had* **been God, he would have found a way**
17   **down off that cross.**
18 **JOSES:** **Wait a minute, Jude. There were too many strange**
19   **things going on last week to say God wasn't in the picture**
20   **at all. What about that strange cloud cover on Friday**
21   **afternoon? And the unexpected earthquake? And why did**
22   **our brother die after only six hours, instead of hanging**
23   **there two or three days, like most of the Romans' victims?**
24   **The whole day had an unearthly sense of dread about it. It**
25   **was something I never felt before.** *(Pointing his finger at*
26   *JUDE)* **I tell you, there was a whole lot more going on there**
27   **than just the things we saw.**
28 **JUDE:** **So, what do we have to do to convince you of his**
29   **mortality, Joses? All through our growing up, Jesus bled**
30   **like we bleed. He got thirsty and hungry, just like us. He**
31   **grew tired after working in Father's woodshop all day; he**
32   **slept just like we sleep. Would God come to us in** *that*
33   **complete of a disguise?** *(JUDE points Off-stage in the direction*
34   *of Exit C, through which the two MARYS will soon enter.)* **If you**
35   **think Jesus is God, then death shouldn't keep him in**

1   **Joseph of Arimathea's tomb — guards or no guards. Maybe**
2   **we should all march up there and give it our own final test.**
3   *(He continues baiting JOSES.)* **Is that what you're saying,**
4   **Joses? Huh? Huh?** *(JUDE then buries his head in his hands and*
5   *grows silent. The other three BROTHERS sit motionless for what*
6   *seems like an eternal moment.)*

7 **JAMES:** *(Trying to break the tension)* **We know what you mean,**
8   **Joses. Sure, it would take a lot of bitterness off our backs**
9   **if we thought Jesus could return from the dead, after what**
10   **the soldiers did. But you were there, same as us. You saw**
11   **what we saw. Can the human body sustain that kind of**
12   **mutilation and survive?** *(Pauses, then adds.)* **Do you think our**
13   **world would be any better off if Jesus *did* come back?**

14 **JOSES:** *(Arises and begins pacing.)* **Maybe I'm just restless. But I**
15   **have this feeling something's just not right. I think we**
16   ***should* go back up to Jerusalem, as soon as ...** *(JOSES is*
17   *interrupted by the sudden, unexpected entrance through Exit C*
18   *of the two women — MARY, their mother, and MARY*
19   *MAGDALENE — who both rush toward the four BROTHERS.)*

20 **SIMON: Mother! You're back!**

21 **JAMES: Mary Magdalene?! What are you doing here?**

22 **MARY #1:** *(Excited and out of breath)* **He's alive! Jesus, your**
23   **brother, is alive!** *(The four BROTHERS stare at each other, then*
24   *at the WOMEN, with disbelief and shock. They exchange such*
25   *remarks as: "It can't be!" "Impossible!" "Not our brother!" "Not*
26   *Jesus!" "Things like this don't happen!" "You've got to be*
27   *wrong!" "But we saw him die!" etc.)*

28 **JUDE:** *(Grabbing his MOTHER)* **Are you sure? Are you really sure?**

29 **MARY #1: Yes! Yes! The stone has been dragged aside! He's no**
30   **longer in the cave!**

31 **MARY #2:** *(Breaking into MARY #1's words)* **The guards were**
32   **frightened away! And the tomb is empty, except for his**
33   **grave clothes.**

34 **MARY #1: Simon Peter and others have seen him ...**

35 **MARY #2:** *(Staring at her hands, in amazement)* **... And I *touched* him!**

1 **JOSES:** *(Turning toward the other BROTHERS)* **Now I'm not**
2 **restless. I'm terrified! What if they're telling the truth?!**
3 **JUDE: If it *is* true, it turns my world upside down. If Jesus *has***
4 **come back from the dead, then with God *anything* is**
5 **possible!**
6 **SIMON: Does that mean we won't have to leave Jesus here**
7 **when we go home to Galilee?**
8 **MARY #1: Better than that. It means he'll never leave *us*!**
9 **JAMES: Even if all this is true, who will believe a woman's**
10 **report?** *(Motioning to the other BROTHERS)* **C'mon, let's go.**
11 **I've got to see this for myself!**
12 **JOSES:** *(Rushing toward Exit C, where the two MARYS first entered)*
13 **I'll go saddle the animals.** *(He exits.)*
14 **JUDE:** *(Scooping up the bread, then following JOSES out Exit C)* **I'll**
15 **take these loaves with us.**
16 **SIMON:** *(Confused, he moves toward Exit A.)* **I'll ... I'll tell Martha**
17 **... that we've ...**
18 **JAMES:** *(Following JUDE out Exit C, he motions to SIMON.)* **Never**
19 **mind, Simon. There's no time. Let's go, now!** *(SIMON*
20 *follows JAMES as they both leave through Exit C, the two*
21 *MARYS following. All are buzzing and whispering about the*
22 *events the two MARYS have just reported. As soon as the room*
23 *has emptied and all is quiet again, MARTHA emerges through*
24 *Exit A, wiping her hands on a dish towel. She is completely*
25 *unaware of what has just transpired.)*
26 **MARTHA:** *(Looking around the room)* **What did you all want ... for**
27 **... breakfast? James? Simon?** *(Shaking her head)* **Every time**
28 **I try to help this family, I always end up missing something.**
29 *(She shrugs, turns, and goes back out through Exit A.)*
30
31
32
33
34
35

No Vacancy

The Bethlehem inn revisited — 33 years later
by Tim Lewis

CAST

Benjar
An innkeeper. He is a large man, 39 years of age.
He is gruff and outspoken, but has a soft heart.

Alisha
Benjar's wife. She is 33 years of age.
She is strong-willed, but possesses a tender spirit.

Melchizedek
A mysterious old man.
He is wise and soft-spoken with gentle eyes.

PRODUCTION NOTES

Overview: An Easter drama with a twist: the setting is the Bethlehem inn, 33 years after Christ's birth. The old innkeeper has died and his son Benjar now runs the inn with his wife Alisha. Benjar clearly remembers visiting the baby Messiah as a wide-eyed six-year-old. His belief in Jesus grew over the years. But now, Jesus has been crucified. Benjar's doubts overwhelm him. What if Jesus really isn't the promised King who will save mankind? Then a mysterious old man visits Benjar and Alisha and shows them that the scriptural prophecies were fulfilled in Jesus' death. Their faith is restored when they see that Jesus the King establishes his kingdom within people's hearts.

Set and Props: It is the time of the Jewish Passover celebration in Jerusalem, and Jesus has just been crucified two days previously. The set

234

should be divided into two sections, with Stage Right being the "yard" area of the inn and Stage Left being the "living quarters" of the innkeeper and his family. If possible, place a door between the yard side of the stage and the living quarters side. An Upstage partition will suffice in designating the Off-stage sleeping area.

Props and Set Pieces: The period furnishings should be that of first-century Palestine. Wooden or clay tools and utensils should be used, as iron or precious metals were too expensive for the common man. A sample prop list follows:

Oil-burning lamps — Two crude ceramic bowls with votive candles may be used; however, the bowls must be deep enough to hide all but the flame. These give the appearance of oil lamps and are much safer and easier to use.

Furniture — (1) A crude wooden table with two small benches or stools. (2) A long bench (like that from a picnic table) may be draped with a colorful piece of cloth, thus making an additional piece to give the set more depth. (3) A trunk, table, or bench for storage of food and kitchen utensils.

Kitchen utensils/food — An assortment of wooden or ceramic bowls and cups and a ceramic pitcher, plus a small loaf of dark-colored bread. (Rolls or bagels broken into chunks work great.)

"No Vacancy" sign — Must be made of wood, in the shape of a cross, and tall enough for the audience to read. It should have a small platform to hold an oil lamp and a stand at the bottom. The sign should be constructed beforehand, with the actor merely "banging" on it, then setting it upright.

Wooden hammer

Large staff

Large scroll/cloth bag — May be constructed from wooden dowels and butcher paper; however, it should be as ornate as possible. Cloth bag may be a simple pillowcase with a drawstring.

Optional props — Anything that will enhance the period and make the set more believable, e.g., water jug, baskets of various sizes, braided rugs, etc. Potted palms and various plants may be placed about the "yard" area.

Costumes: Traditional biblical robes, cloth head pieces, and sandals. Benjar and Alisha each should wear an outer covering or traveling cloak that can be removed to reveal night clothes for Scene 3. The colors used for their clothing should be earth tones to depict their working-class status. Melchizedek should also wear a traveling cloak, but his robes should be multicolored or purple, depicting royalty.

Music: Music with a Jewish or Middle Eastern influence will greatly enhance scene changes and help set the mood. Somber tones could be played at the beginning, underneath the hammering, while a lively or victorious melody could be played at the end.

Lights: Pay special attention to "time of day" (dusk, midnight, dawn). An effective technique is to slowly bring up the lights between Scenes 3 and 4, depicting a sunrise. Most church sanctuaries or performance areas have some lighting available that is controlled with dimmer switches. If a light board is available, colored gels greatly enhance the entire production.

Synopsis of Scenes:
        Scene 1 — Yard of the Bethlehem inn. Sunset.
        Scene 2 — Benjar and Alisha's living quarters. After supper.
        Scene 3 — Living quarters. Late into the night.
        Scene 4 — Yard. Early the next morning.

Playing Time: About 20 minutes.

1 **Scene 1**

2

3 *(It is almost sunset [dusk]. A single oil lamp burns inside the*
4 *house at Left. As the lights come up, hammering is heard at*
5 *Downstage Right, where BENJAR is erecting a crude wooden*
6 *sign that reads "No Vacancy." His pounding should represent the*
7 *sound of the nails that were driven into Christ's hands at the*
8 *Crucifixion.)*

9 **BENJAR:** *(Impatiently calling)* **Alisha! Alisha!** *(Enter ALISHA*
10 *Upstage from behind a partition that designates the sleeping*
11 *area. She is carrying an oil lamp. BENJAR calls again, almost*
12 *angry)* **Alisha!** *(ALISHA crosses to door.)*

13 **ALISHA: What is it, my husband?**

14 **BENJAR:** *(Takes brief notice of her, then continues working.)* **Good.**
15 **I see you brought a lamp. Where were you?**

16 **ALISHA: I was putting the children to bed. The journey from**
17 **Passover left them both so exhausted, they weren't even**
18 **hungry. I just hope they're not too upset to sleep because**
19 **of all that's ...** *(She notices the sign and crosses to him.*
20 *Surprised)* **Benjar? The inn is empty. Some weary traveler**
21 **may happen by and need a place to rest his head.**

22 **BENJAR:** *(Not looking at her)* **Then let him rest his head in**
23 **another inn.**

24 **ALISHA: You know this is the only inn in Bethlehem.**

25 **BENJAR: Then let him rest his head upon a rock.**

26 **ALISHA: Must you be so bitter? You are not the only one that**
27 **feels loss and confusion because of what's happened!**

28 **BENJAR:** *(Looking at her)* **All I feel at this moment is the need to**
29 **be left alone so I can think. I want no guests tonight. There**
30 **is no vacancy here.** *(He takes the lamp from ALISHA and sets*
31 *it on the sign.)* **There, now. That should turn away any**
32 **midnight visitors. Besides — only thieves and fools travel**
33 **after the sun has gone down.**

34 **ALISHA: But Benjar, others also may have left the celebration**
35 **early. Couldn't you just ...**

1   **BENJAR: Enough! It's been a very long day. I've fed and**
2   **watered the animals. Let's go now and fill our own**
3   **stomachs.** *(He picks up his hammer and they go inside the*
4   *house. Blackout.)*
5
6   **Scene 2**
7
8   *(Lights up full at Left. BENJAR is just finishing his supper and*
9   *the bowls and bread are still on the table. ALISHA enters from*
10   *the Upstage sleeping area.)*
11 **ALISHA: I think the children are finally asleep.**
12 **BENJAR: They've been pretty excited, haven't they?**
13 **ALISHA: I thought Nathan would never stop talking about those**
14   **soldiers.** *(She begins clearing the table.)*
15 **BENJAR: He's seen Roman soldiers before.**
16 **ALISHA: Yes, but never so many at one time.**
17 **BENJAR: Do you think he knows why they were there?**
18 **ALISHA: No, he was too fascinated with all their armor to think**
19   **about anything else.**
20 **BENJAR: Good. I'm glad he's too young to understand.**
21 **ALISHA: But Sarah's not too young. She knows something is**
22   **very wrong.**
23 **BENJAR: How could she? She didn't see anything. She stayed**
24   **in the city with you and most of the other women and**
25   **children. Someone must have told her!**
26 **ALISHA:** *(Softly)* **Benjar ... she sees all she needs to see in your**
27   **eyes. You know how upset you've been.**
28 **BENJAR:** *(Upset)* **I have not been upset! I've only been thinking**
29   **... and I've just tonight come to the logical conclusion that**
30   **it was a nice story to be believed by small children ... and**
31   **fools! So ...** *(He starts to get up)* **no more talk. It's time for bed.**
32 **ALISHA: Benjar, you mustn't consider yourself foolish.**
33 **BENJAR: But Alisha, you don't understand. You can't understand!**
34   **You weren't even born,** *(A beat)* **but I was. I was six years**
35   **old. I saw him ... I touched him ... I even worshiped him!**

1   ALISHA: They all worshiped him. You were not the only one.

2   BENJAR: But I was the youngest. It was as if I could understand

3   him better than anyone else because I, too, was a child!

4   ALISHA: But he was a baby. He couldn't even talk.

5   BENJAR: Remember the story? *(A beat)* Since the inn was so full

6   at that time of year, it was all my father could do to look

7   after the guests. My job was to feed and tend their animals.

8   ALISHA: *(Encouraging)* Go on.

9   BENJAR: *(Becoming lost in his thoughts)* His parents arrived late

10   in the evening, and the inn was filled. Rather than turn

11   them away, Father let them stay in the stable ... our stable!

12   Earlier that very day, I had placed fresh straw in the manger.

13   *(A beat)* I made his bed! God trusted me to prepare the place

14   for his newborn Son to be laid. *(A beat)* I remember sitting

15   in his mother's lap while the babe was sleeping. She was so

16   beautiful. She seemed to radiate a love that only a mother

17   could give. I thought, "What a lucky boy to have a living

18   mother." *(Smiling)* I even brought him my favorite toy,

19   although he was much too young to play with ... *(Suddenly*

20   *becomes angry.)* What am I saying?! None of that matters

21   anymore! He was no different than you or me ... because he

22   ... because he's dead! They killed him! I saw it! It was all

23   lies! All these years, nothing but lies!

24   ALISHA: *(Almost in tears)* But he was God's Son.

25   BENJAR: His blood was just as red as any man's. I saw the pain

26   in his face and the tears flow down his cheeks. His muscles

27   grew weak, and I heard him gasp for every precious breath.

28   We kept waiting for him to ...

29   ALISHA: *(Pleading)* Benjar, don't do this to yourself ...

30   BENJAR: *(Shouting)* If he had really been the Son of God, he

31   would have saved himself!

32   ALISHA: If he had wanted to. Perhaps he had a good reason to ...

33   BENJAR: *(Interrupting)* A good reason to die? What righteous

34   man ever had a good enough reason to die like a common

35   criminal? *(A beat)* If he had really been God's Son, he would

1   not have been on that cross in the first place ... and he

2   wouldn't have been born in a stable!

3 ALISHA: *(Incredulous)* Oh Benjar, how can you say that? My

4   father has told me time after time about the angel who

5   appeared to him and the other shepherds and told them to

6   go to Bethlehem, to this stable, to see the Christ child!

7 BENJAR: Your father is old and can't remember things

8   correctly.

9 ALISHA: He wasn't old when he first told me.

10 BENJAR: Then he must have been dreaming.

11 ALISHA: Oh, Benjar ... I don't like what's happening to you.

12   You've never spoken like this.

13 BENJAR: Because of what's happened. I've decided that we can

14   only depend upon ourselves and logic. Man will usually be

15   true to his own self; and logic? Logic shall always be ... well

16   ... logical.

17 ALISHA: But what about all the stories we've heard of Jesus'

18   miracles? Miracles are not logical.

19 BENJAR: Of course not, because they are just as you say ...

20   stories — made up, I'm sure, by Jesus or one of his

21   followers.

22 ALISHA: But he shared so many wonderful teachings.

23 BENJAR: As did the prophet Isaiah. Was he the Son of God?

24 ALISHA: *(A little defensive)* He never proclaimed to be.

25 BENJAR: He never proclaimed to be, because he was a wise

26   man. If Jesus had been half as wise, he would have never

27   put himself in a position to be crucified.

28 ALISHA: He had no choice. You saw the angry mob.

29 BENJAR: What I saw was a man that for as long as I can

30   remember has claimed to be the Son of God. And as long

31   as I can remember, I believed he was God's Son. Why? *(A*

32   *beat)* Because my father believed. Through the years, I have

33   heard miraculous stories about Jesus from many different

34   guests. I was proud that he was born in this inn. However,

35   I have decided that I cannot believe in something just

1   **because my father did. I must face life as a man and stop**
2   **living childhood fantasies. I must make my own decision.**
3   *(Becoming lost in his thoughts)* **Two days ago, at Golgotha,**
4   **something died inside of me. Perhaps some silly childhood**
5   **belief,** *(A beat)* **perhaps something much deeper. I just don't**
6   **know. But I do know this: Whatever reason I had for**
7   **believing in him is now completely gone. I lost part of that**
8   **reason when my father died ... but the rest of it? The rest**
9   **of it, my dear wife, I left helpless ... nailed to a cross.**
10   *(Blackout)*
11
12   **Scene 3**
13
14   *(All is dim except for the lighted sign at Stage Right. BENJAR*
15   *enters from the sleeping area dressed in his night clothes. He*
16   *cannot sleep and begins looking for something to eat. After*
17   *much grumbling, he finds the bread left over from supper. On his*
18   *way to the table, he stumbles or stubs his toe, which creates a lot*
19   *of noise.)*
20 **ALISHA:** *(From behind the sleeping partition, in a loud whisper)*
21   **Benjar? Is that you, Benjar?** *(She enters carrying a lamp. The*
22   *lights come up.)* **Eating at this hour?**
23 **BENJAR:** *(Grumpy, with mouth full)* **When a man is hungry, eating**
24   **is very logical.**
25 **ALISHA: But in the middle of the night? Are you still worried?**
26 **BENJAR: I'm not still worried about anyone! Can't a man even**
27   **eat in his own house?** *(He starts to cross Upstage to the*
28   *sleeping area, then remembering his bread, turns back and grabs*
29   *it.)* **Good night!** *(He exits as ALISHA watches.)*
30 **ALISHA:** *(Kneels and prays.)* **Oh, Father in heaven, I'm so scared**
31   **and confused. We all loved Jesus so. Why would anyone**
32   **want to kill him?** *(Becoming intense)* **Why didn't he save**
33   **himself? ... Did he not want to? Please help me to**
34   **understand. And most of all, dear God, help Benjar to**
35   **understand. I know in my heart that he still wants to**

1   **believe. Help him find the reasons to believe. I love him so!**

2   *(She pauses for a moment with her head in her hands as if crying.*

3   *Suddenly a knock is heard at the door. It is MELCHIZEDEK. He*

4   *has appeared in the shadows at Stage Right carrying a large staff*

5   *and a cloth bag. He notices the No Vacancy sign, but pays it no*

6   *heed and knocks softly on the door with his staff. ALISHA*

7   *speaks in hushed tones.)* **Benjar! Benjar!** *(BENJAR enters from*

8   *the sleeping area holding the bread and still eating.)*

9 **BENJAR: Can't a man get some sleep in his own house?**

10   *(MELCHIZEDEK knocks again, a little louder this time.)*

11 **ALISHA: I think there's someone at the door!**

12 **BENJAR:** *(Disgusted)* **A logical conclusion.** *(MELCHIZEDEK*

13   *knocks again, louder still.)*

14 **ALISHA: Oh ... it could be thieves!**

15 **BENJAR:** *(Putting down the bread and crossing to the door)* **Thieves**

16   **don't knock! The wind must have blown out my lamp.**

17 **ALISHA: Then perhaps it is only a traveler.**

18 **BENJAR: Or a fool!** *(MELCHIZEDEK knocks again, this time*

19   *loudest of all.)* **And who awakens me at this midnight hour?**

20 **MELCHIZEDEK: 'Tis only a weary traveler.**

21 **BENJAR: Can't you read the sign? Or has the light gone out?**

22 **MELCHIZEDEK: No, the light has not gone. It is here and will**

23   **always burn in the darkness.**

24 **BENJAR:** *(Opening the door)* **What? Then you must be blind!**

25 **MELCHIZEDEK: No ... I'm afraid it is you who cannot see.**

26 **ALISHA: What's happening? Who is there?**

27 **BENJAR: It is only some blind old fool. Now go back to bed.**

28 **ALISHA:** *(Reprovingly)* **Benjar!** *(BENJAR gives her a very stern look*

29   *and she crosses to the sleeping area.)*

30 **BENJAR: Now, what is it you want?**

31 **MELCHIZEDEK: Sir! I am known as Melchizedek, and I am not**

32   **blind!**

33 **BENJAR: Perhaps not, but very stupid; for no man with any**

34   **sense about him would travel at this dark hour.**

35 **MELCHIZEDEK: "There is a way that seems right to a man, but**

1   in the end it leads to death" *(Prov. 16:25).*

2 BENJAR: What? Whose death? Why do you speak that way?

3 MELCHIZEDEK: I speak only on behalf of the one who sent me.

4 BENJAR: Sent you? Sent you here?

5 MELCHIZEDEK: I go only where I am needed.

6 BENJAR: Then what is your business, old man? For I need no one.

7 MELCHIZEDEK: I have traveled a great distance. I wish only to

8   rest a moment and perhaps eat a bit of your bread. I would

9   be very grateful.

10 BENJAR: Oh ... very well. I cannot sleep anyway. *(MELCHIZEDEK*

11   *enters the house, puts down his staff, removes his outer cloak,*

12   *but holds onto his cloth bag. BENJAR places the bread on the*

13   *table.)* Come and eat, old man.

14 MELCHIZEDEK: The Holy Scriptures say that "good will come

15   to him that is generous" *(Ps. 112:5).*

16 BENJAR: *(Uninterested)* The Holy Scriptures say many things.

17 MELCHIZEDEK: Ah! Then you are familiar with them?

18 BENJAR: Familiar?! Do you think me a fool? I had to memorize

19   them when I was young, as does every Jewish boy.

20 MELCHIZEDEK: Then you must believe in their teachings.

21 BENJAR: Of course I believe. I've never had reason to doubt.

22 MELCHIZEDEK: Until two days ago.

23 BENJAR: What? Why do you say that?

24 MELCHIZEDEK: I know about all his followers.

25 BENJAR: Whose followers?

26 MELCHIZEDEK: Jesus'.

27 BENJAR: Well evidently, old man, you don't know as much as

28   you think. I'm certainly not his follower anymore. Golgotha

29   put an end to that.

30 MELCHIZEDEK: Are you certain?

31 BENJAR: Am I certain? Don't you understand? No man survives

32   the cross!

33 MELCHIZEDEK: I only understand what I read in the Scriptures.

34 BENJAR: Holy Scripture has nothing to do with this man Jesus,

35   or his death.

1   MELCHIZEDEK: "Be them ever hearing, but never understanding;
2   be them ever seeing, but never perceiving" *(Isa. 6:9-10).*
3   BENJAR: You speak the words of Isaiah the prophet. Why?
4   MELCHIZEDEK: Excellent! You are learned of his teachings?
5   BENJAR: I told you ... I memorized them as a boy.
6   MELCHIZEDEK: Of course ... but do you know what they say?
7   BENJAR: *(Getting up)* You seem to talk only in circles, old man.
8   It is late, and I do wish to sleep a few hours before dawn.
9   You may rest in the stable until sunrise, if you wish.
10   MELCHIZEDEK: "He was despised and rejected by men" *(Isa. 53:3).*
11   BENJAR: Now what are you talking about?
12   MELCHIZEDEK: Didn't you memorize that part?
13   BENJAR: I'm no Pharisee. I can't remember everything.
14   MELCHIZEDEK: Then perhaps you would like to read it for
15   yourself? *(He pulls a large scroll from his bag.)*
16   BENJAR: *(Amazed)* A scroll!
17   MELCHIZEDEK: *(Opening the scroll)* A logical conclusion. Read here.
18   BENJAR: *(Reading)* "He was despised and rejected by men."
19   *(Becoming exited)* The Isaiah scroll. Where did you get this?
20   MELCHIZEDEK: Keep reading.
21   BENJAR: *(Reading)* "He was despised and we esteemed him not"
22   *(Isa. 53:3).* Who was despised?
23   MELCHIZEDEK: Why, the King, of course!
24   BENJAR: The King? What King?
25   MELCHIZEDEK: *(Majestically)* The King of Kings!
26   BENJAR: As I remember, the King of which Isaiah prophesied is
27   to establish a kingdom which will last forever. And this King
28   will never die.
29   MELCHIZEDEK: But how might this King live forever? The
30   Scriptures say that all men must return to the dust of the
31   earth *(Gen. 3:19).* Do the Scriptures lie?
32   BENJAR: No, the Scriptures do not lie! There has got to be
33   some logical explanation.
34   MELCHIZEDEK: Perhaps, then, this King is different from other
35   kings.

1   BENJAR: What do you mean?

2   MELCHIZEDEK: *(Reading)* "In love a throne will be established;

3   in faithfulness a man will sit on it" *(Isa. 16:5)*.

4   BENJAR: What throne will be established?

5   MELCHIZEDEK: *(Cutting him off)* "Then he will open the eyes of

6   the blind and unstop the ears of the deaf. Then will the

7   lame leap like a deer, and the mute tongue shout for joy"

8   *(Isa. 35:5-6)*.

9   BENJAR: Jesus did all that... but *(A beat)* there is a cloth

10   merchant who has spent many a night in this inn. His

11   servants would have to lift him from his donkey and carry

12   him about because he was completely lame. Not long ago,

13   his caravan stopped as usual, but this time he climbed

14   down from his own donkey and walked! He said that Jesus

15   had healed him.

16 MELCHIZEDEK: You're saying that perhaps Jesus is this King?

17 BENJAR: I once thought that perhaps it might be true, but now

18   I don't now. Some of it seems to fit ... but it can't fit. I saw

19   him crucified!

20 MELCHIZEDEK: Then read this:

21 BENJAR: *(Reading)* "He was oppressed and afflicted, yet he did

22   not open his mouth" *(Isa. 53:7)*. That's true. When they

23   brought him before the high priest, he said nothing in his

24   defense. *(Reading again)* "I offered my back to those who

25   beat me ... I did not hide my face from mocking and

26   spitting" *(Isa. 50:6)*. Yes! Yes! I was there! I saw it! These

27   words are true!

28 MELCHIZEDEK: So now you understand?

29 BENJAR: No. This is the part I don't understand. Why did they

30   kill him? If he was really the Messiah, they could not have

31   killed him.

32 MELCHIZEDEK: Why do we celebrate the Passover?

33 BENJAR: What does the Passover celebration have to do with

34   the death of Jesus?

35 MELCHIZEDEK: Just answer the question.

1   BENJAR: It's so we Jews won't forget how God delivered our
2   ancestors from Egypt and the Angel of Death.
3   MELCHIZEDEK: So how did he deliver them?
4   BENJAR: By blood — lamb's blood. Each family that believed in
5   God put some lamb's blood on their doorpost. When the
6   Angel of Death saw this blood, he passed over their house.
7   MELCHIZEDEK: Signifying what?
8   BENJAR: Deliverance. Deliverance from the bondage of
9   Egyptian rule.
10 MELCHIZEDEK: So why still sacrifice a lamb at Passover time?
11   Egyptian rule has long been banished.
12 BENJAR: *(Becoming agitated)* But Roman rule has not gone! We
13   still sacrifice the Passover lamb because we look forward to
14   the day when our Messiah, our King, will come and take us
15   out of bondage once again. The lamb's blood is significant
16   of the deliverance we seek, just as it was significant in our
17   ancestors' time.
18 MELCHIZEDEK: Exactly! ... What day of the Passover celebration
19   was Jesus crucified?
20 BENJAR: The same day the Passover lamb was slain.
21 MELCHIZEDEK: *(Reading)* "He was led like a lamb to the
22   slaughter" *(Isa. 53:7)*.
23 BENJAR: Let me see that! Could this mean that Jesus is like
24   that lamb? *(A beat)* That his blood delivers men? *(A beat)* But
25   delivers them from what?
26 MELCHIZEDEK: *(Pointing to a place on the scroll)* Here lies the
27   answer! *(BENJAR picks up the scroll and begins reading. As he*
28   *reads, MELCHIZEDEK gathers his things and slips silently back*
29   *outside into the darkness.)*
30 BENJAR: *(Reading)* "He was pierced for our transgressions" *(Isa.*
31   *53:5)*. *(He looks up.)* He was pierced for our transgressions.
32   Then he had to die. He did not come to deliver us from
33   human bondage, but from inner bondage. *(Reading again)*
34   "We all, like sheep, have gone astray, each of us has turned
35   to his own way; and the Lord God has laid on him" ... on

1 **Jesus ... "the iniquity of us all"** *(Isa. 53:6). (Looking up)* **Then**
2 **because of his blood, we are free. Free from the bondage**
3 **of sin. So the Messiah has come ... and he has delivered his**
4 **people!**

5 *(Blackout)*

6

7 **Scene 4**

8

9 *(It is now daylight. As the lights come up, BENJAR is*
10 *disassembling the No Vacancy sign with a wooden hammer at*
11 *Stage Right.)*

12 ALISHA: *(Enters from behind the sleeping partition.)* **Benjar?** *(She*
13 *hears the pounding and crosses through the door to Stage Right.)*
14 **Benjar? You never came back to bed. The sign ... why are**
15 **you destroying it?**

16 BENJAR: **Because we have no further need for it.**

17 ALISHA: **But when the inn is really full and we have no room?**

18 BENJAR: **There will always be room here.**

19 ALISHA: **How can you be sure?**

20 BENJAR: *(Very excited)* **Because, Alisha — I've seen him!**

21 ALISHA: **You mean that stranger last night?**

22 BENJAR: **His name was Melchizedek, and we talked most of the**
23 **night. Suddenly I turned around, and he was gone. I**
24 **thought that perhaps he had decided to sleep in the stable,**
25 **so I ran out there to look for him. When I reached the**
26 **stable, I saw a man dressed in a white robe.**

27 ALISHA: **The stranger?**

28 BENJAR: **No ... it was ... it was Jesus!**

29 ALISHA: *(Confused)* **But Benjar, Jesus is dead.**

30 BENJAR: **No, Alisha. He is risen from the dead and is very much**
31 **alive!**

32 ALISHA: *(Still confused, but excited)* **Then we must go to him. He**
33 **must be hungry and need a place to rest.**

34 BENJAR: **But he is not there.**

35 ALISHA: **Then where is he? Where has he gone?**

1　BENJAR:　When he was born into this world, there was no room
2　　　　for him. And there was still no room for him when he died.
3　　　　So he established his kingdom in the only possible place ...
4　　　　in our hearts. Over the years, my own heart has become so
5　　　　full of hurt and selfish pride that it held no vacancy for him.
6　　　　However, last night changed all that. I came to understand
7　　　　why he died. But it wasn't until I saw him this morning that
8　　　　I realized the most important thing. He has not only
9　　　　conquered sin, but he has overcome death as well. We live
10　　　　because he lives! As the prophet Isaiah says, "Death has
11　　　　been swallowed up in victory!" *(Isa. 25:8).* So where is he
12　　　　now, you ask? Why ... he is here! *(He places his hand on his*
13　　　　*heart.)* Right here, *living* in my heart ... in your heart ... in
14　　　　any heart that believes, for he has established his throne in
15　　　　love. And on that throne, he will live forever!
16　　　　　　　　　　　　*(Blackout)*
17
18
19
20
21
22
23
24
25
26
27
28
29
30
31
32
33
34
35

Children and Youth

All Things Are Bright and Beautiful

An Easter tableau of children and flowers
by Arthur L. Zapel

CAST

Pastor

Twelve Children

Reading ability is the only talent requisite. The Children may be males or females, 8-14 years of age.

Children's Choir

PRODUCTION NOTES

Overview: Several classes of Sunday school children can participate in this Easter morning program using flowers as the central theme. They may perform as readers, singers in the children's choir, or as bearers of flowers. The symbolism of three Easter flowers is told with Scripture readings. Easter lilies are then added to form first the design of the Holy Trinity, then the design of the Cross. Six or more well-known hymns are used during the program. The script is structured as a total worship service for Easter (a suggested order of worship and a responsive reading are included), or it may be used in place of a sermon.

Program Considerations: The call to worship, invocation, pastoral prayer, and benediction are not included, as these would best be done in the style and words of the pastor. The Scripture selections included are from the *Today's English Version*. It is our feeling that these words are more easily read by children. Scripture readings from any Bible translation may be substituted.

Set: You may wish to use risers for the children's choir. If possible, it is effective if the flowers can be placed on boxes or risers of some sort, the lowest end toward the front pews and the highest toward the altar. This will provide maximum visibility.

Props: One arrangement each of white carnations, violets, and irises, and eleven or more Easter lilies. The cross may be as long as the Easter lilies and space available.

The placement of the flowers to climax this presentation would be as diagrammed here:

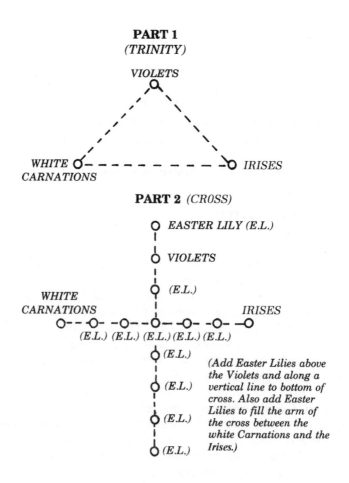

PART 1
(TRINITY)

VIOLETS

WHITE CARNATIONS   IRISES

PART 2 *(CROSS)*

EASTER LILY *(E.L.)*

VIOLETS

(E.L.)

WHITE CARNATIONS   IRISES

(E.L.) (E.L.) (E.L.) (E.L.) (E.L.)

(E.L.)

(E.L.)

(E.L.)

(E.L.)

(Add Easter Lilies above the Violets and along a vertical line to bottom of cross. Also add Easter Lilies to fill the arm of the cross between the white Carnations and the Irises.)

Costumes: No special costumes are needed.

Music: The hymns that may be used during the service are only suggested because of their words relating to the sub-themes of this program. The church music director may have better choices. All of the hymns indicated may be found in most church hymnals.

Playing time: Up to one hour.

SUGGESTED ORDER OF SERVICE

1. **Prelude**

2. **Call to Worship** (Pastor)

3. **Invocation** (Pastor)

4. **Lord's Prayer** (Everyone)

5. **Hymn** (Entire congregation, "Golden Breaks the Dawn")

6. **Responsive Reading:**
   PASTOR: Praise the Lord Jesus.
   CONGREGATION: He is risen; he lives with us today and forever.
   PASTOR: Praise him for his suffering that we are redeemed.
   CONGREGATION: Praise him for his victory over sin and death's dark night.
   PASTOR: Praise him with the flowers of Easter.
   CONGREGATION: Praise him with beauty, color, and song.
   PASTOR: Praise him with lilies, violets, and iris.
   CONGREGATION: Praise him with clover, columbine and daisies.
   PASTOR: Let everything that grows praise the risen Lord.
   CONGREGATION: Praise Jesus, our savior.
   PASTOR: He is risen,
   CONGREGATION: Praise the Lord!

7. **Scripture Lesson:** Matthew 28:5-8

8. **Anthem:** "Christ the Lord Is Risen Today"

9. **Children's Presentation:** "All Things Are Bright and Beautiful"

10. **Offering** (With children's hymn, "Joy Dawned Again on Easter Day")

11. **Pastoral Prayer**

12. **Hymn** (Entire congregation, "Good Christian Men, Rejoice and Sing")

13. **Benediction** (Pastor)

14. **Postlude**

1   PASTOR: On this Easter Sunday we celebrate new life — your
2   new life, because Jesus Christ our Savior died for us and
3   was resurrected. Jesus lived, died, then lived again.
4   Because he lives, you live, redeemed by his love.
5   Easter morning! All things are bright and beautiful.
6   Jesus Christ lives, and rebirth is all about us — in our new
7   life, in our children, in springtime, in all of the wonders of
8   God's creation. In the early hour of dawn, Jesus rose from
9   the dead to free us of our burdens of sin and gave us life
10   eternal. In spirit you were there that morning of wonder.
11   You remember the freshness and beauty lifted out of the
12   dark night. You see the first rays of sunlight piercing
13   through the heavy-laden mists of dawn. You see the gold
14   and silver dewdrops clinging to the grasses. From the
15   petals of flowers, they hang as trembling ornaments. You
16   hear the breath of resurrection and new life in the soft
17   breeze of morning. The sweetest of perfumes encircles your
18   presence, and you know you are part of God's love and
19   redemption. All things are bright and beautiful. Joy has
20   dawned again on Easter day.
21
22 *PROCESSIONAL:* Groups of children enter down the center aisle
23   carrying flowers: Easter lilies, violets, carnations, iris, and laurel.
24   They are singing: "All Things Bright and Beautiful." They take
25   positions at the front of the chancel and turn to place their flowers
26   at their sides, then turn to face the congregation.
27
28 PASTOR: To celebrate this Easter Sunday, several groups of
29   children from our Sunday school department would like to
30   present for you a tableau of children and flowers entitled
31   *All Things Are Bright and Beautiful.*
32 CHILD 1: Flowers and children symbolize our victory over sin
33   and death. In every flower, as in every child, there are seeds
34   of new beginnings. Though beauty and love may wilt away,
35   there is always, in God's world, a new beginning.

1   **CHILD 2:** Jesus taught in parables — short little stories full of
2   meaning for those who would listen carefully.
3   **CHILD 3:** *(Reading from the Bible)* **Mark 4:3-8:** There was a man
4   who went out to sow. As he scattered the seed in the field,
5   some of it fell along the path, and the birds came and ate
6   it up. Some of it fell on rocky ground, where there was little
7   soil. The seeds soon sprouted, because the soil wasn't
8   deep. Then when the sun came up it burned the young
9   plants, and because the roots had not grown deep enough
10   the plants soon dried up. Some of the seed fell among
11   thorns, which grew up and choked the plants, and they
12   didn't bear grain. But some seeds fell in good soil, and the
13   plants sprouted, grew, and bore grain: some had thirty
14   grains, others sixty, and others one hundred.
15   **CHILD 2:** But those who listened did not always hear what
16   Jesus was trying to tell them, so he explained his parable.
17   **CHILD 3:** *(Reading from the Bible)* **Mark 4:14-20:** The sower
18   sows God's message. Sometimes the message falls along
19   the path; these people hear it, but as soon as they hear it
20   Satan comes and takes away the message sown in them.
21   Other people are like the seeds that fall on rocky ground.
22   As soon as they hear the message, they receive it gladly.
23   But it does not sink deep into them ... so when trouble or
24   persecution comes because of the message, they give it up
25   at once. Other people are like the seeds sown among the
26   thorns. These are the ones who hear the message, but the
27   worries about this life, the love for riches, and all other
28   kinds of desires crowd in and choke the message, and they
29   don't bear fruit. But other people are like the seeds sown
30   in good soil. They hear the message, accept it, and bear
31   fruit: some thirty, some sixty, and some one hundred.
32   **CHILD 2:** Flowers are the fruit of the seeds — beautiful symbols
33   of Jesus' lessons.
34   **CHILD 4:** *(Holding up a violet plant or vase of cut flowers for all to
35   see)* The violet is a flower of Easter symbolizing humility —

how Christ humbled himself by dying on the cross. He could have been King of the Jews but he chose, instead, to be "the Son of Man." He could have worn a crown of gold, but he chose to wear a crown of thorns. He taught us that one must be humble to enter the kingdom of heaven.

CHILD 5: Jesus called a child, had him stand in front of them, and said, "Remember this! Unless you change and become like children, you will never enter the kingdom of heaven. The greatest in the kingdom of heaven is the one who humbles himself and becomes like this child. And whoever welcomes in my name one such child as this, welcomes me" *(Matt. 18:2-5)*.

CHILD 6: And all of you must put on the apron of humility, to serve one another; for the Scripture says, "God resists the proud, but gives grace to the humble." Humble yourselves, then, under God's mighty hand, so that he will lift you up in his own good time. Throw all your worries on him, because he cares for you *(1 Peter 5:5-7)*.

CHILD 1: The color violet is made from red and blue. Red represents sacrifice and love. Blue stands for faith and truth. Together they represent the humility of Jesus, our Lord and Savior.

HYMN: The children's choir steps forward and sings the first two verses of "What a Friend We Have in Jesus."

CHILD 2: *(Holding up a carnation plant or vase of cut flowers for all to see)* The carnation is another flower of Easter. It signifies pure love. The kind of love Jesus demonstrated so many times during his ministry.

CHILD 7: With God's power of love expressed through his son Jesus, there were many miracles. Jesus healed a man born blind, he healed a boy troubled by an evil spirit, he healed a paralyzed man, a man who was deaf and dumb, and a man with a crippled hand. He made the lepers clean. So

1   great was his love that he raised people from the dead.

2   **CHILD 8: Jesus told us that we, too, could do great things with**

3   **love. He said, "You have heard that it was said, 'Love your**

4   **friends, hate your enemies.' But now I tell you: love your**

5   **enemies, and pray for those who persecute you, so that you**

6   **will become the sons of your Father in heaven. For he**

7   **makes his sun to shine on bad and good people alike, and**

8   **gives rain to those who do good and those who do evil. Why**

9   **should God reward you if you love only the people who love**

10   **you? Even the tax collectors do that!"** *(Matt. 5:43)*.

11   **CHILD 9: Jesus' lessons of love were told by John in the Bible.**

12   **"God is love, and whoever lives in love lives in God and God**

13   **lives in him. There is no fear in love, perfect love drives out**

14   **all fear"** *(1 John 4:16, 18)*.

15   **CHILD 2: This carnation is the symbol of God's pure love.**

16

17   *HYMN:* Children's choir or entire congregation sings "All Creatures of

18   Our God and King."

19

20   **CHILD 1:** *(Stepping to the front, holding a vase with iris blossoms)*

21   **The iris is the flower that symbolizes Christ's passion —**

22   **how he quietly suffered, then died on a cross for us.**

23   **CHILD 10: John 19:1-3: Then Pilate took Jesus and had him**

24   **whipped. The soldiers made a crown of thorny branches**

25   **and put it on his head; they put a purple robe on him, and**

26   **came to him and said, "Long live the King of the Jews!"**

27   **And they went up and slapped him.**

28   **CHILD 11: John 19:17-18: He went out, carrying his cross, and**

29   **came to "The Place of the Skull," as it is called. There they**

30   **nailed him to the cross ...**

31   **CHILD 12: Matthew 27:45, 46, 50, 54: At noon the whole**

32   **country was covered with darkness, which lasted for three**

33   **hours. At about three o'clock Jesus cried out with a loud**

34   **shout, "Eli, Eli, lema sabachthani?" which means, "My God,**

35   **my God, why did you abandon me?" Jesus again gave a**

1   **loud cry, and breathed his last. When the army officer and**
2   **the soldiers with him who were watching Jesus saw the**
3   **earthquake and everything else that happened, they were**
4   **terrified and said, "He really was the Son of God!"**
5   **CHILD 1: These iris blossoms are the symbol of our Lord's**
6   **passion in his final hours before his earthly death.**
7
8   ***HYMN:*** Children's choir sings "Let Us With a Gladsome Mind."
9
10 **PASTOR:** *(As he or she speaks, three CHILDREN, each carrying a*
11   *flower, step forward to a center position as their flower is named.)*
12   **Church history and tradition have chosen many flowers to**
13   **signify saints, sacraments, and events of early Christianity.**
14   **Today we have shown you three. The violet, which**
15   **symbolizes the humility of Jesus;** *(CHILD WITH VIOLETS*
16   *steps forward)* **white carnations which symbolize the pure**
17   **love of Jesus;** *(CHILD WITH CARNATIONS steps forward)* **and**
18   **the iris, which symbolizes the passion of Christ Jesus.**
19   *(CHILD WITH IRIS BLOSSOMS steps forward.)*
20   **Let us now place these flowers in a triangle representing**
21   **the trinity of our faith — Father, Son, and the Holy Spirit.**
22   *(The three CHILDREN place their flowers in a triangle. See*
23   *diagram on page 252.)* **Let us next place a white lily above the**
24   **triangle of the trinity to represent the resurrection.** *(One*
25   *CHILD places an Easter lily above the triangle — see diagram.)*
26   **This flower is the symbol of Easter. And between them all,**
27   **let us place several Easter lilies to represent the cross of**
28   **Christianity.** *(Several CHILDREN place Easter lilies in position*
29   *to make a cross. See diagram.)* **We live because he lives. He is**
30   **risen and so are we!**
31
32
33
34
35

Jesus Loved Them

A reading for junior- and senior-high youth
by Sally Evans

CAST

John the Baptist — *Reader #1*
A Pharisee — *Reader #2*
John the Apostle — *Reader #3*
Andrew — *Reader #4*
Faith — *Reader #5*
Matthew — *Reader #6*
Judas — *Reader #7*
The Roman Centurion — *Reader #8*
Mary Magdalene — *Reader #9*
Youth Leader

PRODUCTION NOTES

Overview: This is a structured worship service that offers many young people the chance to participate as readers, soloists, members of the choir, or as ushers. A message entitled "Jesus Loved Them" replaces the sermon. Nine biblical personalities who knew Jesus tell their stories. Included are John the Baptist, a Pharisee, John, Andrew, Faith (the woman who touched Jesus' cloak), Matthew, Judas, the Roman Centurion, and Mary Magdalene.

Set: Nothing more than what is likely already in your chancel area, i.e., the pulpit and pew behind or to the side of the pulpit.

Props: None.

Costumes: Contemporary dress is fine.

Playing time: 50 minutes.

OPTIONAL ORDER OF WORSHIP

MOMENTS OF SILENT MEDITATION: There are many rooms in my Father's house, and I am going to prepare a place for you. I would not tell you this if it were not so *(John 14:2).*

ORGAN PRELUDE

THE CHORAL CALL TO WORSHIP: *(YOUTH CHOIR. First speaker goes to pulpit during Introit.)*

CALL TO WORSHIP: *(LEADER and CONGREGATION)* **This is a time to give praise and thanksgiving to God and to Jesus Christ, his only Son, who loved us enough to conquer death and die in our place. This is a time to give praise and thanksgiving to God who raised Jesus from the dead to have abundant life everlasting; and praise to Jesus who gives us the same eternal life in reward for following him!**

HYMN: *(Suggestion)* **"Jesus Christ Is Risen Today"**

THE MORNING WELCOME AND ANNOUNCEMENTS

HYMN: *(Suggestion)* **"Amazing Grace"**

THE DOXOLOGY

THE PRAYER OF DEDICATION: *(LEADER and CONGREGATION)* **Father, all that we have comes from and truly belongs to you. Please accept our tithes and offerings and use them as you see fit. Help us to see how much better our lives will be after we have committed ourselves totally and completely to you. Thank you for wanting us, just as we are, at this moment. Please grant us the faith to meet you half way. In Jesus' name we pray. Amen.**

LORD'S PRAYER

MESSAGE: **"Jesus Loved Them"**

SOLO: *(Optional. Can be an adult soloist or a selection by a youth or the youth choir.)*

BENEDICTION: *(YOUTH LEADER)* **May the grace and peace of our Lord be with us always, and may everything we say and do give honor and glory to his name.**

POSTLUDE: *(Suggestion)* **"Hallelujah Chorus"** from Handel's *Messiah*. **Congregation remains standing until youth leaders leave sanctuary.**

1   *(READERS #1–#3 sit on the pew behind or adjacent to the*
2   *pulpit when the service begins. The rest of the READERS are*
3   *sitting on the front pew. At the appropriate time, READER #1*
4   *stands to speak at the pulpit.)*

5 **JOHN THE BAPTIST:** *(READER #1)* **I am called John, the**
6   **Baptist. This name was well chosen, for that is what I**
7   **do. This is what I am — the baptizer. Prophet? Man of**
8   **God? Yes ... but not God. I am not the Messiah. I will tell**
9   **you as I have told them — I am a mere voice ... a voice**
10   **crying out in the wilderness, "Prepare the way of the**
11   **Lord." My cry is a warning, "Repent! Turn away from**
12   **your sins! The kingdom of heaven is at hand! Prepare**
13   **the way of the Lord! Make straight a highway for our**
14   **God!" And I say to you ... "Hush. Be silent ... and you**
15   **will see God walking ... coming toward you down a**
16   **wilderness road in the desert."**

17   **My disciples have questioned me, "Can God truly walk**
18   **with man?"**

19   **I say to you as I have said to them, "All flesh will see**
20   **it together! The glory of the Lord shall be revealed! The**
21   **rough places shall be made plain!"** *(Isa. 40:4-5, author's*
22   *paraphrase). (READER #1 takes his seat on the front pew.*
23   *READER #2 stands to speak at the pulpit.)*

24 **A PHARISEE:** *(READER #2)* **My name is Gallo. I am a man of**
25   **wealth and position ... owner of a fishing fleet by trade**
26   **and a Pharisee by appointment. As you know, we are a**
27   **highly religious sect ... careful to keep our robes tightly**
28   **about us so as not to touch any unclean thing. We are also**
29   **keepers of the law ... and of order. It was this business we**
30   **were about on this day of which I am to tell you ... a day**
31   **I can never forget. We had been sent by the Sanhedrin to**
32   **hear the preaching of this John ... this menace ... this one**
33   **called the Baptist. We were to travel far, and it was the**
34   **fourth day when our commission reached the wilds of the**
35   **Jordan. The preacher's commanding call could be heard**

1   from afar, demanding repentance. His message was
2   awesome. His appearance, wild and unforgettable. So this
3   was the man so notorious throughout Palestine. The voice
4   that had called so many sons away from home and family.

5   But suddenly, my eye was caught unexpectedly by a
6   figure standing some distance away in the large
7   congregation. The man was a young Jew, perhaps in his
8   early thirties. A light woolen mantle covered his head, but
9   a smooth forehead and regular features were visible
10   beneath. From what I could tell, his hair and beard were
11   light brown with glints of auburn. His tanned skin
12   indicated that he had spent a good deal of time outdoors.
13   He was not unusually tall and his rolled sleeves exposed
14   arms apparently used to hard labor. But it was something
15   in his bearing that captured me. He was part of, yet apart
16   from, the others. The preacher's call came again. The
17   young Jew made his way toward the Baptist. The Baptist
18   looked up and tears of joy filled his eyes. "I need to be
19   baptized by you," John said, bewildered, "and you come
20   to me?" *(Matt. 3:14, author's paraphrase)*.

21   The stranger looked upon the Baptist, and said, "Allow
22   it to be so now, for thus it becomes us to fulfill all
23   righteousness" *(Matt. 3:14, author's paraphrase)*.

24   The crowd watched as the pilgrim went through the rite
25   of baptism. What happened then, I can't explain. As the
26   man came up from the rushing waters and looked high
27   into the sky, a brilliant light, almost tangible in its outline
28   and energy, surrounded the stranger. The heavens
29   rumbled, and the crowd fell back. Fear and awe gripped
30   our very souls. Then a voice came from the heavens,
31   saying loudly, "This is my beloved Son, in whom I am well
32   pleased" *(Matt. 3:17, KJV)*. The shaft of light slowly
33   disappeared, and the stranger lowered his eyes and
34   bowed his head. Then slowly, he rose. Hesitating only
35   momentarily, his bearing marked with a mixture of

1   intense inner struggle, he returned from the river and
2   passed silently down the shore. All eyes followed his
3   determined stride until he was lost from sight in the wilds
4   of Jordan.
5   I shook my head and rubbed my eyes. For a moment,
6   I thought I had seen God walking down the road into the
7   wilderness. There were no more baptisms that day; it
8   would be sunset before the crowds dispersed. We
9   returned home and were told to remain silent on the
10 issue. But my mind would not remain silent. God
11 walking as a man? Impossible! Reason will not let me
12 believe what my heart is telling me is true. During the
13 daylight hours, I can almost forget what happened that
14 day. But when the night falls and I am in darkness, I see
15 the face of the stranger, and a curious unrest burns
16 within me. Again, I hear the warning cry of the Baptist
17 — "Repent! The kingdom of heaven is at hand! Make
18 straight a highway for our God!" Has the Baptist robbed
19 me of my worldly peace? Or have I only stolen from
20 myself? I cry to the gods, beseeching them to still my
21 soul; but in response, I receive only a vision of the
22 stranger ... walking ... into the wilderness. Why will the
23 gods not answer my plea? Why are they deaf to my cry
24 for peace? *(READER #2 takes his seat on the front pew.*
25 *READER #3 stands to speak at the pulpit.)*
26 **JOHN THE APOSTLE:** *(READER #3)* My name is John. I sat
27 alone that night, awaiting the Master's return. He had
28 gone off to pray in the wilderness, and hours had passed
29 since his leaving. The uneven snoring of the other men
30 could be heard in the distance, and I knew they were all
31 sleeping ... all but me. Sleep eluded me now, and had
32 for several days. I thought of the others who followed
33 Jesus ... of Peter ... of Andrew ... of James, my brother.
34 Why? I questioned myself. Why couldn't I be of a more
35 simple faith like them? Why did doubts and fears keep

1   me awake nights while the others slept? Resting my
2   head on my knees, I wept bitterly, not caring, for once,
3   whether the others heard me or not. Then suddenly, a
4   soft footfall startled me. Looking up, I saw Jesus headed
5   my way. "It is a warm night," the Master called.
6   "Yes," I nodded.
7   He took a place next to me and we sat in silence until
8   the Lord said, "It seems to be your custom to always be
9   waiting for me apart from the others."
10   I turned my head, not wanting him to read my
11   thoughts. "I guess I like to think alone sometimes," I
12   offered.
13   "And what are your thoughts tonight?" Jesus
14   questioned.
15   "Master," I answered, "they are many. Too numerous
16   to mention." Jesus smiled compassionately and placed
17   an arm around my shoulders. I felt myself enveloped in
18   the warmth of his love.
19   Calluses of pride began to fall away from my heart.
20   "My Lord," I confessed, "I have so many questions. I
21   have hidden them for days, trying myself to find the
22   answers."
23   "I know," Jesus said gently.
24   "You know, Master?" I said.
25   Jesus nodded with understanding. "But tell me of
26   them, John, for it is well for you to do so."
27   A great weight lifted from my soul as I put into words
28   all the doubts and fears that had been plaguing me for
29   so many days and nights. "My Lord, I am a sinful man. I
30   have never felt more unworthy of anyone's love than I
31   feel of yours. You know my nature. I feel that somehow
32   you know me better than anyone else ever has. And yet
33   ... you love me. In spite of my tendency to rebellion and
34   anger; in spite of my stubborn pride; and in spite of all
35   the times I have failed to do as you have taught ... you

1   love me just the same. Master, I love your words; but
2   they do not seem to grow in me. I must be bad soil,
3   because I do not bring forth the fruit of peace which you
4   said I should." The night grew totally dark, and it
5   seemed the world awaited the Master's reply.
6   He turned to me and, taking my face in his hands,
7   gently lifted my head so that my eyes met his. He studied
8   me a moment, and then smiled with compassion. "John,
9   have you failed to see what I have been trying to teach
10   you? Did I not tell you but to ask and it would be given
11   you? To knock and the door would be opened to you? If
12   no man can keep the law of Moses, how can he keep the
13   law of the spirit in his own strength? It is not the seed
14   alone, nor the soil which is of consequence. It is the
15   Master who must bring them together and tend to their
16   husbandry. The part of the soil is to yield to the Master's
17   plow." Had I understood correctly? The lesson was
18   clear, but still hard to accept. Did I simply have to yield
19   to Jesus? The Lord's words, "the part of the soil is to
20   yield to the Master's plow," came back to me. This
21   single condition was required of the man wanting to
22   change. With what faith I had been given, I clung to
23   those words, and found that Jesus, who could heal
24   disease and had the power to forgive sins, was also
25   Master over the character of the human heart. *(READER*
26   *#3 introduces hymn. During the hymn, READER #3 takes his*
27   *seat on the front pew, and READERS #4–#6 sit on the pew*
28   *by the pulpit. Following the hymn, READER #4 stands to*
29   *speak at the pulpit.)*
30 **ANDREW:** *(READER #4)* My name is Andrew. I am usually
31   referred to as Simon Peter's brother ... and I am proud
32   to be known as such. I would like to take this
33   opportunity to speak to those of you who feel you live
34   your lives in the shadow of another. No, it is not easy to
35   live out your life day after day in a subordinate position

1   while someone else gets the notice, the publicity, the
2   credit, the praise, and perhaps ... to the mind's eye ...
3   the rewards. I understand these feelings, and I have
4   good news to tell you. Though it is true that I was not
5   given the gift of being the great preacher Peter was, and
6   I am not the great missionary who helped churches
7   spring forward like flowers in the desert, and though it
8   was not I who gave the sermon at Pentecost that was to
9   turn the whole world upside down ... even though I was
10   none of these, God used me in a very special way. You
11   see ... though it was not I who led thousands to Christ
12   as my brother did ... it was I, Andrew, who led my
13   brother to Christ. *(READER #4 returns to his seat on the*
14   *front pew. READER #5 stands to speak at the pulpit.)*
15 FAITH: (READER #5) I am the woman who touched his cloak.
16   I had often heard of the great teacher and his wonderful
17   works. I had heard of all he had done for others ... his
18   power to heal ... the power of his love. As a last resort,
19   I had come to sit by the roadside where he was to pass
20   that day. For years I had been ill with a disease that you
21   would call a type of cancer. All the money I had had been
22   spent on various physicians, and each was to diagnose
23   the   same: "Hopeless" ... "Incurable" ... "There   is
24   nothing we can do." "Incurable." The word sounded its
25   verdict within me. "No!" I replied aloud, startled at my
26   own determination. No, not today. Today I would have
27   hope. One last hope in the person of Jesus of Nazareth.
28   Closing my mind to doubt, I opened my heart to faith.
29   "Sir," I prayed, "if you will just look upon me, I know I
30   will be made well. I know all of what you have done for
31   others, and I believe you will do the same for me." A
32   peace such as I had never known came over me then,
33   flooding my very soul with radiant joy. And it was then
34   that I knew ... beyond all doubt ... that I would witness a
35   miracle that day.

1   Then, suddenly, a great crowd was upon me. In my
2   fervor of hope and prayer, I had not heard the multitude
3   approaching that now pressed in on me from all sides.
4   Fear gripped me as I reached in the dust for my cane and
5   found that someone had evidently kicked it aside.
6   Without my cane, I was unable to stand. I could only
7   huddle in the dirt and hope that I would not be trampled.
8   But then ... I saw him! In the midst of the clamoring
9   crowd, I saw Jesus. He was drawing near! My heart
10 sank, and the joy and assurance I had known earlier
11 vanished. How could he help me if he could not see me?
12 It was then that the thought came to me ... "If I can just
13 touch him, I know I will be made well!" I scrambled to
14 my knees, unmindful of the crowd, keeping my eyes
15 focused only on Jesus. It seemed that time stood still as
16 I waited there in the dust for Jesus to draw close
17 enough. But then he was upon me! So close that I could
18 see his face; and so taken was I with that face, that I
19 momentarily forgot the mission on which I had come ...
20 for it was in his face that I saw my freedom.
21   Someone brushed against me, and immediately I was
22 jolted back to reality ... to the crowd ... to the confusion.
23 It was then that I spotted my cane only a short distance
24 away. I made a move toward it, but stopped. If I chose
25 to retrieve my cane, I would lose the chance to touch
26 Jesus — for it lay in the other direction. I looked up and
27 saw that the Lord had almost passed. With one last
28 desperate gesture, I reached out and touched the hem of
29 his garment. Instantly amid the throng, he turned. "Who
30 touched me?" he asked. Something like an electric
31 shock surged through my veins. I stood to my feet, and
32 his eyes met mine. "Daughter," he said, almost in a
33 whisper, "thy faith has made thee whole *(Matt. 9:22,
34 KJV)*. Go in peace and be healed of thy plague." My
35 lifetime passed before me as I looked into his eyes. The

part of me that had been diseased melted under his gaze, and new life was born within me. Yes, I was truly whole. What I tell you is true. I did not have money — only faith. I did not come to him in the synagogue — but yet, he met me in the street. I had not private counsel with the Lord — for I met him in a crowd. Truly I say to you — the human touch is able to arrest God. *(READER #5 returns to her seat on the front pew. READER #6 stands to speak at the pulpit.)*

MATTHEW: *(READER #6)* **I am Matthew Bar Alpheus; also called Levi. Before I met the Master, I held the position of a tax collector. As tax collectors, we were among the most despised men of Israel, for not only did we support Rome, but we were also notorious for overcharging the people and keeping the extra revenue for ourselves. This was my life before ... before I met Jesus. I still remember that day as if it were yesterday. The Master and his followers had to go by the custom seat where the tax collectors scrutinized all traffic that passed. That day, I was in charge. Considered a traitor by my fellow countrymen, I had built up a stony facade. Arrogance and pride were my shields of armor. But that day was to be different from all others, for Jesus had stopped at my table. Knowing he was a rabbi, I looked up with disdain, prepared for the usual judgmental reproach. But as his gaze caught mine, there was no condemnation in his eyes to be found. Only love. "Follow me," he commanded in a gentle, yet compelling, way. I turned from the money table, stepped down from the customs house, and followed after Jesus. Ahead walked the Master of a new life.** *(READER #6 introduces anthem. During the anthem, READER #6 returns to his seat on the front pew, and READERS #7–#9 sit on the pew by the pulpit. Following the anthem, READER #7 stands to speak at the pulpit.)*

JUDAS ISCARIOT: *(READER #7)* **I am Judas of Iscariot. You**

1   may not want to hear what I have to say. I know the
2   disgust you must feel when you think of me. But you can
3   think no worse of me than I do of myself. I will not ask
4   you to understand or accept my feelings of grief and
5   remorse. They go far beyond human comprehension.
6   But I do ask you not to judge me so harshly that you fail
7   to heed the warning I am to give you. We are all given a
8   choice ... for we are all given free will. It is by free will
9   that we choose to follow Jesus. It is by free will that we
10   choose to follow the world. At some point in our lives,
11   we all come to this fork in the road where we have to
12   make this decision. Almost two thousand years ago, the
13   choice I made led to my end. I turned my back on Jesus
14   and chose to follow the world and what seemed to be its
15   riches. I didn't know the price to be paid for such a
16   decision: disillusionment, regret, remorse, and death.
17   Or maybe I did know and just refused to listen. *(READER*
18   *#7 returns to his seat on the front pew. READER #8 stands*
19   *to speak at the pulpit.)*
20 **THE ROMAN CENTURION:** *(READER #8)* **I am a Roman**
21   **centurion. Little is said of me in the Scriptures. I am the**
22   **Roman centurion who rode at the head of the tragic**
23   **procession which escorted Jesus to Calvary. The heat**
24   **was oppressive that day, and a mysterious hot yellow**
25   **light pervaded the earth. A strange odor hung in the**
26   **steaming air, and heat waves shimmered all about,**
27   **giving things a look of instability. Beyond Golgotha, red**
28   **and purple clouds streamed up into the sky like**
29   **flickering tongues, spreading themselves over hot, white**
30   **heavens. Several of the soldiers cursed, trying to keep at**
31   **bay the large crowd that had gathered. One man**
32   **muttered an incantation against evil spirits. A young**
33   **soldier drew up next to me, sweat pouring down his face**
34   **from under his helmet. He looked at me with dismay.**
35   **"Who is it we are to execute?" he asked.**

1   "Only three criminals," I replied, careful not to let my
2   own fear enter my voice.

3   The young officer fingered an amulet and shook his
4   head. "I don't like this. There are portents here," he said.

5   The eerie light increased like a threatening glare from
6   Olympus. I reached within my armor to clutch my own
7   amulet, but the hot metal burned my fingers, and it was
8   wet with sweat. Fear such as I had never known raced
9   through my being. "In the name of the gods, let's be
10   done with this matter!" I shouted.

11   The opium boy sat crouched behind a large boulder.
12   He rose and stared blankly at me for a moment and then
13   brought forth the crude goblet. I then approached the
14   condemned man. Standing before Jesus, I looked fully
15   into his face. The godlike eyes regarded me straight on,
16   as if probing my very soul. I remember thinking in
17   bewilderment, "Who is he?"

18   "Drink," I stammered, "it will help you." The words
19   died in my throat. Jesus shook his head slightly, but he
20   inclined his head gratefully. His eyes had been lowered,
21   but now he raised them to meet mine. The look he gave
22   me was tender beyond all tenderness I could imagine ...
23   and incredibly kind and gentle. In terror and awe I fell
24   back from that look, stumbling into my horse. "Let it be
25   consummated!" I cried, in a voice I didn't recognize as
26   my own. Burying my face in my horse's neck, I heard the
27   sound of hammering; but aside from that ... silence.
28   Complete silence.

29   I heard the cross enter its foothold. The earth stood still,
30   and then he spoke. "Father, forgive them; for they know
31   not what they do" *(Luke 23:34, KJV)*, he said. Despite the
32   unrelenting heat, a horrible chill crept up my spine.

33   "Why?" I asked myself, in the roaring confusion of my
34   mind. "Why should any man forgive his enemies, or
35   implore his God to do so, when death was upon him?

Especially to ask forgiveness for the very men who had taken such a vital part in establishing his death! Why would any man ..." the word caught in my throat. No man would. No mere man could. Slowly, I turned and lifted my eyes to the central cross. The unearthly light pulsed out more blindingly than before ... as if gathering itself for one huge conflagration. I looked at Jesus. He was speaking to the man on the cross next to him. I crept closer, crawling on my hands and knees. Fear and awe kept me from standing. The other man was straining to look at Jesus.

"Remember me, Jesus, when you come as King!" *(Luke 2:42)*, he asked.

For several moments Jesus gazed at him with unearthly compassion, and then he smiled and said, "I tell you this: today you will be in Paradise with me" *(Luke 23:43)*.

Uncounted time passed. I seemed to fall into a dream-like state. I felt frozen into eternity, and never would I leave this place and never would I know anything else. I would always be here, watching boiled clouds ascend like steam from a hot earth. I crept even closer to the central cross. Complete despair overcame my soul. Then suddenly — the light was gone. It was gone as completely as if midnight had settled on the earth. The kneeling and betting soldiers jumped to their feet with terrified cries. Someone gripped my shoulders and tried to pull me back. "No," I said. The word, in a moan, escaped my lips. I lurched forward, grasping a large rock, and moved farther up the steep incline. How I wished the whole mountain would fall on me ... and would hide me from what I did not want to know.

At that instant, the ground rose like a ship on a gigantic wave, and a sound like thunder struck the darkness. The air was then pervaded by a voice ... by a mighty voice, ringing strong and full of exultation.

1   "Father! In your hands I place my spirit!" *(Luke 23:46).*
2   he cried out.
3   The darkness deepened ... the soldiers stammered
4   incoherently. The Pharisees and scribes retreated
5   backwards down the hill, grasping at each others' arms.
6   I turned to find a young officer trembling at my side. His
7   voice shook as he spoke, "Truly, this was a just man!" I
8   turned and walked the few remaining steps to the
9   central cross. I looked down to where the friends of
10   Jesus sat, huddled together ... comforting one another.
11   A greater emptiness filled me than I had ever known,
12   and I wished above everything else that I were one of
13   them. Turning back to the cross, I placed my hands upon
14   its roughness and bitterly wept.
15   There were rumors that on the third day Jesus had
16   risen from the dead. It was then that I became
17   desperately ill, and finally, bedridden. I knew that he,
18   who had power over death, had surely condemned me to
19   death for my part in his execution. Many physicians tried
20   to help me, but no cure could be found to relieve the all-
21   consuming pain within my stomach. Then, finally, I was
22   visited quite unexpectedly by a physician who had heard
23   of my case. A dear and glorious physician! I felt
24   compelled to tell him of that day and of the fears that
25   have hounded me since. "No," he proclaimed. His voice
26   was warm and soothing. He continued, "How could God
27   condemn you? It was prophesied ages ago that he would
28   die in that manner, for the salvation of all men! Did he
29   hate you? No! He loved you! And I tell you that he loves
30   you now and is with you always."
31   I closed my tired eyes. "Is it true?" I urged ... "Is it
32   really true? He has risen? And he loves even me?"
33   "Yes," Luke assured me. "It is true. He has risen from
34   the dead! And he not only loves you ... he lives for you."
35   Opening my eyes, I looked into the face of my

1   wonderful friend. I saw there the compassion that had
2   etched Jesus' face on that day long ago. "And he was
3   surely God?" I whispered.
4   Luke smiled and said, "He is surely God." I slept
5   peaceably then and glorious health returned to me ...
6   health to proclaim the wondrous news of the resurrection
7   ... that Jesus Christ lives ... and because he lives, we will
8   live also! *(READER #8 returns to his seat on the front pew.*
9   *READER #9 stands to speak at the pulpit.)*
10 **MARY MAGDALENE:** *(READER #9)* I am Mary Magdalene.
11 When the full realization had come to me that Jesus was
12 really dead, I wept at great length, not knowing where
13 to turn for comfort. Joseph of Arimathea had gone to
14 Pilate, requesting the body of our Lord. Pilate then
15 summoned the centurion to confirm the statement that
16 Jesus had died. Being completely satisfied, Pilate
17 granted Joseph's request. Joseph, with Nicodemus to
18 help him, gently took the body of our Lord and wrapped
19 it in strips of linen with spices between the layers. Then
20 they carried the body to a newly made tomb in the
21 counselor's garden. Mary, Jesus' mother, and I watched
22 from a distance. We had seen the hasty anointing of the
23 Lord's body and had vowed, at the first possible
24 moment, to complete the task. So, before light dawned
25 on the Sabbath, Mary, Salome (the mother of James and
26 John), and I were on our way to this tomb where Jesus'
27 body had been laid.
28   There was one problem that deeply concerned us. A
29 huge stone had been rolled in front of the doorway of
30 the sepulcher, and a seal had been placed on it to
31 prevent tampering. Also, Pilate had ordered guards to
32 keep a constant vigil at the gravesite, and no one would
33 be allowed entrance. But even as we wondered — we
34 looked, and saw that the great stone had been rolled
35 away! There were no guards present to prevent us from

1   drawing closer; yet, in fear, we kept our distance, gazing
2   in momentary shock and confusion. Deeply frightened,
3   we did not wait to investigate. We fled. Upon reaching
4   Peter and John, I told them that someone had evidently
5   stolen the body of our Lord and laid him elsewhere. A
6   strange look passed between the two men, and though I
7   knew them well, I could not discern what it was. Then
8   they were running ... running as fast as they could in the
9   direction of the garden. John, younger and more agile
10   than Peter, reached the tomb ... and I, following,
11   lingered near the edge of the garden. I saw John enter
12   the doorway and then stop, in obvious amazement at
13   what he found. Peter, momentarily forgetting his
14   ingrained fear of the dead, went fully into the cave-like
15   structure ... with John following close behind. In
16   seconds the two men emerged, talking in excited voices
17   that I could not understand. I started toward them, but
18   in their haste to leave the garden, they didn't see me
19   approaching. I turned to follow them, but something
20   within me drew me deeper into the garden.
21   Drawing near to the entrance of the tomb, I fell to my
22   knees, overcome with grief and loneliness. It was then
23   that I heard a voice from behind me say, "Woman, why
24   are you crying? Who is it that you are looking for?"
25   Shocked at being found there, I kept my place ...
26   covering my eyes with my hands and bowing my head.
27   "If you took him away, sir, tell me where you have put
28   him, and I will go and get him" *(John 20:15).*
29   I heard a rustling of his robe, and I knew that the man
30   now stood in front of me. The voice came softly ...
31   barely above a whisper, calling, "Mary."
32   I lifted my head with a jerk, blinking back the tears,
33   and found myself staring into the eyes of my beloved
34   Master! The loneliness and grief I had felt earlier
35   vanished as I looked from the darkness of death into the

1   glorious light of life. "Teacher!" The word escaped my
2   lips. I wanted to rush to him, but his gaze held me back.
3   Instantly, I knew that his love was no longer limited to
4   physical restrictions, but that his love would be within
5   me ... always ... throughout eternity. His light would
6   shine through me and others down through the ages ...
7   even until the end of the world. His love ... a candle in
8   the darkness of the tomb ... a glowing, reaching, loving
9   light that would never be extinguished by anything in
10   this world. I had come to weep — now I could worship.
11   I had come expecting him to be in the darkness of the
12   tomb. But, instead, I found him walking in the newness
13   of the Resurrection. He is with us always ... alive ...
14   forevermore! *(READER #9 introduces solo, then returns to*
15   *her seat on the front pew. Following the solo, YOUTH*
16   *LEADER goes to the pulpit to say the benediction, with*
17   *READERS #1–#9 [and any other youth participants in the*
18   *service] standing behind him or her.)*
19
20 *BENEDICTION*
21 **YOUTH LEADER:** May the grace and peace of our Lord be
22   with us always, and may everything we say and do give
23   honor and glory to his name.
24
25 *POSTLUDE*
26   *(Suggestion)* **"Hallelujah Chorus"**
27   *(YOUTH LEADER leaves first, followed by the READERS*
28   *and other YOUTH, two at a time. The congregation remains*
29   *standing until all participants leave the sanctuary.)*
30
31
32
33
34
35

The Sycamore Cross

A one-act Easter legend for children
by Myrtle L. Forsten

CAST

Narrator

Mulberry

Apple

Ash

Sycamore

Choir of Trees
(Unlimited number of children)

Boy

Girl

First Woodsman

Second Woodsman

Butterfly
(Off-stage voice)

PRODUCTION NOTES

Overview: A spirited play about the hope of Easter based on a traditional folktale. A forest of trees mourn as their friend, the wise old Sycamore, gives his crooked and twisted trunk — indeed, his very life — to serve as

278

the cross for Jesus' crucifixion. But suddenly, a few days later, Jesus is alive again! The trees experience the renewal as spring awakens: a butterfly breaks free of his cocoon, and a new shoot miraculously grows from the stump of the Sycamore, echoing the resurrection of Jesus. The presentation highlights the victory of the cross and its transformation from an emblem of guilt and shame to a symbol of beauty and power. Suggested songs are included. May be performed for a sunrise service.

Set/Staging: A forest between Bethlehem and Jerusalem around the time of the first Easter. A bare stage is adequate, but if you wish you may use a backdrop painted with a simple scene of three crosses on a hill and a tomb. To add to the outdoor effect, you may wish to scatter some hills around your playing area. A hill may be formed by draping a brown blanket over a bench and stuffing crumpled newspapers behind it to give it shape.

The main tree characters are placed in a row Center Stage Front in the following order (Stage Right to Left): Sycamore, Ash, Mulberry, and Apple.

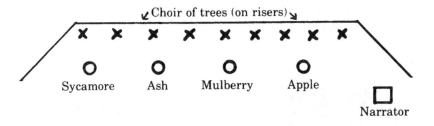

The Choir of Trees stands on risers behind the main tree characters. The Narrator stands at a podium with a microphone at Stage Left.

Props: A butterfly for the Apple character. It may be constructed of cardboard or Fome-Cor (a lightweight, durable material found in art supply stores) and attached to a dowel. Use the illustration on the following page as a guide. Color or paint the finished butterfly brightly. Place behind the Apple tree for quick access at the appropriate time.

A hatchet for First Woodsman. Use a plastic toy one if available. If not, improvise with gray construction paper cut into a hatchet shape and taped to a stick.

A lunch basket for the Boy and Girl containing a small loaf of bread or a roll.

279

A self-standing Fome-Cor or cardboard stump for the Sycamore. Make a leafy shoot and put Velcro on the stump and shoot for later attachment. Hide the shoot behind the stump until needed.

Fake bird attached to a dowel for Mulberry. It may be hidden behind the tree for easy access at the appropriate time. Fake birds are available from craft or hobby stores.

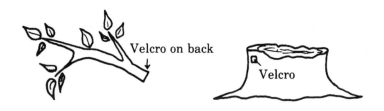

Velcro on back

Velcro

Costumes: The Choir of Trees wears green posterboard cutouts of fir trees. The trees have a cord which goes around the children's necks so the tree hangs down in front. Leave the tips of the trees off below the children's faces as shown in the costume illustration on the next page. (Optional: Each child may wear a green cone-shaped hat on his or her head as the top of the tree.)

The Mulberry, Ash, Sycamore, and Apple characters each stand behind a self-standing, cardboard or Fome-Cor cutout of a tree. This allows them to freely move their arms for expression. A hole is cut out for the children's faces, as pictured on the following page. Paint the trunk brown and leaves green.

The Sycamore's trunk should be crooked. It may have gnarled, twisted branches. Hidden behind the Sycamore should be a stump, which will remain when the woodsmen "cut down" the tree. (See props.)

The Apple tree should have pink and white silk blossoms glued to its branches. A brown construction-paper cocoon should also be glued in the leafy green part of the tree — toward the top. Cardboard bees may be added, if desired.

The Mulberry tree needs a nest at the top of the leafy part of the tree. The nest may be made of twigs or grapevine (available in craft stores). It should be fashioned into a half-circle shape.

The First and Second Woodsmen, Boy, and Girl should wear biblical costumes, i.e., simple robes in earth tones made of a rough weave of cloth belted with a cord or strip of the same fabric as their robes. Their matching headpieces should be tied to their heads with cord.

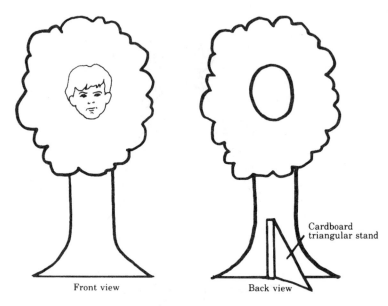

Front view   Back view

Cardboard
triangular stand

Lights: Normal lighting is adequate — simply turn the lights off and on as indicated. If your sanctuary does not have a dimmer switch, simply turn some but not all of the lights off when the directions call for the lights to dim.

Sound effects: An audio tape of bird sounds or someone to whistle into a microphone Off-stage. You may also wish to have someone Off-stage striking a hammer on a board when the Sycamore tree is chopped down.

Music: Although songs are suggested throughout the script, you are encouraged to feel free to substitute songs of a similar theme from your church's own music library. Collections of children's songs are a good place to start.

The author has suggested several songs from *Scripture in Song, Volumes 1 and 2*, published by Benson Music Group, Zondervan Direct, Attention B34, 5300 Patterson Avenue SE, Grand Rapids, MI 49530. These songs may also be found in a number of contemporary collections of songs and choruses, or you may choose the alternate selection or your own selection.

1. "Beauty for Ashes" by Bob Manzano, *Scripture in Song, Volume 1*. Alternate suggestion: "This Is My Father's World" by Maltbie D. Babcock and Franklin L. Sheppard (found in most hymnals), or any song about nature or creation.

2. "King of Kings" by Sophie Conty and Naomi Batya, *Scripture in Song, Volume 2*. Alternate suggestion: "Come, Thou Almighty King" by Felice de Giardini, in most hymnals, or any song that refers to Christ as King.

3. "Lift Jesus Higher," composer unknown, from *Scripture in Song, Volume 1*. Alternate suggestion: "Jesus Loves Me, This I Know" or any song that talks about God's love.

4. "The Old Rugged Cross" by George Bennard. May be found in most hymnals. Alternate suggestion: "Jesus, Keep Me Near the Cross" by Fanny J. Crosby and William H. Doane, found in most hymnals, or any song with the theme of the cross.

5. "Our God Reigns" by Leonard Smith, Jr., from *Scripture in Song, Volume 1*. Alternate suggestion: "Christ the Lord Is Risen Today" by Charles Wesley, in most hymnals, or any triumphant Easter song.

6. "He Rolled the Stone Away," words by M.L. Forsten, adapted to the chorus of "We Shall See the King" by J.B. Vaughn. (Words and actions on the following page.) It may be found in *Assembly Songs*, published by Gospel Publishing House, 1445 Boonville, Springfield, MO 65802-1894. If this tune is unfamiliar, you may wish to have the children simply recite the words as a poem done with the accompanying actions.

7. "He Is Lord," composer unknown, from *Scripture in Song, Volume 1*. Alternate suggestion: "Fairest Lord Jesus," composer unknown, found in most hymnals.

8. Optional: "Let the Heavens Be Glad" by Rod Wallace, *Scripture in Song, Volume 1*. Alternate suggestion: "The Day of Resurrection" by John of Damascus (translated by John M. Neale) and Henry Smart, found in most hymnals, or any triumphant Easter song.

"He Rolled the Stone Away"

Verse 1

(He) rolled the stone away,
Rolled the stone away,
An angel came and rolled it
  away!

*(Fisted hands rolled over each
other; right hand sweeps out
and away. Repeat.)*

Christ lives forevermore,
Our victory to secure,
An angel came and rolled it
  away!

(Pointing up)
(Right hand with "V" fingers)
(Rolled as above)

Verse 2

Jesus gives us life,
Jesus gives us life,
The grave can never hold the
  Lord our King!

(Point up, then to self)
(Repeat ...)
(Point down, then up)

For the Song of God arose,
Triumphant o'er his foes,
An angel came and rolled the
  stone away!

(Arms up in air)
(Stretch arms)
(Rolled as above)

Playing Time: About 20 minutes.

1   *(CHOIR OR TREES and CAST members are in place [as shown*
2   *on the diagram on page 279] when the play begins.)*
3   **SONG:** "Beauty for Ashes" *(CHOIR OF TREES sings.)*
4   **NARRATOR: There was a time on earth when Jesus walked in**
5   **old Judea. Between Bethlehem and Jerusalem was a lovely**
6   **forest where all the trees were dressed in their finest green.**
7   **Many were adorned with sweet-smelling blossoms, for it**
8   **was springtime in the valley. The lilies were abloom. The**
9   **cooing of doves could be heard, and the babbling of sheep**
10   **and goats. If you listened carefully, you could hear the**
11   **stirring conversation of the trees as they chatted with one**
12   **another.**
13   **MULBERRY: I'm so-o-o excited!** *(Pointing to nest)* **I'm wearing a**
14   **new nest! That means the birds will start serenading me**
15   **every day. Their singing is beautiful!**
16   **APPLE: Yes it is, Mulberry. The birds really love your branches.**
17   **But I am bothered with bees again this spring. They dance**
18   **in and out of my blossoms and tickle me down to my toes!**
19   **Ha-ha-ha!** *(Laughs and moves arms all around as though tickled.*
20   *CHOIR OF TREES giggles and laughs along.)*
21   **ASH: And what's that brown thing snapped to your hair, young**
22   **Apple Tree? Is that a cocoon I see?**
23   **APPLE: It sure is. I know it looks really funny, but the Sycamore**
24   **tells me it's a good sign.**
25   **SYCAMORE: That's right, fair lady. It's a sign of better things**
26   **to come. There's life inside that brown lump — just wait**
27   **and see.** *(Sighs.)* **Oh, sweet Apple Tree, you *do* remind me**
28   **of Little Fir who blessed us all some time ago. I'm sure the**
29   **noble Ash remembers her.**
30   **ASH: I sure do. Little Fir gave her life to the Lord of the Trees**
31   **to become a manger for the Baby King — the King born in**
32   **Bethlehem. What a delight she was!**
33   **CHOIR OF TREES:** *(Reciting in unison)*
34   **Little Fir was kind of heart**
35   **So gentle and so good.**

1   To be the manger for the King

2   She gave of her own wood.

3 SYCAMORE: Tell me, noble Ash, have you heard the news of

4   this king? He's no longer a tiny baby. He walks the streets

5   of our cities, healing the sick and causing the blind to see

6   and the deaf to hear. This great Man is doing miracles

7   everywhere.

8 ASH: Yes, Sycamore. I hear he calmed the stormy sea of Galilee

9   with his voice. And do you know what ship he sailed on?

10 CHOIR OF TREES: *(Ad-lib)* **Ah-h-h-h! Yes! We know!** *(TREES nod*

11   *knowingly. A single voice from the CHOIR OF TREES says:)* **Our**

12   **friend, the mighty Oak, was there.**

13 ASH: Of course, Mr. Oak was the mast for that strong ship. But

14   this Man who calmed the sea, who healed the sick and

15   raised the dead, isn't this Jesus the one who will rule the

16   earth?

17 CHOIR OF TREES: *(Ad-lib while waving arms)* **Yes! Yes! Jesus will**

18   **reign!**

19 *SONG:* "King of Kings" *(CHOIR OF TREES sings in a round.)*

20 SYCAMORE: But this Jesus is not accepted as a king by his

21   people. There's a lot of trouble in the land.

22 ASH: I have heard that the time will soon come for Jesus to die.

23   Do you think this is true, old wise one?

24 SYCAMORE: Yes, I do. And I shall go to him. I will give him as

25   much comfort and support as I can.

26 CHOIR OF TREES: *(Ad-lib)* **Jesus will die? Oh! Oh! It can't be**

27   **true!** *(Holding up arms, shaking)*

28 SYCAMORE: You know that I've been chosen by the Lord of the

29   trees to be made into a cross. It is on this cross that Jesus,

30   the son of God, will die. I am ready to do this for him.

31   Though I am the ugliest of all the trees, I am honored to

32   serve him in this way. For I know that when Jesus is lifted

33   up, then people will be drawn to him. They will begin to

34   understand how much God loves them when they see that

35   he sent his Son to die for them.

1   **SONG:** "Lift Jesus Higher" *(CHOIR OF TREES sings reverently,*
2   *lifting hands, palms up, on "Lift ...")*
3   **APPLE:** I wish I could be there to see Jesus lifted up. But it
4   would hurt to see him suffer. He doesn't deserve to die.
5   **ASH:** Don't worry, little Apple Tree. The Lord of all the earth
6   cannot be held forever on a cross. See that nest in Miss
7   Mulberry's hair? It holds three bird eggs. And there is life
8   inside those eggs. Soon baby birds will break out through
9   those shells. The living Son of God will also break forth in
10   great power, for no grave can hold the Lord of all the earth!
11   **APPLE:** I wonder how it will happen.
12   **SYCAMORE:** These are exciting times, little Apple. You were
13   just a sapling when the Baby King was born. That was a
14   time of great joy. But now you will see even greater things.
15   *(BOY and GIRL enter. BOY carries lunch basket.)*
16   **BOY:** I love to come to this forest, especially when the trees are
17   in bloom.
18   **GIRL:** Me too. Here's an apple tree loaded with blossoms.
19   Doesn't it smell good? Let's sit here and eat our lunch.
20   *(They sit by the APPLE TREE.)*
21   **BOY:** *(Pulls out a roll and breaks it, giving the GIRL half.)* **My**
22   **mother's good bread always reminds me of the time I**
23   **shared my lunch with Jesus when all the people gathered**
24   **on the hillside to hear him preach. Remember that? Jesus**
25   **fed more than five thousand people with those five loaves**
26   **of bread and two little fish.**
27   **GIRL:** He really is amazing. I'd follow him everywhere if I could.
28   I'll never forget last Sunday, when we got to follow him
29   through the streets of Jerusalem. It was so exciting to see
30   Jesus on that donkey. He seemed like a king on a throne.
31   **BOY:** He really did. All the children were singing to him and
32   waving palm branches. People called him the Son of David.
33   And he is! Won't it be great when they really crown him
34   king?
35   **GIRL:** But what if the people don't want Jesus for their king?

1 BOY: Well, who else could be such a great leader for our
2   people?
3 GIRL: I don't know, but my father is worried about the Jewish
4   leaders who are angry with Jesus. Maybe they will be nicer
5   to him when we have the Passover celebration. Oh my! I
6   forgot I told my father I would help to get everything ready.
7   We'd better get back.
8 BOY: Maybe I can help, too. *(They gather things and exit.)*
9 NARRATOR: It is beginning to get dark as two woodsmen
10   approach the forest. They don't know the importance of
11   their mission, but the old Sycamore does. He bows in
12   submission when his name is called. *(WOODSMEN enter.*
13   *FIRST WOODSMAN carries an axe.)*
14 FIRST WOODSMAN: Well, here we are on another errand for
15   those cruel Roman soldiers. I don't like making crosses.
16   Why should *we* take part in their dirty work?
17 SECOND WOODSMAN: Cutting the trees isn't as bad as hanging
18   prisoners on their crosses.
19 FIRST WOODSMAN: Well, that's true. Look, let's just get this
20   over with. *(Pointing)* There's a tall, straight tree beside that
21   twisted Sycamore. *(ASH shakes in fright.)*
22 SECOND WOODSMAN: Nah — save the good tree. Let's just
23   cut down that old Sycamore. It's a miserable-looking tree,
24   all knotted and crooked. But who cares? They're only going
25   to make a cross out of it.
26 FIRST WOODSMAN: *(Putting hand on SYCAMORE's trunk)* It's
27   good and strong. It'll do. *(Character playing the SYCAMORE*
28   *slips Off-stage as unobtrusively as possible. Optional: Sound effect*
29   *to suggest the chopping down of the tree as FIRST WOODSMAN*
30   *pantomimes the act. They exit, with SECOND WOODSMAN*
31   *dragging the tree Off-stage, leaving in its place the stump which*
32   *was hidden behind it.)*
33 APPLE: Oh! Oh! I can't bear to look. *(Covers eyes with hands,*
34   *sobs.)* Our old friend is gone. What will we do without him?
35 ASH: Don't cry, Apple Tree. This is a great victory! Remember

1   **what the Sycamore said? He will become the cross on**
2   **which the Lord of the earth will be crucified. His death will**
3   **lift up Jesus and bring life to many people. This is really an**
4   **honor for him — and it's happening right before our eyes,**
5   **just like he said.**
6   ***SONG:*** "The Old Rugged Cross," verses 1 and 3 *(CHOIR OF TREES*
7   *sings.)*
8   **MULBERRY: Remember, dear Apple, what the Ash told us? The**
9   **Lord of the earth cannot be held on a cross for very long.**
10   **He is the living Creator of all things.**
11   **APPLE: Oh yes, now I remember. This is just the beginning —**
12   **not the end.** *(Lights dim to signify nighttime, then come up again.*
13   *BOY and GIRL enter.)*
14   **GIRL: I'm so scared. Father said they have taken Jesus away to**
15   **be judged. Many of the people have asked the governor to**
16   **crucify him. How could they do such a thing? I thought they**
17   **loved Jesus.**
18   **BOY: The people in the crowd were just listening to the Jewish**
19   **leaders, but they'll be very sorry they did.**
20   **GIRL:** *(Interrupting)* **Oh, look, that beautiful sycamore tree is**
21   **gone. Remember how we used to climb in its twisted**
22   **branches?**
23   **BOY: You're right! I wonder why they cut it down.**
24   **GIRL: Let's go to Jerusalem. Maybe someone there can tell us.**
25   *(BOY and GIRL exit left. FIRST WOODSMAN enters from right*
26   *and walks slowly into the forest with his head down. He*
27   *approaches the stump of the SYCAMORE.)*
28   **FIRST WOODSMAN: I'm sorry, friend. I'm *so* sorry. I didn't**
29   **know they were going to crucify *Jesus*, the Son of God! He**
30   **didn't deserve to die, nor did you, old Sycamore. But for a**
31   **crooked old tree, you were just beautiful as you held him**
32   **high in proud rebuke of their cruelty.** *(He exits slowly.)*
33   **MULBERRY: Wasn't that awesome?! There are people who**
34   **loved the old Sycamore as much as we did. And they loved**
35   **Jesus, too.**

1   **APPLE: Oh, yes! My heart is sad, but I believe that old**
2   **Sycamore, our friend, gave himself for something that will**
3   **be remembered always.**
4   ***SONG:*** Chorus of "The Old Rugged Cross" *(CHOIR OF TREES sings*
5   *softly. Lights dim to simulate nighttime. FIRST WOODSMAN*
6   *enters and stands at Center Stage, head up, gazing at sky. Then*
7   *SECOND WOODSMAN enters slowly.)*
8   **SECOND WOODSMAN: Well, Jonas, what are *you* doing here?**
9   **FIRST WOODSMAN: I might ask you the same thing, friend.**
10   **SECOND WOODSMAN: Me? I came here to escape the mess in**
11   **Jerusalem. I can't believe they would crucify Jesus, of all**
12   **men.** *(Stops, puts head in hands, continues sadly.)* **And on a**
13   **cross that we helped build, too. Jonas, I really believe that**
14   **he was the Messiah come to rule Israel.**
15   **FIRST WOODSMAN: I know. I feel the same way. But why did**
16   **you come here, where we chopped down the tree for his**
17   **cross? Doesn't it make you sad?**
18   **SECOND WOODSMAN: Yes, it does, but at least it's peaceful**
19   **here. In Jerusalem, the Roman soldiers are guarding the**
20   **tomb where they laid Jesus' body. The rulers fear his body**
21   **will be stolen, and then his disciples will claim Jesus rose**
22   **from the dead.**
23   **FIRST WOODSMAN: But if he really *is* the Son of God, he**
24   ***could* rise from the grave, couldn't he?**
25   **SECOND WOODSMAN: I suppose so, but he would have to**
26   **push that heavy stone door away, and ...**
27   **FIRST WOODSMAN:** *(Interrupting)* **I'm going back to Jerusalem.**
28   **Come along and show me where they buried Jesus. I want**
29   **to be there if he does rise again.** *(WOODSMEN exit. Lights*
30   *come back up to represent daylight.)*
31   **APPLE:** *(Excitedly, raising arms)* **Oh-h-h-h! Oh-h-h-h! There's**
32   **something different in the air — like God's presence is all**
33   **around us.**
34   **MULBERRY and ASH:** *(Together, lifting arms)* **We feel it, too!**
35   **CHOIR OF TREES:** *(Reciting in unison)*

1   **There's a stillness in the air,**
2   **Warmth and love are everywhere.**
3   **It must be like the woodsman said,**
4   **The Lord has risen from the dead!**
5   ***SONG:*** "Our God Reigns," verses 2 and 5 *(GIRL enters on verse 2,*
6   *weeping and covering her face with her hands. On verse 5 she*
7   *looks up with wonder, putting both hands on chest. BOY enters*
8   *at the close of verse 5, runs to GIRL, and shakes her lightly.)*
9   **BOY: Jesus *is* alive!**
10   **GIRL: Wh-what?! Jesus is *alive*?! How do you know?**
11   **BOY: People all over Jerusalem are talking about it. I heard**
12   **that Jesus appeared to some of his disciples. And I saw for**
13   **myself that the tomb is empty. The people say an angel**
14   **came and rolled away the stone!**
15   ***SONG:*** "He Rolled the Stone Away" *(CHOIR OF TREES sings with*
16   *actions.)*
17   *(After the song, the sound effect of chirping birds begins.*
18   *MULBERRY character takes the bird on a stick and holds it*
19   *above the tree, waving it back and forth as if the bird is flying.*
20   *APPLE character takes the butterfly on a stick and makes it*
21   *"dance" above the cocoon. When bird sound effect is over, the*
22   *Off-stage voice of the BUTTERFLY is heard.)*
23   **BUTTERFLY:** *(From Off-stage)* **I'm so happy! Jesus gave me**
24   **wings.** *(BUTTERFLY perches atop APPLE TREE.)*
25   **GIRL:** *(Clapping hands)* **This is wonderful! The whole world is**
26   **happy!**
27   **BOY: Remember how Jesus gave Lazarus life again? It wasn't**
28   **possible for death to hold either one of them down. I knew**
29   **he had to be the Messiah!** *(FIRST and SECOND WOODSMEN*
30   *enter, talking.)*
31   **FIRST WOODSMAN: That was some earthquake when the angel**
32   **came and rolled away the stone. Awesome!**
33   **SECOND WOODSMAN: Imagine how those women felt when**
34   **they saw that mighty angel. Even the guards were shaking**
35   **with fear.** *(BOY, GIRL, and FIRST WOODSMAN position*

1　*themselves in front of the Sycamore stump to shield it from the*
2　*audience's view.)*
3　**SONG:** Verse 5 ("He Is Alive") of "Our God Reigns." *(During the song,*
4　*SECOND WOODSMAN attaches the leafy shoot to the stump,*
5　*then rejoins the others.)*
6　**BUTTERFLY:** *(Dancing to Off-stage voice)* **Alive! Alive! Alive!**
7　**APPLE: Oh, Mr. Ash! Everything makes sense now. The old**
8　**Sycamore told us about the cocoon — that it was a sign of**
9　**good things to come. The cocoon was dead, but a living**
10　**butterfly came out of it. The bird hatched from the egg, and**
11　**now it's learning to fly.** *(Pauses, gasps.)* **And look — a new**
12　**shoot is even growing out of the Sycamore's stump! It's a**
13　**miracle!**
14　**ASH: That's right, little Apple Tree. The tomb was also a dead**
15　**thing, but the living Son of God broke forth from it. That**
16　**cruel cross that he died on will now be seen as a thing of**
17　**beauty. Our friend the Sycamore, though he seemed**
18　**twisted and useless, will be remembered for lifting up**
19　**Jesus, the Son of God. His life was beautiful, too — and**
20　**now he lives again!**
21　**MULBERRY: The Lord of all the Earth could not stay in a tomb.**
22　**He is the One who gives life to all of us!**
23　**CHOIR OF TREES:** *(Together)* **He is Lord!**
24　**SONG:** "He Is Lord" *(All cast and CHOIR OF TREES sings. BOY,*
25　*GIRL, and FIRST and SECOND WOODSMEN join hands in*
26　*front of the trees as they sing.)*
27　**OPTIONAL CLOSING SONG:** *(With congregation)* "Let the
28　Heavens Be Glad."
29
30
31
32
33
34
35

Three Gifts From Gentle Jesus

A children's Easter presentation
by Arthur L. Zapel

CAST

Pastor

Child Reader 1

Child Reader 2

Child Reader 3

Child Reader 4

Child Reader 5

Children's Choir

PRODUCTION NOTES

Overview: Many Sunday school children and the junior choir can participate in this program of short readings and music. The title song, which is an original choral theme, punctuates the presentation of three gift boxes representing Jesus' greatest gifts to the world: The Promise, The Sacrifice, and The Fulfillment (Resurrection). In each box there is a symbolic object. The third box reveals a surprise. Biblical readings accompany the Easter message narrative. A suggested order of worship with a responsive reading is included. All those present are given a seed as a symbolic gift as they leave the church. The script is structured as a total worship service, or it may be used in place of a sermon.

Casting Considerations: Though the script indicates five child readers, you may cast as many or as few as you like. Depending on the reading ability of your choices, you may be required to use older children as readers.

Some of the words, like Tiberius, Gethsemane, Barabbas and Golgotha, may be difficult for the younger participants. Unfortunately, there are no easy substitutions for these words except to delete them.

To keep a lively pace to the presentation, we suggest that the readers speak from more than one place in the chancel. This avoids the delay of each child exchanging positions with the next reader. The pastor may speak from a third place, if possible.

Set: All that is needed is an altar table to hold the three gifts and possibly risers for the children's choir.

Props: Three gifts from Jesus enclosed in three brightly wrapped boxes: a small box containing a chalice, a medium-sized box containing a wooden cross encircled by a crown of thorns, and a large box containing a tiny seed packet. (Having the last gift of Jesus be in a large box will dramatize the emptiness of the tomb.) When the large box is first opened, no one should see the seed packet that it holds. This is a found object after careful reexamination of the box.

The gift of a single tree seed in a packet to everyone as they leave the church can be a fellowship project for the Sunday school classes. We suggest purchase of a quantity of small glassene packets or paper coin envelopes from a stationery or office supply store. The tree seeds may be purchased from a nursery. A maple tree seed is perhaps the most unique in appearance because of its spiral wing, but any available tree seed will do. Only one to a packet is needed. Children of various ages can be positioned at each of the exits to distribute the seed packets, or they may stand beside the pastor as he gives his farewell to the church members and guests.

Costumes: No special costumes are necessary. The children may wear choir robes if desired.

Music: The hymns that may be used during the service are only suggested because their words relate to the sub-themes of this program. The church music director may have better choices. All of the hymns indicated can be found in most church hymnals.

Music for the title song, "Three Gifts From Gentle Jesus," is included on page 298. You may reproduce as many copies as necessary for the junior choir. We recommend that all four verses of the words be printed in the church bulletin so the entire congregation can see the words as they are sung by the children. This will also permit the entire congregation to sing the fourth verse at the end of the presentation. Since the melody will have been sung four times by the children, we do not feel that the congregation will have any trouble singing it without musical notation.

Playing time: Up to one hour.

SUGGESTED ORDER OF SERVICE

1. **Prelude**

2. **Call to Worship** (Pastor)

3. **Invocation** (Pastor)

4. **Lord's Prayer** (Everyone)

5. **Hymn** (Entire congregation: "All Glory, Laud and Honor")

6. **Responsive Reading:**
> PASTOR: Praise the Lord Jesus.
>
> CONGREGATION: He is risen; he lives with us today and forever.
>
> PASTOR: Praise him for the gifts of his teachings, his example, his life, and his death.
>
> CONGREGATION: Praise him for his victory over death.
>
> PASTOR: Praise him with music and the voices of children.
>
> CONGREGATION: Praise him for our victory over sin.
>
> PASTOR: Praise him for the promise of salvation.
>
> CONGREGATION: Praise him for eternal life.
>
> PASTOR: Let everything we say and do praise the risen Lord.
>
> CONGREGATION: Praise Jesus, our Savior.
>
> PASTOR: He is risen.
>
> CONGREGATION: Praise the Lord!

7. **Scripture Lesson:** John 15:11-17

8. **Anthem:** "O Sons and Daughters, Let Us Sing"

9. **Children's Presentation:**
> Verses to title song, "Three Gifts From Gentle Jesus," sung during presentation (music on page 298):
>
> 1. Thank you, gentle Jesus, for gifts from God above.
>   Thank you, Lord and Shepherd, for your golden gift of love.
>   Faith and hope you give me to live with every day.
>   Thank you, King and Father, for showing me the way.

2. Thank you, gentle Jesus, for the life you gave for me.
   Thank you Lord, my Holy Lamb, for helping me to see
   salvation's joy, God's endless gift for every day.
   Thank you, sweet and giving Lord, for teaching me the way.

3. Thank you, gentle Jesus, from death you returned to give.
   Thank you, Holy Savior, for the path of how to live.
   Your life is my example, and so it shall always be.
   Thank you, friendly Jesus, please walk each day with me.

4. Thank you, gentle Jesus, for the gifts you gave to me.
   Thank you, Christ, for faith, death, and life — these three.
   They are my rock, my sea — so beauteously divine.
   Thank you, Savior Jesus — hold me, I am thine!

10. Offering (With children's hymn: "This Is My Father's World")

11. Pastoral Prayer

12. Hymn (Entire congregation: "The Whole World Rejoices Now")

13. Benediction (Pastor)

14. Postlude

Three Gifts From Gentle Jesus

Music by Robert Crowder / Lyrics by Arthur Zapel

1   *PROCESSIONAL* Children's CHOIR and CHILD READERS walk up
2   aisle to the chancel singing "I Love to Tell the Story." There are
3   among them three children bearing brightly wrapped gifts: one
4   large, one medium and one small size. They deposit the three gifts
5   on the altar table and retire to their places.

6   **PASTOR: Today, in celebration of our Lord's life, death, and**
7   **resurrection, the children of our church have asked if they**
8   **could tell the Easter story. I know each of you, as I,**
9   **welcome their participation and the message they bring.**
10   **Their special Easter presentation is entitled *Three Gifts***
11   ***From Gentle Jesus.***

12   **CHILD READER 1: Our Lord and Savior lives! He is with us**
13   **today. He may be invisible, but he is with us. These are his**
14   **words from John 14:19: "In a little while the world will see**
15   **me no more, but you will see me; and because I live, you**
16   **also will live."**

17   **CHILD READER 2: The proof of Jesus' continuing presence is**
18   **the truth of his life. He gave us the three most beautiful**
19   **gifts that the Son of God could give** *(Gestures to the three*
20   *boxes on the altar table)* **— Promise, Sacrifice and Fulfillment.**

21   **CHILDREN'S CHOIR:** *(Sings the fourth verse of "Three Gifts From*
22   *Gentle Jesus.")*

23   **Thank you, gentle Jesus, for the gifts you gave to me.**
24   **Thank you, Christ, for faith, death, and life — these three,**
25   **They are my rock, my sea — so beauteously divine.**
26   **Thank you, Savior Jesus — hold me, I am thine!**

27   **CHILD READER 3: In the fifteenth year of the Roman rule of**
28   **Emperor Tiberius** *(Ti-BEE-ree-us),* **John the Baptist was**
29   **baptizing the hopeful and prophesying the coming of the**
30   **Messiah — the Lamb of God. As Jesus came to his cousin**
31   **John, in Bethany at the Jordan River, John knew that the**
32   **moment for which he had been born had arrived. At first he**
33   **was not willing to baptize Jesus, for he felt that he should**
34   **be baptized by Jesus. But Jesus said, "Let it be as I ask, for**
35   **in this way we shall do what God requires." John agreed,**

1   **and Jesus was baptized. Immediately the heavens opened**
2   **and the Spirit of God in the form of a dove came down and**
3   **rested on Jesus' shoulder. A voice was heard from heaven:**
4   **"This is my own dear Son, with whom I am pleased"** *(Matt.*
5   *3:15-17, author's paraphrase).*

6   **CHILD READER 4: So began the ministry of our Lord. He now**
7   **began traveling among the men, women and children of**
8   **Galilee to tell them of the Promise, the good news about**
9   **the kingdom of heaven.**

10 **CHILD READER 5: He was a teacher who taught about God's**
11   **love with stories called "parables." He was a healer who,**
12   **with miracles, made the lame walk and the blind see. He**
13   **was the Promise and the Salvation, for he would redeem all**
14   **sins.**

15 **CHILD READER 1:** *(He/she walks to altar table and takes the*
16   *smallest of the three boxes.)* **This is our first gift from Jesus.**
17   *(He/she unwraps and opens the first box. Inside is a chalice,*
18   *which he/she holds up for all to see.)* **This chalice represents**
19   **God's first gift to us — the promise of forgiveness of our sins.**

20 **CHILD READER 2: Matthew 26, verses 27 and 28: "Then he**
21   **took a cup, gave thanks to God, and gave it to them. 'Drink**
22   **it, all of you,' he said; 'this is my blood, which seals God's**
23   **covenant, my blood poured out for many for the**
24   **forgiveness of sins.' "**

25 **CHILDREN'S CHOIR:** *(Sings first verse of "Three Gifts From Gentle*
26   *Jesus.")*

27   **Thank you, gentle Jesus, for gifts from God above.**
28   **Thank you, Lord and Shepherd, for your golden gift of love.**
29   **Faith and hope you give me to live with every day.**
30   **Thank you, King and Father, for showing me the way.**

31 **CHILD READER 3: The last supper took place in a house**
32   **appointed in Jerusalem. Afterward, the Lord led his**
33   **disciples to Gethsemane** *(Geth-SEM-annie),* **where he told**
34   **them to wait. Alone, Jesus went farther and fell on his face**
35   **and prayed. He asked his Father if he could be spared his**

1   cup of suffering, but if not, he would drink it — God's will

2   to be done.

3   **CHILD READER 4:** Soon thereafter came a band of men and

4   officers from the chief priests. They were led by Judas, who

5   betrayed Jesus with a kiss. Jesus was then taken prisoner

6   to the rooms of the chief priests, who found him guilty of

7   blasphemy *(BLAS-fem-ee)* and condemned him to death.

8   Next he was taken before the Roman governor, Pilate, who

9   said that he found no fault in him. Then he was taken

10   before King Herod, who mocked him but did not believe he

11   should be killed.

12 **CHILD READER 5:** The chief priests and elders suggested that

13   Jesus be brought before the people with the prisoner,

14   Barabbas *(Buh-RAB-bus)*. One would be released. The crowd

15   chose Barabbas and shouted, "Crucify Jesus!"

16 **CHILD READER 1:** Bearing his cross, Jesus walked quietly to

17   the place of the skull, called Golgotha *(Gahl-GOTH-uh)*,

18   where he was crucified. The prophecy had been fulfilled.

19   Jesus, the Lamb of God, had been sacrificed.

20 **CHILD READER 2:** *(He/she walks to the altar table and takes the*

21   *middle-sized box.)* **Our second gift from Jesus.** *(He/she opens*

22   *the box. Inside is a wooden cross encircled by a crown of thorns.)*

23   This cross and crown of thorns represents the sacrifice of

24   Jesus. For our salvation he suffered mockery, pain, and

25   death.

26 **CHILD READER 3:** Matthew 27, verses 35 to 37: "They

27   crucified him and then divided his clothes among them by

28   throwing dice. After that, they sat there and watched him

29   die. Above his head they put a mocking notice of the

30   accusation against him: 'This is Jesus, the King of the

31   Jews.' "

32 **CHILDREN'S CHOIR:** *(Sings the second verse of "Three Gifts From*

33   *Gentle Jesus.")*

34   Thank you, gentle Jesus, for the life you gave for me.

35   Thank you Lord, my Holy Lamb, for helping me to see

1 Salvation's joy, God's endless gift, for every day.

2 Thank you, sweet and giving Lord, for teaching me the way.

3 CHILD READER 1: When it was close to evening on the day of
4 the crucifixion, a rich man from Arimathea *(AIR-uh-muh-thee-*
5 *ah)* named Joseph went before Pilate and asked for the
6 body of Jesus. Permission was granted, and Joseph and
7 another member of the council, Nicodemus *(Nicko-DEEM-*
8 *us)*, took Jesus down from the cross. Together they bound
9 Jesus' body in linen cloths with myrrh and aloe. Then they
10 carried the body to Joseph's own tomb, which had been
11 carved as a cave in the rock.

12 CHILD READER 4: A great stone was rolled against the mouth
13 of the cave, and the Roman officers sealed it tight. Guards
14 were left to watch, so that the friends of Jesus could not
15 steal the body and say he had risen.

16 CHILD READER 5: In the early morning hours of the third day,
17 Mary Magdalene, Mary, the mother of James, and Salome
18 *(Suh-LOW-me)*, who had followed Jesus across Galilee, came
19 to the tomb. They were carrying spices and ointments to
20 anoint the body of Jesus, according to the custom of the
21 Jews.

22 CHILD READER 1: They were wondering who might roll back
23 the stone so they could enter the tomb.

24 CHILD READER 2: When they arrived in the garden, they were
25 greatly surprised. The stone had already been rolled back,
26 and they could see inside the cave. The body of Jesus was
27 no longer there.

28 CHILD READER 3: *(He/she walks to the altar table and takes the*
29 *largest of the three boxes.)* This is our third gift from Jesus.
30 *(He/she unwraps and opens the box. There appears to be nothing*
31 *in it.)* An empty box! Can this be the same as the empty
32 tomb? But where is the third and greatest gift of Jesus?
33 *(He/she looks again into the box and after a moment holds up*
34 *the seed of a tree.)* Here it is! A seed! This seed of a tree
35 symbolizes the fulfillment of his promise — the Resurrection!

1 He was crucified on a wooden cross, but he rose again on
2 the third day.
3 CHILD READER 4: Mark 16, verses 4 to 6: "...Then they
4 looked up and saw that the stone had already been rolled
5 back. So they entered the tomb, where they saw a young
6 man sitting at the right, wearing a white robe — and they
7 were alarmed. 'Don't be alarmed,' he said. 'I know you are
8 looking for Jesus of Nazareth, who was crucified. He is not
9 here — he has been raised!' "
10 CHILDREN'S CHOIR: *(Sings the third verse of "Three Gifts From*
11 *Gentle Jesus.")*
12 Thank you, gentle Jesus, from death you returned to give.
13 Thank you, Holy Savior, for the path of how to live.
14 Your life is my example, and so it shall always be.
15 Thank you, friendly Jesus, please walk each day with me.
16 CHILD READER 5: We have received — all of us — the three
17 gifts of Jesus: *The Promise, The Sacrifice, and The*
18 *Fulfillment.* Jesus lives, and because he lives, we live also
19 in his salvation! We ask now that everyone sing with us the
20 fourth verse of "Three Gifts From Gentle Jesus." The words
21 are in your program. *(The entire congregation sings with the*
22 *children.)*
23 Thank you, gentle Jesus, for the gifts you gave to me.
24 Thank you, Christ, for faith, death, and life — these three.
25 They are my rock, my sea — so beauteously divine.
26 Thank you, Savior Jesus — hold me, I am thine!
27 PASTOR: In addition to this inspiring Easter presentation, the
28 children have another gift for you today. As you leave the
29 sanctuary, you will receive a small packet from one of the
30 children of our youth ministry. It contains the seed of a
31 (maple) tree, which symbolizes the Resurrection. Plant this
32 in your yard as a remembrance of how Christ has given us
33 eternal life.
34
35

Monologs

Faces of the Cross

The Crucifixion story in six monologs
by Ronnie Hill

CAST

Jewish Religious Leader

Pilate

Thief at the Right Hand

Roman Soldier

Mary, Mother of Jesus

Apostle John

PRODUCTION NOTES

Overview: Six personalities who participated in the crucifixion of the Lord reveal their inner feelings about the happenings on Good Friday in these dramatic monologs. The characters' stories range in emotion from despair to joy as they encounter first the crucified, then the risen Christ. The monologs may be presented together or sequentially, as interludes during a worship service. They may be read, with the characters sitting on stools and using scripts in Readers Theatre fashion, or acted, with the lines memorized. They have been written to give the director as much room for imagination as possible as far as how simply or elaborately (i.e., stage makeup, lighting, audiovisual aids, etc.) they will be staged.

Set: A bare stage is fine.

Props: None needed.

Costumes: Biblical robes, headpieces, and sandals may be used if desired; however, special costuming is not essential.

Dedication: To the youth of the First Baptist Church, Brownfield, Texas.

Playing time: Approximately five minutes per monolog.

Jewish Religious Leader

It's hard to believe that one man can cause such a big stir. I'm glad it's over. Even now it's hard to believe all that went on. I can relax today because I know he's dead. You see, I stayed around till I was sure he was dead. In fact, I watched Joseph of Arimathea take his body to Joseph's tomb. *(Puzzled)* Why Joseph wanted to waste his tomb, I don't understand. I say I can relax today because at times I wasn't sure if he really was the Messiah or not. But now he's sealed away in a tomb, and Pilate has seen to it that guards are at a constant vigil so none of his followers can steal his body and start rumors. I'm also sure that Jehovah God would've never abandoned his son — and let the real Messiah die.

No, he never even looked like a Messiah! We Jewish religious leaders have been anticipating the arrival of our true Messiah. Jesus didn't even look like a king. Many have claimed the Messiahship, but their faults have always been easy to find, and we've exposed their real nature. I will admit that this Jesus was not like that; he was a smart one. I'm not sure that anyone ever exposed his faults or contradictions. Many times we tried, but he always stayed about one pace ahead of us. A smooth operator! But the important thing is that he was not what we were looking for. He didn't have the appearance nor the power. You know, I never knew a time that he ever grasped for power. The Lord will raise his Messiah through the established order of the Sanhedrin, and this Jesus never seemed even one bit interested! Can you imagine that? And he still tried to tell us he was the Christ, God's chosen one. Ha!

I will admit, though, that he has followers. There must have been thousands. I have journeyed to simple countrysides where he was teaching, and the hillsides would be covered with not hundreds, but thousands of

1   friendly and interested listeners. The crowds seemed to be
2   growing, too! That began to worry us. How can so many
3   people be fooled?

4   We finally decided that enough was enough, and we
5   would go though whatever measures necessary to get rid of
6   this blemish on our religious order. Now aren't you glad we
7   did? Anyway, one of his own was bought off for thirty pieces
8   of silver — that's loyalty, isn't it? Shows you the respect his
9   "disciples" had for him. Then the events moved ever so
10   swiftly. First the trials and meetings of the Sanhedrin.
11   Sometimes we had to pay off a false witness, but who cares,
12   as long as justice is accomplished as the final result?! Then
13   we sent him to Pilate. You see, we as Jewish leaders have a
14   lot of authority in ruling our people — but not to execute;
15   that is Roman responsibility. Pontius Pilate, our governor,
16   would be the proper channel to convict Jesus. And we
17   wanted this conviction as correct in format as we could get
18   it. We must be convincing, or all his many followers would
19   be after us. That is what we were trying to avoid, so we were
20   working overtime to "do this up good." Why not? We just
21   couldn't afford to slip up. Besides, if it were the Roman
22   leaders who sentenced him, the burden of execution and
23   guilt would be completely off us. And I know for a fact we
24   could put some deadly pressure on the Roman rulers!

25   This time I don't know what got into that devilish Pilate,
26   but he put on his "righteous cloak" and pronounced Jesus
27   "not guilty" — however, he did give us counsel with Herod.
28   Herod happened to be in Jerusalem, but thought he would
29   appease us by simple punishing Jesus. Well, it didn't work.
30   So he sent us back to Pilate. I personally was getting sick
31   and tired of being pawned back and forth. So we pressured
32   Pilate. I, myself, called him aside and told him I'd travel to
33   Rome and seek counsel with Caesar himself. I would accuse
34   him of conspiring with Jesus to commit treason if he did
35   not show us favor. Our charge was that Jesus professed to

1 be King of the Jews. Any king could be a threat to Caesar.
2 Pilate unwittingly disapproved of my offer, and obnoxiously
3 demanded Jesus simply be whipped and released. But we
4 persisted. When he saw our determination, I could almost
5 read his mind. He would have the crowd release a prisoner.
6 But we anticipated that, and so we won. The taste of victory
7 had never been so sweet.
8   I remember his hanging on the cross. Some friends of the
9 council and I made our way close to him. The crowds were
10 thick and angry, and I was pleased. I was confident enough
11 then to shout, "If you are the Christ — save yourself and
12 come down from the cross" *(Mark 15:30, author's paraphrase).*
13 We laughed. *(Mockingly)* And to think Jesus said he would
14 "destroy the temple and rebuild it in three days!" What a
15 joke. That's tomorrow, and he can't even move. *(Mockingly)*
16 What can he do for us now?
17
18
19
20
21
22
23
24
25
26
27
28
29
30
31
32
33
34
35

1	<div align="center">**Pilate**</div>
2	
3	I did all I could. I, Pilate, the governor *(Emphasis, almost*
4	*irritated)* did all I could. Why should anyone even murmur
5	my name in connection with that awful murder of their
6	prisoner? I even washed my hands of the matter —
7	remember? *(Pause)* Those dreadful members of the
8	Sanhedrin, it's their fault, those pigeons! Now that he's out
9	there hanging on the cross, they should be happy. Always
10	protecting their own interest!
11	I'll tell you exactly as it really was. *(Pause)* They wanted
12	him dead from the beginning. Of course I had heard of
13	Jesus — who hasn't? He was well-known around these
14	parts for his "do-goods" — and what, may I ask, is wrong
15	with that? He kept the public happy. Rumor has it he even
16	healed a lame man, and could make the blind see. But they
17	say his greatest miracle was not of the physical. Most
18	reliable sources have told me that he preached the
19	renewing of man's inner soul to satisfaction and peace
20	within. *(Almost staring into space as in deep thought)* I do
21	understand why people would listen to him. I, too, have
22	longed for such inner control. So often I find myself in need
23	of trust of a further power to calm my inner self. Outwardly
24	I possess a strong sense of power, but inwardly I am not so
25	sure. Can you understand that? It is not easy for me to
26	admit my faults — but after the meeting with this
27	carpenter's son, I really need someone to talk to. *(Quickly)*
28	Don't get me wrong — I was ready for him! I was aware of
29	what was going on between the Sanhedrin and Jesus. I
30	knew by inside sources that Jesus' teaching did not jibe
31	with the Jewish leaders. Of course, that doesn't break any
32	Roman law. These people must understand that the power
33	vested in me is Roman — not of a religious order. The man
34	Jesus had to be harmless — you could tell by looking! In
35	fact, he looked rather tattered to me, sort of worn out. Of

1   course, the chief priests and scribes had everything so well
2   planned. Even the prosecution lawyers had their remarks
3   well-prepared. Even the flattery. *(Mocking fashion)* *"Our most*
4   *glorious leader and ruler, we, your beloved countrymen*
5   *and subjects, come to you for counsel."* Of course, their
6   intentions were not so honorable. I almost laughed when the
7   lawyer suggested that Jesus was perverting the nation.
8   *(Almost laughing)* That's not what the rumors indicate. In fact,
9   quite the contrary. Then came a real accusation: *"He*
10   *professes to be a king — Christ the King."*

11   *(Confidently)* I suppose they thought this would
12   jeopardize my government position if I didn't act on such a
13   treasonous account immediately. So I asked him if he was
14   King of the Jews. Jesus was too smart to give direct
15   answer, and he gave the question to me, with "That's what
16   you say." I suppose he thought if I was convinced enough
17   to ask such a preposterous question, then I must have
18   some definite thoughts about it. His answer was enough for
19   me. I informed them I could not sentence him for their lack
20   of evidence presented. You could feel the roomful of Jewish
21   leaders glaring, and the air took on an icy chill.

22   I found an easy out when one of the leaders shouted that
23   he was stirring up the populace, beginning with Galilee.
24   You see, my jurisdiction does not extend to Galilee; that's
25   Herod's job. Convenient, too, 'cause Herod just so
26   happened to be in Jerusalem for other matters. *(Proudly)*
27   They agreed to a trial by Herod, seeing how much power I
28   had and knowing I would not budge in my decision of "not
29   guilty." *(Subdued)* I will admit to you, though, that I was
30   deeply relieved that they were gone.

31   I should have known my luck; Herod sent him back to
32   me. I had never liked Herod up to that day, but he and I
33   saw eye to eye here, and both of us knew of the Jews'
34   conspiracy in the making. Herod had Jesus of Nazareth
35   mocked and beaten, but the council was not satisfied, so

guess who they came back to?

Why were they so set in getting rid of this man? If his teachings were fake, why should they worry? If he was the Messiah, why didn't they listen to test him out? The lawyers didn't accuse him of faking miracles. Could it be the people knew better? The lawyers accused him of being King of the Jews — a Messiah. Isn't that what they've been waiting for? Could it be that these leaders were threatened by his power over the people?

(Trying to discard the responsibility) I don't understand their bickering over religion. But I do understand the political implications. These Jewish leaders have been most cooperative with Caesar and the Roman government. We must not have these people angry with us now, even if it costs one good man. Insurrection is difficult and would look bad on my record as governor.

I did try, though. When they brought Jesus back, I knew they wouldn't settle for anything less than what they wanted. One leader even suggested he would go see Caesar in Rome and report me as guilty of treason. *(Brightly)* I thought of the answer! I would bring out the meanest criminal in all the land and let the people choose between Jesus or the criminal to be set free. Setting a prisoner free was our generous custom during the Passover season. But the leaders got wind of my idea, and I don't know how they did it, but when I went out to present the two prisoners, the crowd shouted, Give us Barabbas, give us Barabbas," and then the chant turned to "Crucify Jesus." The noise almost burst my eardrums, but the silence of Jesus almost burst my heart.

What else could I do? I washed my hands of the matter. What else could I do? *(Nervously)* I did all I could! *(Shouting)* What else could I do?

Thief at the Right Hand

This crowd didn't show up on my account. That would be asking too much. I'm not that well-known, at least by the people. The judges and the courts know me well. I am a thief by profession. I have always been fairly proud of that fact. My only problem is that I have had the misfortune of being caught once too often.

Jesus of Nazareth, they call him. He is why the crowds are gathered. How do I know? News travels fast in towns like this. I almost burst out laughing when I found out Pilate, not Herod, could pin anything on him. It was that Jewish council, the Sanhedrin. You get them on your back, and you've had it! I even heard they've been after him for three years. Well, that's where he went wrong. He should have agreed to do whatever they wanted him to — you know, "compromise." I've done that all my life, and must say I've done well with it — well, almost.

Soon the Roman soldiers will come to take us to that place called Golgotha. *(Looking out the "jail window")* The road seems narrow. Jesus is ahead of us. It looks like he has been beaten worse than I have. Oh, he fell. Someone in the crowd has come to help him. Why are the mobs on the sides of these streets so angry? Their thoughts appear to contradict their actions. The faces of the crowd are different, yet they all seem to melt together. A question each is asking, I now ask myself: Why Jesus? I, too, have heard of his teachings and his "wonder" miracles. How would this get him into so much trouble? All I've ever heard is the good that he's done. This must be a political execution. *(As if trying to forget all that is said)* But why should I worry and waste my time on him? Soon, I will die myself.

I should think of my own neck. *(Long pause. Subdued)* But even when I try, I end up looking at him. Maybe, for the first time in my life, I know what compassion is.

1   **When I hang on this cross, the suffering will not come**
2   **easy for me, for I usually find a way to escape.** *(Almost in*
3   *anger)* **To kick a Roman soldier would make this easier, but**
4   **I believe they were anticipating my trying to escape, 'cause**
5   **the guard was much too heavy. But several times I did try**
6   **to fight the soldiers that had me bound. If I could have only**
7   **—** *(Sudden stop)* **You know, I never saw Jesus of Nazareth**
8   **struggle even once.**

9   *(Hanging from the cross)* **The salty sweat from the day and**
10   **my forehead drips in my eyes, but I can still see and hear**
11   **the crowd. My pain seems to hurt less compared to his. At**
12   **least I wasn't spit upon, or jeered, or mocked. All of the**
13   **attention is now on that center cross. People are still**
14   **laughing and shouting.**

15   **Hear my friend shouting to Jesus? He cries,** *(Mockingly)*
16   **"Aren't you really the Christ? Save yourself and us." He's a**
17   **fool! I know we deserve what we're getting, but Jesus has**
18   **done nothing wrong. Can't he realize that?**

19   **My head is beginning to swim. Why have I taken up for**
20   **this man? Oh yes, I remember all the stories of a Messiah**
21   **coming to save the people. Could this man, hanging on the**
22   **cross, humiliated by these people, be God's chosen one?**
23   *(Pleading)* **Jesus, remember me when you come into your**
24   **kingdom** *(Luke 23:42)*. *(Long pause)* **And he answers that**
25   **today I will be with him in paradise.**

26   **I can hardly believe it. I feel peace and security in my life**
27   **— something I've never known before. It sweeps through,**
28   **like cool water on hot sand.**

29   *(Excited)* **Look, the sun is hiding; it is dark everywhere.**
30   **For the first time, the crowd is quiet. It may be dark there.**
31   **But where I am now, I can feel warm sunlight and great**
32   **love. Yes, such a wonderful feeling. Beautiful!**

33

34

35

Roman Soldier

I don't understand people — or politics. I don't understand life or death. What I mean is, well, like yesterday, Friday. I, as a loyal Roman soldier, have been in charge of the execution of criminals many times. It brings a little extra pay and besides, if one is sentenced to die at the hands of the Romans, he deserves the penalty. At least I used to be sure of that.

But now I look for the reasoning behind the crucifixion of this Jesus of Nazareth. The events are so muddled. My mind wants to push out all thoughts about it. That is, my mind wants to, but it can't.

I realize it was unusual and beyond the call of duty to mock him and put a purple robe and a crown of thorns on him before leading him out to be crucified. We were only having fun. Besides, it is peculiar to get the order to execute one who is referred to as "King of the Jews."

His attitude, his face, his words were all so unusual. How can anyone suffer having nails driven through his hands and feet and flesh torn from his body without fighting back? I thought I could never wash the blood from my hands. The more I scrubbed, the more the blood seemed to hold to my flesh.

I remember lifting the cross with four other soldiers and, as the cross pounded downward into the hole, I could feel the downward thrust of his body weight. I feared that he might be ripped from his own cross. My friends laughed, and I did too — proudly in my shining uniform; *(Sarcastically)* my facade. Inside, my stomach grew sour. I suppose it was only pride that kept me from running then. Why were there so many people?

We nailed the sign that said "King of the Jews" above him, and everyone laughed. I joined in the frolic until I glanced at his face. The glance turned into a gaze, and then

1   a cold stare. *(Pause)* **Then his look. I believe he was looking**
2   **at me when he said something like** *(Almost in trance)* **"Father,**
3   **forgive them; for they know not what they do"** *(Luke 23:34,*
4   *KJV)*. **Can you understand that? Who was he talking to?**
5   **Why was he so willing to die? Why did he seem to be saying**
6   **that to me?** *(As if defending)* **I didn't wager on dividing his**
7   **clothes. Besides, who wanted an old robe?**

8   **Father, forgive them; for they know not — what — they**
9   **do!** *(Perplexed)* **Why would he say that?** *(Long pause)*

10   **Then I was excited because this man named Jesus called**
11   **out to Elijah. He said, "Eloi, Eloi, lama sabachthani?" I then**
12   **yelled,** *(Excited)* **"Listen, he is calling for Elijah." I knew then**
13   **if anyone was to save this mysterious person, it would be**
14   **the Jews' Elijah. Even as a small boy, I remembered hearing**
15   **the Jews say Elijah would come help God's people in**
16   **distress. This was the test — would Elijah really come? I**
17   **quickly dipped a sponge in some cheap wine that the soldiers**
18   **had brought for themselves and stuck it on a pole. Then I**
19   **raised it to his lips.** *(Still excited)* **I had to make sure he**
20   **would stay alive long enough for the test to see if Elijah**
21   **would come and deliver him. I waited —** *(Long pause, then*
22   *subdued)* **and he didn't. I don't even know if I was**
23   **disappointed.**

24   **The most important thing that happened is that he then**
25   **cried out in a loud voice and bowed his head. I think it was**
26   **then that he died.** *(Long pause)*

27   **Darkness came quickly over the skies. It was now three**
28   **o'clock. The earth began to tremble, then quake restlessly.**
29   **The mob was yelling, but this time not for the man on the**
30   **cross, but for themselves. I wish I'd never spit upon him.**

31   **I was in awe. The people were now trying to save**
32   **themselves.**

33   **Truly, I believe, this was the Son of God.**

34

35

Mary, Mother of Jesus

I have cried until I can't cry anymore. Yet I can't do anything else.

As his mother, I find it a difficult thing to give up my child. Or did I ever really have possession? I don't really know! I do know that my life dwells within his. My sadness is not just for the years of labor and teaching and suffering that we went through together, but for the good moments of love we shared.

The unbelievability of having our God's Son was an unusual event within itself. But I never wanted that thought to interfere with my raising of this Christ-child as any of my children. An honor, yes, but also a responsibility.

I knew when Jesus was ready for the ministry and John, his cousin, went about preparing his way. That was an exciting time, but I remember I cried then, too, both for sadness and joy. I knew his ministry would bring heartaches, but it was also the beginning of God's masterful plan of salvation for each of us. *(Pause)* Those days were very difficult. Many times I would go see him and help in any way that I thought I could. He always worked so hard. A masterful Father must have designed the love Jesus had for people whom he had never seen before.

Many times throughout his ministry, he would say things I wasn't sure I understood. That was not his fault. It could be that I didn't want to accept some of the things he said would happen. My protective instinct wanted to shield him from danger, from being hurt by just anyone or anything. I knew that was wrong, too, but sometimes I couldn't help myself.

(Saddened) Now that I look back, he tried to prepare us for this very event. I didn't understand — mainly because I refused to. I loved my son too much. I have never questioned God to this point, but I cannot understand the

1   usefulness of this mockery and humiliation. Crucified
2   among thieves! Look at the soldiers laugh and carry on as
3   if a Roman circus were about. *(Pause)* Among criminals. Oh,
4   how my heart weeps at this sight.
5   But I also remember the joyful days. Jesus was always
6   ready to heal the sick. To know some had the full faith of
7   his healing made him happy. *(In retrospect)* The day the blind
8   man returned to thank Jesus for giving him his sight — that
9   was an exceedingly happy time. The boy that gave up his
10   lunch to Jesus, so Jesus could feed others — five thousand
11   others — and did. The woman who had been bleeding for
12   seven years simply touched Jesus' garment and was made
13   whole. Some of these exciting times I heard about, and
14   many I witnessed myself. Oh, how his ministry was blessed.
15   I thank God for my son and his ministry.
16   But now it is over. This day soldiers have mocked him,
17   tortured him, reviled him, and crucified him. Jesus, my son,
18   and the Son of God.
19   After all his suffering, he did not forget me. Some of his
20   last words were for my protection.
21   Then he spoke to John and said, "There is your mother."
22   He was saying that I should live in the home of John whom
23   he loved, and whom he knew would love and care for me
24   until I shall see him again.
25
26
27
28
29
30
31
32
33
34
35

Apostle John

"Life is but a vacuum, waiting for time to march through and erase the importance of the events of the past."

"Purpose is a never-ending reward, and subsequence of Truth!"

Christ Jesus was — and is — our Lord. He said he was the Truth. I will never forget the day Jesus looked into my eyes and said, "John, I love you — follow me, and doubt not the things that I say or do, no, not even the events to come." I have not been the follower of Jesus he would've probably liked for me to have been. There were times when I argued and questioned. But through it all, I know my life is changed. His life and teachings have had such an impact on my life that I shall never forget them. In fact, I won't let myself forget.

The day-by-day life with Jesus was exciting and comforting. I have never known such security. When he spoke, multitudes listened to the challenging words and comforting thoughts. I've seen miracles occur that I can scarcely describe. Children love Jesus. Women and men cry with tears of joy because they were healed of their affliction. I've even seen the dead rise to make life anew. But the part I loved most was the renewing of oneself in the eyes of our God, because of his son, Jesus. I have discovered that everyone is in search of life — real life — life within that produces outward joy. Jesus said he was the Life — *(Pause)* and you know — he was. Whoever came to him and reached out — he always met their reach and supplied their needs. I know — he met mine, too!

Jesus was enjoyable to be with always. He never failed to do and say the right thing at the right times. But I will admit

1   that I never fully recognized the urgency of his ministry
2   until the day before yesterday, Friday, when he was
3   hanging on the cross. To me, the urgency appeared to be
4   suspended in mid-air, as if time were no longer the villain.
5   Jesus had foretold of that event, but hearing of it and
6   witnessing it are totally different. We, his "faithful"
7   followers, assured him of our support, and that we would
8   never leave him nor deny him. *(Pause)* We've done all that
9   we said we wouldn't.

10   Mary, his mother, and Mary Magdalene and my mother
11   and myself went to the cross where Jesus was crucified.
12   The ugly sight was deplorable. We knew that any friends of
13   those convicted by the Romans were not welcome, but that
14   didn't matter. As I looked in my dear Jesus' face, I knew he
15   was suffering in my place. Why couldn't we trade places? I
16   could hear the sobs of his mother; she was broken in spirit
17   as she bent to the ground, seldom looking at her son. My
18   heart was filled with the desire to kill the soldiers who were
19   enjoying their job, and yet I felt love for those who were my
20   enemies.

21   The three women's loud cries must have echoed to
22   heaven, and as I looked on the bruised body of Jesus, tears
23   washed my cheeks. Is love so dangerous that we must beat
24   it and kill it? Or is it that our lives are so impure that we
25   can't stand for beautiful love to encounter us — because we
26   might have to clean up our lives?

27   I suddenly wanted to cry for myself, for all the times my
28   heart wanted to burst open with love and tell Jesus that I
29   loved him — and didn't. Why have I been so incapable of
30   sharing that love?

31   Then Jesus did a most beautiful thing. He called to his
32   mother and, even in this great hour of suffering in his life,
33   he told her to look to me and then he told me to look to
34   her. As far as I was concerned, at that very moment his
35   mother was my mother, and I would watch over her as if I

were her eldest son. But the important fact is that in that very hour of deadly strain, he was thinking of the sorrow of others — the loneliness of his mother. Remarkable? That was Jesus.

(Long pause) Today is Sunday. Everything is bright, but my spirit is still dampened. Peter and I are walking along a road to Jerusalem. The sun is rising and seems brighter than usual. Peter and I are trying to straighten out some of the events and tie them in with Jesus' teaching.

Wait, listen — I hear the cry of a small voice. It's getting closer. It's Mary Magdalene. She's yelling that Jesus is alive! *(Louder and louder)* He has risen from the grave! He is alive! Jesus is alive!

About the Playwrights

William D. Blake and Cynthia H. Blake *(Jesus Our Brother Is Alive!)* of Asheville, North Carolina, are the parents of three grown children. Cyndi, a registered nurse for twenty-five years, paints watercolor florals in her off hours. Bill holds a master's in theological studies from Wheaton College. He worked for seventeen years in Christian education and youth ministry within the United Presbyterian and United Methodist denominations. He is currently the owner of a commercial printing company and a freelance writer on the side.

The late **George W. Crumley, Jr.** *(Death Day — Life Day)* was pastor of the Levittown (New York) Community Church for sixteen years. He served as minister of several Reformed churches, where his ministry included innovations in youth programs and worship, as well as a jail chaplaincy program. He held a degree in physics and two master's degrees, in divinity and religious education. He served on the editorial council of *The Church Herald*. He was the author of numerous published articles, study guides, sermons, and religious dramas, as well as a book, *People at Worship*.

Michael E. Dixon *(Into the Light)* enjoys teaching the Bible through drama. He was a Christian Church (Disciples of Christ) minister for twelve years. He is currently an editor at Christian Board of Publication, where he has worked for twenty years. His published works include two books, *Bread of Blessing, Cup of Hope* and *Fed by God's Grace*, and several plays. Michael, his wife, beagle Maddie, and grown children all live in the St. Louis, Missouri area, where he is active in community theatre.

Sally Evans *(Jesus Loved Them)* has always loved to write. Her varied efforts include poetry, short stories, music lyrics, and short plays. She has lived in the Chicago area her whole life. Among her hobbies are the outdoor pursuits of gardening and raising rabbits. She hopes to eventually retire to an area with an abundance of wildlife. She has three grown children.

Myrtle L. Forsten *(The Sycamore Cross)* is retired from full-time teaching, having taught in a number of elementary schools in Michigan. She still substitute teaches occasionally. She has extensive experience in many children's ministries, including Sunday school, puppet ministry, and vacation Bible school. In addition, she has directed programs and plays. She is the author of several published works.

John Gillies *(Give Us a Sign)* is the author of nine books, including two novels. He wrote several published plays and an outdoor musical drama, *The Firemakers,* based on the life of Jean duSable and the Potawatomi Nation. He authored over forty dramatic series for *Stories of Great Christians* (Moody Radio Network) and radio docudramas for *Unshackled!* (Pacific Garden Mission). He was a lay missionary in Brazil and Lithuania through the Presbyterian Church, USA. He is the father of three adult children and currently lives in Austin, Texas.

Linda M. Goens *(Resurrection on Trial)* is Director of Creative Worship Arts at Church of the Savior in Indianapolis, where she writes and directs drama and clown sketches for worship in addition to choreographing and performing liturgical movement. She facilitates workshops in spiritual journaling and creative worship and is the author of chancel dramas and a book, *Praising God Through the Lively Arts.*

Ronnie Hill *(Faces of the Cross)* — Information unavailable.

LeRoy Koopman *(It Is Finished)* of Wyoming, Michigan has worked as an editor and writer for the Reformed Church in America for twenty years. He is the author of thirteen books, including *Guide to Ecclesiastical Birdwatching,* and approximately 300 articles in numerous publications. He previously served as a pastor for sixteen years and as Associate Editor of *The Church Herald.* He has two adult children.

Tim Lewis *(No Vacancy)* of Canyon, Texas, is the published author of fifteen plays/musicals and two novels. He is also a cowboy poet, singer, and songwriter, with a degree in music education. He recently released a new CD entitled *Comanche Free.* His musical, *Can't Get Enough of Texas,* explores ethnic and other influences on the music of Texas.

Joanne Owens *(To Serve One Another)* is a writer for a national farm magazine. Her past positions include Manager of the Gordon County Chamber of Commerce and Director of Program at her hometown church, Calhoun, Georgia's First United Methodist. She was named Writer of the Year by the North Georgia Writers Association, with a wide range of articles, curriculum materials, and plays, as well as a book, *The Official Sunday School Teachers Handbook,* to her credit. She has three grown children.

Beverly Guyton Rhymes *(The Way of the Cross)* is an artist who combines painting with writing, seminars, and retreat work in her home state of Louisiana. She holds a master's degree in religious studies from Loyola University. She has also completed a program in spiritual direction with the Shalem Institute. She is active in the Episcopal church locally and on the diocesan level. She has seven grown children.

Jon McCauley Smith *(This Is My Story),* an ordained minister in the Christian Church (Disciples of Christ), has served as pastor of seven churches and is currently the pastor of Broadway Christian Church in Wichita, Kansas. He holds a doctorate degree in Church Revitalization. He is the author of several published plays. His other involvements include ministry to those living with HIV/AIDS, the mentally or physically challenged, the imprisoned, and those dealing with grief. He has four children.

Alison Spitz *(Christus),* a native of New Zealand, currently lives in Oxford, Massachusetts, where she was a teacher until her recent retirement. She is active in theatre and playwriting, with six published plays to her credit. She was a three-time first-place winner in the Massachusetts State Federation of Women's Clubs drama contests. She has three grown children.

Ernest R. Stair *(Parade Without a Permit),* an ordained minister in the United Methodist Church, served as pastor of a congregation in Evansville, Indiana for twenty-five years. He recently took an early retirement to pursue full-time freelance writing. He holds degrees in philosophy and English literature, as well as a degree in theology from Yale University. In addition, he has completed numerous writing courses.

Nancy Thum *(The Carpenter and the Cross)* is retired from her position as head of the private Foothill Country Day School but continues to volunteer at public and private schools. She received an Ed.M. from Harvard University. A lifelong Presbyterian, she has been active as an elder, deacon, and Sunday school teacher. She has lived in Claremont, California for thirty years and has two adult children.

Nancy G. Westerfield *(The Morning of the Marys)* was Nebraska's first National Endowment Fellow for the Arts, in poetry. She has twice won the National Catholic Prize in poetry. She was a two-time resident fellow at the artists' colony of Saratoga Springs, New York. She has been active in the Episcopal church, from the parish to the national level. In 1998, she was named Central Nebraska Region Humanitarian for the Year for community service. All her activities are carried out on foot — the Westerfields have never owned or driven an automobile.

Arthur L. Zapel *(Who Am I? All Things Are Bright and Beautiful, Three Gifts From Gentle Jesus)* has had a lifetime career as a writer/editor of plays, documentaries, and advertising for radio, TV, and film. Fine art painting became the passion of his senior years. His oil paintings are sold in galleries and are exhibited at major art shows in the West. He lives and works in Colorado Springs and Westcliffe, Colorado.

Scripture Permissions

Many of these plays contain Scripture quotations. In some instances, the author has quoted from the King James Version (KJV) or used his or her own paraphrase. These are noted in the text. Many playwrights, however, chose to use one or more of the versions used widely today. Following is a listing of the predominant versions used in their plays. We gratefully acknowledge these publishers for the use of their respective Scripture versions.

New International Version — *Into the Light*

Unless otherwise indicated, based on Scripture taken from the HOLY BIBLE, NEW INTERNATIONAL VERSION®. NIV®. Copyright © 1973, 1978, 1984 by International Bible Society. Used by permission of Zondervan Publishing House. All rights reserved.

The "NIV" and "New International Version" trademarks are registered in the United States Patent and Trademark Office by International Bible Society. Use of either trademark requires the permission of International Bible Society.

Revised Standard Version — *It Is Finished, The Way of the Cross*

Unless otherwise marked, all Scripture quotations are from the Revised Standard Version, copyright © 1971 by the Division of Christian Education of the National Council of Churches of Christ in the USA. Used by permission.

The Living Bible — *To Serve One Another*

Unless otherwise stated, all Scripture quotes are taken from The Living Bible © 1971. Used by permission of Tyndale House Publishers, Wheaton, IL 60189. All rights reserved.

Today's English Version

All Things Are Bright and Beautiful
Jesus Loved Them
Three Gifts From Gentle Jesus

Unless otherwise noted, all Scripture is taken from the Today's English Version — Second Edition Copyright © 1992 by American Bible Society. Used by permission.

Order Form

Meriwether Publishing Ltd.
P.O. Box 7710
Colorado Springs, CO 80933
Telephone: (719) 594-4422
Website: www.meriwetherpublishing.com

TM

Please send me the following books:

_____	**The Drama of Easter #BK-B235**	**$15.95**
	edited by Rhonda Wray	
	An anthology of royalty-free Easter plays for all ages	
_____	**Christmas on Stage #BK-B153**	**$15.95**
	edited by Theodore O. Zapel	
	An anthology of Christmas plays for performance	
_____	**Joy to the World #BK-B161**	**$14.95**
	by L.G. Enscoe and Annie Enscoe	
	A variety collection of Christmas programs	
_____	**Costuming the Christmas and Easter Play #BK-B180**	**$10.95**
	by Alice M. Staeheli	
	How to costume any religious play	
_____	**Service With a Smile #BK-B225**	**$14.95**
	by Daniel Wray	
	52 humorous sketches for Sunday worship	
_____	**Divine Comedies #BK-B190**	**$12.95**
	by T. M. Williams	
	A collection of plays for church drama groups	
_____	**Isaac Air Freight: The Works #BK-B215**	**$15.95**
	by Dan Rupple and Dave Toole	
	Sketches from the premier Christian comedy group	

These and other fine Meriwether Publishing books are available at your local bookstore or direct from the publisher. Use the handy order form on this page.

Name: _____

Organization name: _____

Address: _____

City: _____ State: _____

Zip: _____ Phone: _____

❑ **Check Enclosed**

❑ **Visa or MasterCard #** _____

Expiration
Signature: _____ *Date:* _____

(required for Visa/MasterCard orders)

Colorado Residents: Please add 3% sales tax.
Shipping: Include $2.75 for the first book and 50¢ for each additional book ordered.

❑ *Please send me a copy of your complete catalog of books and plays.*

Order Form

TM

Meriwether Publishing Ltd.
P.O. Box 7710
Colorado Springs, CO 80933
Telephone: (719) 594-4422
Website: www.meriwetherpublishing.com

Please send me the following books:

_____	**The Drama of Easter #BK-B235**	**$15.95**
	edited by Rhonda Wray	
	An anthology of royalty-free Easter plays for all ages	
_____	**Christmas on Stage #BK-B153**	**$15.95**
	edited by Theodore O. Zapel	
	An anthology of Christmas plays for performance	
_____	**Joy to the World #BK-B161**	**$14.95**
	by L.G. Enscoe and Annie Enscoe	
	A variety collection of Christmas programs	
_____	**Costuming the Christmas and Easter Play #BK-B180**	**$10.95**
	by Alice M. Staeheli	
	How to costume any religious play	
_____	**Service With a Smile #BK-B225**	**$14.95**
	by Daniel Wray	
	52 humorous sketches for Sunday worship	
_____	**Divine Comedies #BK-B190**	**$12.95**
	by T. M. Williams	
	A collection of plays for church drama groups	
_____	**Isaac Air Freight: The Works #BK-B215**	**$15.95**
	by Dan Rupple and Dave Toole	
	Sketches from the premier Christian comedy group	

These and other fine Meriwether Publishing books are available at your local bookstore or direct from the publisher. Use the handy order form on this page.

Name: _____

Organization name: _____

Address: _____

City: _____ State: _____

Zip: _____ Phone: _____

❑ **Check Enclosed**

❑ **Visa or MasterCard #** _____

Signature: _____ Expiration Date: _____

(required for Visa/MasterCard orders)

Colorado Residents: Please add 3% sales tax.
Shipping: Include $2.75 for the first book and 50¢ for each additional book ordered.

❑ *Please send me a copy of your complete catalog of books and plays.*